BLOOMSBURY
GOOD MUSIC GUIDE

Bloomsbury
Good Music Guide

Neville Garden

BLOOMSBURY

For Jane, Vanessa, and David
with my love

First published 1989.

Copyright © Neville Garden 1989

British Library Cataloguing in Publication Data

A CIP catalogue record for this book is available from the British Library

ISBN 0 7475 0310 9

10   9   8   7   6   5   4   3   2   1

Designed by Malcolm Smythe
Typeset by Alexander Typesetting, Inc., Indianapolis, IN
Printed in Great Britain by
Butler & Tanner Ltd, Frome, Somerset

CONTENTS

PRELUDE

Over the years, a veritable army of people have beaten a track to my door on matters musical. Sometimes — and this is becoming more and more common thanks to television advertisements — it's a tune they want identified. (They usually whistle or sing it in a way which would baffle the composer himself!) Sometimes it's information on a composer they have just discovered. What else did he write? Sometimes it's just help with building a record library. Who are the best composers to start with, and so on. If I am able to be of some assistance, they invariably say: 'You should write a book — get all that down on paper.'

Well, now I have, and I hope they're happy. What is in these pages is not musical Holy Writ. It's not a dictionary, nor an encyclopedia. It's a guide, pure and simple, aimed at everyone who likes music but doesn't know much about it and would like a way in. There's nothing remotely technical about it. So the reader who wouldn't know a *tierce de Picardie* if it got up and bit him need have no fears. I tend to side with the Australian composer Percy Grainger, who didn't approve of 'fancy' musical terms. He never wrote the word 'crescendo' on any of his scores, for example. He merely said 'get louder'.

Some 300 composers are dealt with in the book. I've tried to give a quick idea of what their music is like — whether it falls easily on the ear, or whether it's hard work. Their main works are discussed; and in some cases I have suggested a 'key' work in their output to which I've given extra attention. Here and there I recommend pieces that would make a good starting-point: and, equally important, ones that wouldn't.

The choice of composers is highly personal, so the guide is bound to be idiosyncratic. It may even be eccentric. The selection is certainly catholic. You will find the Beatles sitting comfortably next to Beethoven. Cole Porter is rubbing shoulders with Francis Poulenc. The reader who wonders why I included Lord Berners and not Buxtehude has every right to do so. But he does not need this guide.

The length of an entry is not in itself significant. The reason Malcolm Arnold has a longer entry than John Cage does not, necessarily, mean that I consider Arnold a more important composer than Cage. It means, simply, that I believe more people will derive more enjoyment from Arnold's music than Cage's. But, naturally, I could be wrong. I am aware that some composers over whom I have enthused are considered unimportant by musicologists. That is their opinion. I believe these composers are undervalued and grievously neglected. All I hope is that readers will investigate for themselves — and agree with me! In stressing the fact that this guide is primarily for the interested rather than the informed, I nevertheless hope the informed will also enjoy reading it.

It may just be that the Mahler buff who loves *Das Lied von der Erde* has not tried Zemlinsky's *Lyric Symphony*. If, after reading the Zemlinsky entry here, he does—then my writing will not have been in vain. In most cases, the music mentioned in the book has been recorded and you can track it down in a good record shop or by rummaging in the second-hand establishments which abound in most cities and towns. (If you haven't tried it, I can assure you that a 'find' will make you feel as elated as a lucky prospector in the Californian Gold Rush!)

Not all the entries in the book are concerned with composers. The instruments of the orchestra are tackled individually, as are the different ranges of the human voice: and, dotted about, are sections with lighted-hearted headings such as 'Rogue's Gallery' — a list of compositions dealing with likable scamps.   NOW LISTEN ⟩ points to works that relate in one way or another to the composer about whom you have just read. They may be similar in style to his output. They may have inspired him, or been inspired by him. Or they may reflect one aspect of him. In the entry on the Brazilian composer Heitor Villa-Lobos, for example, you will read that he wrote a piece describing a little train puffing through his native land. The NOW LISTEN ⟩ section lists pieces about trains written by other composers. The object of the exercise is simple. As the father of the American composer Charles Ives put it so memorably: 'It's to stretch the ears!'

● usually precedes a piece of general information connected with the foregoing entry. In writing about the Polish composer Witold Lutosławski, I observe that he is a particularly fine conductor of his own music. The ● section tells of other composers who knew how to wield the baton. The composers arrowed thus ▷ have an entry to themselves.

There are several people I must thank in connection with this guide. My wife Jane for her constant, cheerful and valuable encouragement; my daughter Debbie for casting a professional musician's eye over the manuscript and making helpful suggestions; Betty Kirkpatrick for being the one who actually got me started; Kathy Rooney of Bloomsbury for her enthusiasm and lack of hassle; and my mother, Doris, for nurturing in me a love of music in the first place. For me, music has always been a way of life. A day without at least a few minutes of it is a day incomplete. I hope some of that feeling comes through as you read this and that, above all, you will have fun.

Neville Garden,
October 1988

ADAM, Adolphe (1803–1856)

It took the Frenchman Adolphe Adam less than one month to compose the complete score for the ballet *Giselle*. But those few weeks of toil ensured him a place in musical history. *Giselle* remains one of the most popular ballets ever conceived. It's the tale of a peasant girl who is deceived by her lover, loses her reason and kills herself. Thereafter, she joins the ranks of the Wilis, the ghosts of maidens who have died before their wedding day. (We recall these hapless ladies every time we say that something has 'given us the willies'.) Adam's music is often very pretty, in the best sense of the word. But it can be dramatic when required (Giselle's mad scene is punctuated by wisps of melody taken from earlier, happier scenes in the ballet). Adam was a busy man. He was a professor of composition in Paris and wrote nearly 40 operas. But apart from one, the jolly *Postillon de Longjumeau* which has a popular tenor aria, his fame rests on *Giselle*.

- A plot similar in outline to *Giselle* was used by ▷Puccini in his first opera *Le villi*. Other classical ballets with supernatural elements are ▷Tchaikovsky's *Swan Lake* (in which a group of girls is turned into swans by an evil magician) and Herman Lovenskjold's *La sylphide* (set in Scotland and revolving around a woodland sprite who ensnares a Highland lad; the male dancers are required to wear the kilt!).

ADAMS, John (born 1947)

The American John Adams writes what is known as 'minimalist' music: short themes are repeated many times, changing very slowly and very slightly. (Mike Oldfield's popular success 'Tubular Bells' is a good example of the genre at its most basic.) But Adams is a lot more interesting than many minimalists such as Steve Reich and Philip Glass who now have a cult following. Adams's works fall attractively on the ear, and far from being boring in their melodic and rhythmic repetition are surprisingly stimulating.

If *Harmonium*, a splendid work for chorus and orchestra, appeals to you, try his opera *Nixon in China* which tackles the unlikely subject of the visit by the American president to Mao Tse-tung in 1972; it's a rich, warmly-coloured score with brilliant orchestral writing, exciting choruses and 'arias'.

ALBÉNIZ, Isaac (1860–1909)

Isaac Albéniz had a short but colourful life: a journey from Spain to Buenos Aires as a boy stowaway, a spell travelling to South America and the USA as a bar-room pianist, finally acceptance as a pupil of ▷Liszt. Most of Albéniz's music was for the piano (as was the case with ▷Chopin and ▷Alkan among others) and it breathes the atmosphere of his native Spain. It can be as bright and colourful as the Iberian sunshine or as dark as the scowl on a Flamenco dancer's face. His most memorable works are the piano suite *Iberia* and the *Suite española*, both of which have been effectively orchestrated by other hands.

ALBERT, Eugen d' (1864–1932)

Eugen d'Albert was an international figure in every way. He was German by adoption, of Italian and French descent, was born in Scotland and died in Russia. (The building in which he first drew breath now houses the offices of Scottish Opera in Glasgow.) He spent much of his life getting in and out of marriage – he had six wives. But he also found time to compose 20 operas, the best being *Tiefland* ('Lowland'), for which he is remembered. Its music is rooted in the

NOW LISTEN ▷

Some fine 'Spanish' works by non-Spaniards: ▷Emmanuel Chabrier, *España*; ▷Claude Debussy, *Ibéria*; ▷Ferenc Liszt, *Rapsodie espagnole*; ▷Jules Massenet, *Don Quixote*; ▷Nikolay Rimsky-Korsakov, *Capriccio espagnole*.

German tradition but there's an Italian influence – a mixture that actually works well. *Tiefland* makes attractive listening. It's about an unscrupulous landowner who tires of his beautiful lover and tries to foist her on a young shepherd. Blood flows before the final curtain.

- Other operas involving peasant passions and sudden death are ▷Delius's *A Village Romeo and Juliet*, ▷Janáček's *Jenůfa*, ▷Mascagni's *Cavalleria rusticana* and ▷Puccini's *Edgar*.

ALFORD, Kenneth (1881–1945)

Under the name Kenneth Alford, Major Frederick Joseph Ricketts wrote some of the finest military marches ever to grace the parade ground. His music is as British as that of ▷Sousa is American. Many of Alford's marches are splendid, swaggering affairs: *Colonel Bogey*, which achieved additional fame in the film *The Bridge on the River Kwai*, is among the best examples. But quite often Alford reflects the tragedy of war as much as the glory. His *Vanished Army* is almost poetic in its tribute to 'the first hundred thousand' who died in World War I.

ALKAN, Charles-Valentin (1813–1888)

One of the most enigmatic French composers was Charles-Valentin Alkan, who shunned public adulation to the point of becoming a recluse. When a government official brought him news of a state honour, Alkan slammed the door in his face, saying he was having his dinner. Alkan's music, almost exclusively for the piano, is enormously original – sometimes looking back to the 18th century but in several ways anticipating 20th-century music (▷Bartók's *Allegro barbaro* for piano was inspired by Alkan's piece of the same name).

The Concerto for solo piano is probably Alkan's masterpiece, a tour de force in which one pair of hands is called on to act as soloist and orchestra combined.

NOW LISTEN ▷

▷Ferruccio Busoni, Piano Concerto; ▷Louis Moreau Gottschalk, *Tournament Galop*; ▷Ferenc Liszt, Sonata in B minor; Ronald Stevenson, *Passacaglia on DSCH*.

The music is very exciting to listen to but a nightmare to perform.

ARENSKY, Anton (1861–1906)
Anton Arensky wrote music which was admired by his fellow Russian ▷Tchaikovsky and dismissed by ▷Rimsky-Korsakov, his teacher. 'He will soon be forgotten', said Rimsky-Korsakov on Arensky's early death. Arensky's talent was not large, but his work is full of charm and his melodies have elegance and colour. He's best remembered for a delightful waltz from his First Suite for two pianos. But his Variations on a Theme of Tchaikovsky should be performed more often: it is a fine example of writing for string orchestra. The Piano Concerto, too, is unjustly neglected; the Violin Concerto even more so, with its central waltz movement which so delighted the great violinist Jascha Heifetz that he had it arranged with piano accompaniment so he could play it in recitals. For a sample of Arensky's small but lovable contribution to musical heritage, try the first of his two orchestral suites: the 'Basso ostinato' movement would become a hit were it given more airings (it is perhaps a 19th-century answer to the celebrated 'Pachelbel Canon').

ARNOLD, Malcolm (born 1921)
The British composer Malcolm Arnold has written a number of jolly, tuneful works which have endeared him to the public. They have reminded people that music is still being written which can actually be understood and enjoyed. Because of this, some critics have tended to dismiss him as facile, which is unfair, for the vast majority of his works are far from empty. The symphonies, for example, reveal a man who thinks deeply even if he does not subscribe to today's more extreme and 'fashionable' ideas on composition. The concertos, written for various instruments, are by no means vapid, and many of his chamber works demand careful listening. Nor are Arnold's more 'popular' works mere fripperies. The sets of characteristic dances – English, Scottish and Cornish – are composed with the greatest care and affection and are bril-

NOW LISTEN
▷Alexander Borodin, *Petite suite*; ▷Alexander Glazunov, *Scènes de ballet*; ▷Anatol Lyadov, Eight Russian Folksongs; ▷Camille Saint-Saëns' Piano Concerto no. 2 in G minor; ▷Igor Stravinsky, Symphony in E flat op.1.

NOW LISTEN
Some 'Scottish' music by non-Scots: ▷Ludwig van Beethoven, *Ecossaises*; ▷Hector Berlioz, *Rob Roy*; ▷Arthur Bliss, *Miracle in the Gorbals*; ▷Max Bruch, *Scottish Fantasia*; ▷Claude Debussy, *Marche écossaise*; ▷Percy Grainger, *Strathspey and Reel*.

liantly scored for the orchestra (Arnold was principal trumpet in the London Philharmonic Orchestra for some time).

The overture *Beckus the Dandipratt* (an old word for urchin) is worth its place at the head of any concert: and if anyone doubts Arnold's ability to write with a gentle and charming gravity, the tiny Serenade for guitar and strings is the perfect answer. *Tam o'Shanter* is probably Arnold's most immediately enjoyable work, though by no means his most substantial. It's a superb overture, based on the Robert Burns poem retailing the adventures of a drunken layabout who clashes with a crowd of witches in an old churchyard. Bassoons and trombones lurch and stagger, the strings do an uncanny imitation of bagpipes, the piccolo plays the cheekiest of tubes as a pretty witch dances in a short skirt and the composer's comic genius shines out of every bar. Arnold's many film scores include the Oscar-winning *The Bridge on the River Kwai*, which makes telling use of ▷Alford's march *Colonel Bogey*.

BACH, Carl (sometimes Karl) Philipp Emanuel (1714–1788)

C.P.E. Bach, the third son of ▷J.S. Bach, is frequently said to have inherited 'the lion's share of his father's genius'. His works are undoubtedly adventurous and original, and have a strong personality. The Sinfonias, which are strong on instrumental colour, are often unexpected and sharply arresting; concertos for flute and for cello are rewarding, as are the so-called 'Hamburg' Concertos for harpsichord. The second of these, in D major, contains an early musical shock. The orchestral introduction is suddenly interrupted by a low, 'rude' noise – after which the soloist rhapsodises in a slower tempo. Then everything returns to normal. Probably the best of C.P.E. Bach is contained in the keyboard sonatas – more than 200 of them – which are mostly fresh and invigorating.

BACH, Johann Christian (1735–1785)

J.C. Bach was the 18th child of ▷J.S. Bach and because of a long stay in London, where he established a famous series of public concerts with C.F. Aisel, he became known as 'the English Bach'. His music points the way to ▷Haydn, ▷Mozart and ▷Beethoven, all of whom expressed their admiration for his work. Some indication of the esteem in which he was held can be gained from the fact that, when he died penniless, the British royal family helped to pay for his funeral and gave his widow a pension.

Johann Christian wrote a number of operas, which were popular in their day and decidedly innovative.

One of them, *Orione*, featured clarinets which were unknown to English orchestras at that time. His many concert works include many fine Sinfonias and 40 piano concertos, whose elegance and graceful melodies undoubtedly influenced ▷Mozart. Several little 'symphonies' for wind sextet, probably written to be performed in London's Vauxhall gardens, and certainly 'outdoor' music, are slight but charming and make a good introduction to the music of this interesting member of the Bach brood.

BACH, Johann Sebastian (1685–1750)
J.S. Bach is the composer for all seasons. Many find his music a source of great spiritual and religious strength; others regard it as an intellectual challenge because of Bach's supreme craftsmanship and elaborate forms and techniques; still others love it on the most basic level – because it so often falls sweetly on the ear. (His most popular piece, the so-called 'Air on the G String', must have helped to sell millions of cigars through a television advertisement.) He composed prolifically, in a wide variety of forms, bringing to each his extraordinary artistry. His influence on later composers is incalculable (several from the 19th century and later wrote pieces in his honour); ▷Wagner described him as 'the most stupendous miracle in all music'.

For most of his life, Bach worked as an organist, choirmaster and teacher in Leipzig, where his duties included composing cantatas for the major feastdays. He wrote over 200 as well as the celebrated *St John* and *St Matthew Passions*, which contain some of his finest music. A renowned organist, he wrote numerous organ pieces of which the most famous is the powerfully dramatic Toccata and Fugue in D minor. But he also wrote much chamber music, including suites for unaccompanied cello (among the finest works for the instrument) and for violin, and keyboard music, notably the Goldberg Variations and the 48 Preludes and Fugues (two books of 25 pieces each of the major and minor keys).

Of his orchestral music, the Brandenburg Concertos are a good introduction to Bach. There are six,

NOW LISTEN ▷

Some 20th-century works in which Bach's music, style or influence is reflected: ▷Alban Berg, Violin concerto; ▷Ernst Bloch, *Concerti grossi*; ▷Ferruccio Busoni, *Fantasia contrappuntistica*; ▷Percy Grainger, *Blithe Bells*; ▷Dimitry Shostakovich, Preludes and Fugues; ▷Heitor Villa-Lobos, *Bachianas brasileiras*; ▷William Walton, *The Wise Virgins*.

each for a different group of soloists set against the main body of players (Bach's title for the set was 'Concertos with several instruments'). The first highlights some exciting passages for horns, the second has an important part for trumpet, the third is for strings alone, and so on. Such is their variety and many attractions it is remarkable to think that the man for whom they were written, the Margrave of Brandenburg, never heard them.

Some purists are fussy about performances of Bach's music, preferring the keyboard works played on a clavichord or harpsichord and not on the piano. They prefer period instruments to be used in the orchestral music to re-create the kind of sound Bach must have envisaged when he wrote it. I incline to the view that Bach's music is great enough to withstand almost any treatment.

BAGPIPES

Bagpipes are not normally found in a symphony orchestra. They are, after all, heard to their best advantage in the open air across a loch or in the depths of a Highland glen. But the Scottish composer Ian Whyte, founder of the BBC Scottish Symphony Orchestra, made musical history by writing a special part for the pipes in his ballet *Donald of the Burthens* which was produced at Covent Garden, London, in 1951. More recently, ▷Peter Maxwell Davies used the pipes in his witty and delightful orchestral piece *Orkney Wedding with Sunrise.*

BALAKIREV, Mily (1837–1910)

Mily Balakirev, who is remembered as leader of the 19th-century Russian nationalist school of composers, worked so hard that he had a nervous breakdown. For a time he left the musical scene to become a railway clerk and then a schoolteacher, living in virtual seclusion. But at the height of his powers, the advice he passed to contemporaries laid the foundations of Russian music as we know it. He might have written more had he not been so concerned to guide others. What he did leave is of high quality. The two symphonies, par-

NOW LISTEN ▷

▷Hector Berlioz, *Te Deum*; ▷Alexander Glazunov, Symphony no. 1; ▷Nikolay Rimsky-Korsakov, *Sheherazade*; ▷Peter Tchaikovsky, *Manfred.*

ticularly the first, are memorable and inventive. The symphonic poem *Tamar* is a marvellously erratic, not to say erotic, portrait of a temptress out of the *Arabian Nights*. The oriental fantasy *Islamey* is among the most brilliant and technically demanding piano pieces in the repertory.

- Balakirev was a member and mentor of the group known as 'The Five' (or 'The Mighty Handful') who wanted to create a distinctive school of Russian music. The other members were ▷Borodin, Cesar Cui, ▷Musorgsky and ▷Rimsky-Korsakov.

BANTOCK, Sir Granville (1868–1946)
Few concert-goers will be aware of the name of Granville Bantock, let alone his music. He is not fashionable and his music is only occasionally revived. Yet in earlier times, Sir Thomas Beecham was one who conducted Bantock's scores with relish; Sir John Barbirolli was another. Bantock spent much of his life as a conductor and in that role was extremely adventurous. He was one of the first to recognise the gifts of ▷Sibelius. As a composer, he was more conservative but his music is not lacking in colour or effectiveness. On the contrary, it is well made and would make a pleasant change from some of the 'war-horses' trotted out with regularity in our concert halls. The orchestral poem *Fifine at the Fair*, after Browning's poem about inconstancy, contains a wealth of lovely writing (the sequences when the hero meets Fifine amidst the trappings of a carnival are scintillating); the *Celtic Symphony*, based on Hebridean melodies, is equally fine.

- ▷Sibelius dedicated his Third Symphony to Bantock, the Englishman who fought his corner so diligently.

BARBER, Samuel (1910–81)

Samuel Barber is among the best-known composers from the USA this century. His music is thoroughly romantic and is easily approached even by those who imagine they do not enjoy contemporary works. Unlike his compatriots ▷Copland and ▷Bernstein, Barber never sought to find a 'national' style. His melodies and rhythms are not especially 'American'. They are more cosmopolitan, though the musical voice with which he speaks is highly individual. The short and poignant Adagio for strings is his most frequently played work. It is also probably his most typical. It finds strong echoes in the symphonies and in the Cello Concerto and the even lovelier Violin Concerto (written on the death of his much-loved mother). The neglected Piano Concerto is more extrovert, though its slow movement features a melody that could be a contender for inclusion in anyone's hundred best tunes.

Vanessa is a super-charged, atmospheric opera with a libretto by Barber's friend ▷Menotti, himself a composer. Its central character is an ageing woman who has locked herself away for years, awaiting the return of her errant lover. He never comes back: but his son makes a surprise appearance. Vanessa falls in love with the young man, only to face competition from her niece, Erika. The story is a brooding, rather unpleasant one. But such is Barber's skill that he carries us along, making us care about characters who don't deserve our sympathy. His use of the orchestra, especially in its depiction of the snow and ice surrounding Vanessa's house, is masterly. Other works by Barber include *Knoxville: Summer of 1915* for soprano and orchestra, the ballets *Medea* and *Souvenirs* and a scintillating Piano Sonata.

Barber was a baritone of no mean ability and recorded his setting of Matthew Arnold's *Dover Beach*. The disc offers a rare example of a singing composer.

BARITONE

The tenor may have all the best tunes, but the baritone has all the best parts. So runs the old opera adage. Certainly it is often the baritone's contribution to an evening in the theatre that is most vividly remembered.

NOW LISTEN ▷

Howard Hanson, 'Romantic' Symphony; Roy Harris, Symphony no.3; ▷Erich Wolfgang Korngold, Violin Concerto; ▷Gian Carlo Menotti, *The Consul*; ▷Walter Piston, *The Incredible Flutist*.

Baritones have voices with a range lying roughly between tenor and bass. They often play villains in the opera house: the evil Scarpia in ▷Puccini's *Tosca* and the title role of ▷Verdi's *Macbeth* are good examples. But they can be sympathetic (Sharpless in another Puccini opera, *Madam Butterfly*), flamboyant (Escamillo, the toreador in ▷Bizet's *Carmen*), tragic (Wozzeck in ▷Berg's opera) and funny (Figaro in ▷Rossini's *The Barber of Seville*). Among the greatest baritones of recent times are Ettore Bastianini (Italy), Sir Geraint Evans (Britain), Dietrich Fischer-Dieskau (Germany), Tito Gobbi (Italy) and Gérard Souzay (France).

BARTÓK, Béla (1881–1945)

It it exciting to get to know the music of the Hungarian composer Béla Bartók. His style is plainly derived from the folk music of his native land (which, with his compatriot ▷Kodály, he collected, studied and arranged); much of his music combines distinctive folklike melodies with energetic dance rhythms. Bartók established an international reputation, both as a composer and a fine pianist. The political situation in Europe forced him to leave Hungary in 1940 and he reluctantly settled in the USA, spending his last years ill and in financial difficulty. His stature and his influence on 20th-century music has been immense.

No-one should perhaps try to reach Bartók through certain works. His six string quartets, for instance, are tough and uncompromising though richly rewarding for those attuned to his idiom. The Duos for violin are similarly astringent and much of Bartók's piano music is challenging. But several of his works are much more accessible and offer a key to understanding his world. The Third Piano Concerto, his last, is full of beautiful writing and its slow movement suggests a ▷Bach chorale. The Dance Suite is an exciting sequence of folklike tunes and the early ballet *The Wooden Prince* is attractively uncomplicated. On a basic level, the *Romanian Dances*, in their version for strings or for full orchestra, are charming. Anyone receptive to these pieces could progress to the Violin Concerto no.2 which, for me, is among the most wonderful works of

NOW LISTEN ▷

Some composers and works which influenced Bartók: ▷Claude Debussy, *Pelléas et Mélisande*; ▷Ferenc Liszt, *Mephisto Waltzes*; ▷Maurice Ravel, *Daphnis et Chloé*; ▷Richard Strauss, *Also sprach Zarathustra*; ▷Igor Stravinsky, *The Rite of Spring*.

its kind and which would have to accompany me to a desert island.

Bartók's Concerto for Orchestra (1943), one of his last works, is, as its title suggests, designed to highlight the various sections of the orchestra, and this colourful, brilliant score demands virtuoso playing. It has many highlights: a movement that evokes the sounds of nocturnal creatures (Bartók often includes nighttime buzzing, chattering and rustling in his works); another in which a broad, beautiful melody is interrupted by snarling, sniggering brass (a parody of a German march used in ▷Shostakovich's 'Leningrad' Symphony).

Other works by Bartók include the atmospheric, skilfully constructed Music for Strings, Percussion and Celesta, a haunting Viola Concerto, the short opera *Duke Bluebeard's Castle* (a two-character work of immense power) and the ballet *The Miraculous Mandarin* (a bizarre shocker about a Chinaman who is beaten up by thugs but refuses to die until he has been embraced by a prostitute).

BASS

The bass voice, the lowest in the human range, has been well served by many composers. There are fine bass arias in ▷Handel's *Messiah* and in ▷Verdi's Requiem (Verdi, indeed, loved the bass voice: he wrote marvellous roles for no fewer than three in his opera *Don Carlos*). The title role in ▷Musorgsky's opera *Boris Godunov* is for a bass, as is Konchak, the amiable villain of ▷Borodin's *Prince Igor* (Russian opera seems to exist for basses). The humorously horrid harem guard Osmin in ▷Mozart's *Die Entführung aus dem Serail* is a bass; so is the oily singing-teacher Don Basilio in ▷Rossini's *The Barber of Seville*. Great basses include Norman Allin (Britain), Feodor Chaliapin (Russia), Boris Christoff (Bulgaria), Nikolay Ghiaurov (Bulgaria), George London (Canada) and David Ward (Britain).

BASSOON

The bassoon is the lowest of the woodwind instruments in the orchestra. Its chuckling sound has often been employed to create a comic effect. ▷Beethoven used it to punctuate his 'village band' music in the 'Pastoral' Symphony. In his popular and entertaining orchestral poem *The Sorcerer's Apprentice*, ▷Dukas made it represent an enchanted broom stumping down to the river to collect buckets of water. But its more poignant side is regularly used by ▷Tchaikovsky, notably at the start of the 'Pathétique' Symphony; and it creates an atmosphere of primeval bleakness in the opening moments of ▷Stravinsky's *The Rite of Spring*. There are fine bassoon concertos by ▷Mozart and ▷Weber among others. Its larger brother, the double bassoon, has a moment of glory in ▷Ravel's Mother Goose ballet when it portrays the Beast in the sequence devoted to 'Beauty and the Beast'.

BAX, Sir Arnold (1883–1953)

Arnold Bax is a difficult composer to categorise. He was a dreamer whose music often appears to have neither shape nor form. His style is rhapsodic, much influenced by the landscapes and seascapes of Ireland and Scotland. His scoring is luxuriant, the effect picturesque – but in the manner of a fine painter and not of a chocolate box. 'More musing than music', was how an unsympathetic critic once described Bax. It's easy to understand the impatience felt by those to whom logical development in music is essential. But Bax has many followers, and, once hooked by his particular bait, it is well-nigh impossible to wriggle away.

Bax's seven symphonies contain his essence and are wonderful outpourings. But investigate first the tone poems *Tintagel* (the Cornish stronghold of King Arthur) and *The Garden of Fand* (a poetic name for the sea). Those seeking a way into Bax's world will also find two of his shortest orchestral works helpful – the aptly named *Dance in the Sunlight* and *Mediterranean*, a warmly evocative piece suggested by a holiday in Spain. For the 11 years before his death, Bax was Master of the King's Musick: an odd post for a man to whom ceremony was anathema. He wrote scores for

NOW LISTEN ▷

▷Frederick Delius, *North Country Sketches*; ▷Hamilton Harty, *In Ireland*; ▷John Ireland, *Mai-Dun*; ▷E.J. Moeran, *Lonely Waters*.

two films – David Lean's *Oliver Twist* and the documentary *Malta GC* – but didn't enjoy the experience. His piano works are rewarding: a favourite of mine is *Hardanger*, a gentle tribute to the home of the Norwegian fiddle, in which Bax subtly mimics the style of ▷Grieg.

BEASTS AND BEASTIES
▷Eric Coates, *The Three Bears*
▷Charles Koech in *Les bander-log* ('The monkeys')
▷Alan Rawsthorne, *Practical Cats*
▷Nikolay Rimsky-Korsakov, *Flight of the Bumblebee*
▷Albert Roussel, *Le Festin d'araignée* ('The Spider's Feast')
▷Ralph Vaughan Williams, *The Wasps*.

BEATLES
The Liverpool pop group who called themselves the Beatles (John Lennon, Paul McCartney, George Harrison and Ringo Starr) were a phenomenon of the 1960s, and though they had disbanded by 1970, the popularity of their music is still high worldwide. Most of the best Beatles songs were by Lennon and McCartney and include *Yesterday, Please, please me, Eleanor Rigby* and *Hey Jude*. The *Sergeant Pepper* album has been described by one learned reference book as 'a genuine song-cycle' in that it was the first rock album to be conceived as a unit, or cycle, and not just as a random collection of songs. The Beatles achieved the distinction of being worshipped by the pop fraternity and enjoyed by people who don't usually like pop music. It seems likely that their songs will endure, like those of ▷Gershwin, ▷Kern and ▷Porter, among others. Lennon died at the hands of an assassin outside his New York home in 1981.

BEETHOVEN, Ludwig van (1770–1827)
The figure of Beethoven towers over all music. Super-ficially, at least, he is the best-known composer. Most people know what he looked like: his haunted face and tousled hair were captured in many portraits. They know about his tragic deafness. They know some of his music: *Für Elise*, the tiny piece handed out by so many piano teachers; the Fifth Symphony, whose opening 'hammer blows' are supposed to represent 'Fate knocking on the door'; the 'Moonlight' Sonata; and the 'Ode to Joy' from the Ninth Symphony, which has become the anthem of the European Community.

But those who care to go deeper into Beethoven's music will find it enriches their lives beyond measure. His works range from the *Missa solemnis*, a 'solemn mass' of epic proportions, to frivolous little marches for military band. But in each genre or form that he used, Beethoven broke new ground, and none of his works is without significance. Even the piano pieces he called *Bagatelles*, or 'trifles', show his originality and indeed they are useful introductions to his piano sona-tas. Beethoven wrote piano sonatas throughout his creative life and they demonstrate well some of his extraordinary innovations: they are on a larger scale than any keyboard sonatas written before, they exploit the power and full range of the instrument (piano mak-ing at this time was undergoing rapid development and pianos were larger and stronger) and they explore new emotional areas.

24 years separate the first of Beethoven's symphonies from the last, no. 9, but they are light years apart in terms of musical expression. The First and Second Symphonies date from Beethoven's early years but al-ready show him beginning to tread new paths. No. 3, 'Eroica', was written in Beethoven's 'middle period' when he wrote many noble, heroic works; it enters a new world, with a funeral march of profound depths. The Fourth and famous Fifth continue to establish a unique personality. The Sixth, 'Pastoral', takes us into an unexpectedly gentle world of babbling brooks, peasants having fun and running from a storm. No. 7 dances its way dynamically towards no. 8, which is charmingly personal. The Ninth, the Choral Sym-phony, with its solo singers and chorus, dates from

> **NOW LISTEN** ▷

Music which either influenced or was influenced by Beethoven: ▷Johannes Brahms, Symphony no. 1 in C minor; ▷Luigi Cherubini, Symphony; ▷Muzio Clementi, piano sonatas; Ferdinando Paer, *Leonora*.

Beethoven's late period, when he was composing works of the utmost intensity, often on a large scale.

Beethoven's piano concertos date from his early and middle periods. The first two are conventional but the third speaks with a highly individual voice. No. 5, 'Emperor', is by far the grandest and most immediately impressive. But it is perhaps no. 4 in G major that best embodies two great features of Beethoven's music, dramatic strength and gentle poetry, juxtaposed here to particularly fine effect. It opens unconventionally not with an orchestral statement of the main themes but with a quiet, pensive solo for the piano. The slow movement lasts only a few minutes and is a kind of contest between the piano and the orchestra, which the soloist wins. (▷Liszt described it as 'Orpheus taming the wild beasts'.) The finale follows without a break and is alternately boisterous and delicate.

Beethoven composed one Violin Concerto (unusual in that it begins with five solo taps on the timpani), an opera *Fidelio* (a 'rescue' opera about a woman who risks her life to free her husband, a political prisoner) and a ballet *The Creatures of Prometheus* (which contains some delightful but relatively unknown music). The chamber music, a subject of endless study, includes 17 string quartets which, for many, are the best of Beethoven. Their invention, intensity and infinite variety make them enormously enriching but it is better to broach them after much exposure to the composer's music.

BELLINI, Vincenzo (1801–1835)

The short life of Vincenzo Bellini was a fruitful one. He composed 11 operas, of which four are firmly in the repertory, distinguished by long, elegant melodies and passages of great floridity, making huge demands on singers. *I puritani* is based on a play after Sir Walter Scott's novel *Old Mortality* and is about the rescue of Charles I's widow from prison. During the action, the heroine goes mad but regains her sanity in time for the final curtain. *La sonnambula* features a heroine who doesn't lose her reason but walks in her sleep; and *I Capuleti e i Montecchi* is a version of Shakespeare's *Romeo and Juliet*.

NOW LISTEN ▷

▷Hector Berlioz, *Roméo et Juliette*;
▷Gaetano Donizetti, *Lucia di Lammermoor*;
▷Ferenc Liszt,
▷Fryderyk Chopin and others, *Hexameron*;
▷Richard Wagner, *Tannhäuser*.

Norma (1831) is, however, Bellini's masterpiece. Its story is strong, about a Druid priestess who has an affair with a Roman pro-consul, admits the liaison and is condemned to death. He is moved to die with her (a similar twist is found in ▷Verdi's much later *Aida*). Bellini's music is powerful and dramatic. Norma's aria 'Casta diva', in which she prays to the moon for peace between Gaul and Rome, is one of the greatest operatic showpieces and is often sung by sopranos in the concert hall.

BENJAMIN, Arthur (1893–1960)

The Australian Arthur Benjamin will forever be remembered for one tiny piece, the *Jamaican Rumba*, written originally as a piano duet. Perhaps some day attention will be paid to his more important works, notably the opera *A Tale of Two Cities* which retells Charles Dickens's story of the French Revolution in music that is strong and approachable. Another, shorter opera, *Prima donna*, is most attractive and very funny; it's about two rival sopranos who have a vocal duel on stage. Benjamin composed for the cinema, his best score being for Oscar Wilde's comedy *An Ideal Husband*.

BENNETT, Richard Rodney (born 1936)

Richard Rodney Bennett is a British composer who is also a fine pianist with a penchant for jazz. His own music often reflects that interest but his versatility is enormous: he was able to write a film score for *Murder on the Orient Express* (which has a wonderful 'popular' waltz tune) with the same skill and enthusiasm as *Spells*, a choral work in an advanced idiom which calls for great concentration from singers and audience alike. Bennett has composed several operas, including the effective *The Mines of Sulphur*, a ghost story involving the strange events which take place when some strolling players arrive at a house with a secret. Perhaps the piece which offers the best entré to Bennett's music is the *Aubade* for orchestra (an aubade is a morning song). Its colours are bright and its style attractive.

- ▷Britten wrote two operas set in haunted houses, both based on stories by Henry James – *The Turn of the Screw* and *Owen Wingrave* (the latter was composed for BBC television).

BERG, Alban (1885–1935)

Alban Berg belongs to the Second Viennese School, a group of composers who worked in Vienna, including ▷Schoenberg and ▷Webern. But Berg is more 'acceptable' to the public than either of his colleagues. He used 'advanced' techniques, including the 12-note method devised by Schoenberg. But he was plainly a romantic, and his music speaks as much to the heart as to the intellect. No-one needs expect to leave a concert hall or a theatre humming a Berg tune. But a listener with an open mind who does not know any of his music will find it arresting, fascinating and ultimately indispensible. Berg's two operas, *Wozzeck* and *Lulu* are 20th-century masterpieces, powerfully affecting in the opera house or on disc. The first is almost unbearably moving in its sympathetic depiction of the suffering of a half-witted soldier; the second is a hypnotic account of the downfall of a good-time girl who ends up a victim of Jack the Ripper. Of his other works, the Three Orchestral Pieces are thoroughly stimulating even on first acquaintance. An impressive string quartet is one of a handful of chamber pieces.

The Violin Concerto (1935) is, for me, Berg's most remarkable work. It was written when the composer heard of the death of 18-year-old Manon Gropius, daughter of the widow of ▷Mahler. Berg loved the girl as his own daughter and the concerto is dedicated 'to the memory of an angel'. It was to be his last completed work: he died of blood-poisoning shortly after. From the concerto's opening, a gently rocking motif played by the clarinet and solo violin, to its wrapt final pages, it has a magical atmosphere. The moment where Berg introduces ▷J. S. Bach's chorale *Es ist Genug* ('It is enough') into his highly personal web of sound is heart-stopping. There is nothing to compare with it in all music.

> **NOW LISTEN** >
>
> ▷Gustav Mahler, *Kindertotenlieder* ('Songs on the Death of Children') and Symphony no. 4.

● Berg's style is closer to that of Mahler than that of his associates in the Second Viennese School. It's interesting to compare Berg's Violin Concerto with Schoenberg's, and Berg's Three Orchestral Pieces with Webern's Five Orchestral Pieces. The essential differences are plain to hear.

BERIO, Luciano (born 1925)

Humour is not high on the agenda of the avant-garde. But the Italian Luciano Berio has never been afraid to offer an audience the chance of a few smiles. Because of this, his music – though often 'difficult' – has a humanity about it and often appeals to listeners who don't expect to like it. Berio draws on many sources and techniques, including tapes, other people's music – even newspapers read aloud. The Sinfonia, which is his most enjoyable work, quotes from works by several other composers. *Laborintos II*, a music-theatre piece, sees Berio blending madrigals, elements of jazz and street cries with his own highly individual sounds. Perhaps Berio's most arresting works are the *Sequenze*, a series of short pieces for different solo instruments including the oboe, trombone and harp. Berio arranged some folksongs for his wife, the soprano Cathy Berberian, to sing with an instrumental ensemble, and these are delightful.

BERKELEY, Sir Lennox (born 1903)

Lennox Berkeley is often described as one of Britain's most 'fastidious' composers. Presumably the word is intended as a compliment, but it does suggest a rather precious and over-careful approach to writing music. There is, to be sure, nothing slap-dash or haphazard about Berkeley's work. But neither does it lack spontaneity, colour or inner life. There are touches of ▷Stravinsky about some of it, and French leanings here and there. But any influences are skilfully absorbed and the resulting musical voice is original and individual. Berkeley's First and Second Symphonies are elegant, civilised works and are among the com-

NOW LISTEN ▷

Works quoted in Berio's Sinfonia: ▷Ludwig van Beethoven, 'Pastoral' Symphony; ▷Gustav Mahler, Symphony no. 2; ▷Maurice Ravel, *La valse*; ▷Richard Strauss, *Der Rosenkavalier*; ▷Richard Wagner, *Das Rheingold*.

poser's best. But the listener coming fresh to Berkeley should do so via the charming Serenade for Strings (how English composers love writing for strings!) and the piquant Sonatina for flute and piano, a favourite of James Galway's. The Guitar Concerto is a refreshing work which doesn't, happily, pretend to be in any way Spanish. I am especially fond of *Antiphon*, a piece for strings reflectively based on plainsong.

The one-act operas *Ruth* (based on the biblical character) and *A Dinner Engagement* (a witty romantic comedy) show Berkeley's skill in theatre pieces.

● Michael Berkeley (born 1948) is Sir Lennox's son. His works include *Or Shall We Die* and *Meditations* which, like his father's *Antiphon*, is for strings and has links with plainsong.

BERLIN, Irving (born 1888)

Irving Berlin celebrated his centenary in the certain knowledge that he was the reigning king of Tin Pan Alley. The man often called the 'Father of American popular song' was in fact born a Russian Jew (his real name was Israel Baline) whose family emigrated to the USA to escape the persecution of the Tsarist guards. He could neither read nor write music, and his ability to play the piano by ear was limited. But he quickly showed he had a heaven-sent gift of melody. His first hit was *Alexander's Ragtime Band*; thereafter he fed the world a non-stop stream of songs, for most of which he provided his own words. *Easter Parade*, *White Christmas*, *Always* and *Putting on my Top Hat* are some of them. His Broadway musicals included *Annie Get your Gun* and *Call me Madam* (both of which were filmed) and a patriotic song, *God Bless America*, has become almost a second national anthem in the USA.

- Other gifted American songwriters include
▷Gershwin, ▷Kern, ▷Porter, ▷Rodgers, Jule
Styne and ▷Sondheim.

BERLIOZ, Hector (1803–69)
One of the most misunderstood of the great composers is the Frenchman Hector Berlioz. He did cut a
somewhat wild, Byronic figure: when a lady jilted him,
for instance, he set out to follow her carrying pistols
and poison! But such tales obscured for many years his
imagination and originality as a composer. His extravagant gestures – a brass band at each corner of the
platform for his monumental Requiem – deflected
people's attention from the fact that much of his work
is reflective, even intimate. (One caricature of the day
shows Berlioz using a sword to conduct thousands of
musicians.) It hurt him deeply that his music was
neither appreciated nor properly played. (He commented on a performance of his *King Lear* overture
that the orchestra had got it 'more or less right', adding
that that was not enough.) He soldiered on almost until
the end of his life. But what virtually destroyed him was
the lack of interest in what he considered his masterpiece, the opera *Les Troyens* ('The Trojans'). It is in two
massive parts; during his lifetime only the second was
performed, and that in a drastically cut version. It was
not until 1969 that a complete performance of *Les
Troyens* was given in Paris for the first time.

Berlioz's dramatic symphony *Roméo et Juliette* and
La damnation de Faust (a concert work but occasionally
staged) are splendid examples of the vision of this
wonderful composer. So are the *Te Deum* and *L'enfance
du Christ* with its popular chorus, the Shepherds'
Farewell. *Les nuits d'été* ('Summer Nights'), a song cycle with orchestra, paved the way for ▷Mahler's cycles. *Harold in Italy*, inspired by Byron, is for viola and
orchestra and is as close as Berlioz came to composing
a concerto. But the listener is more likely to come upon
performances of Berlioz's overtures, of which the dazzling *Le carnaval romain* and *Le corsaire* are the most
immediately enjoyable.

NOW LISTEN
▷Ferenc Liszt, 'Dante'
Symphony; ▷Gustav
Mahler, *Lieder eines
fahrender Gesellen*
(Songs of a Wayfarer);
▷Peter Tchaikovsky,
Hamlet; ▷Richard
Wagner, *Tristan und
Isolde*.

Berlioz's most popular work is the *Symphonie fantastique* (1830). Its five movements tell a story tracing the hopeless love of an artist for a mysterious, enigmatic lady. She has a theme of her own, heard in different guises throughout the work. Towards the end, the artist takes opium, hallucinates and imagines he has been executed for her murder. The symphony ends with a wild Witches' Sabbath. The tale is clearly told. But it shouldn't blind anyone to the purely musical qualities of the work, which are breathtaking and ahead of their time. (The artist in the symphony is Berlioz and the lady is the Irish actress Harriet Smithson, with whom he was in love and eventually married, though he lived to regret it.) ▷Liszt made a piano transcription of the symphony. Other works by Berlioz include two operas, *Béatrice et Bénédict* (after Shakespeare's *Much Ado about Nothing*) and *Benvenuto Cellini* (about the Italian sculptor and writer).

BERNERS, Lord (1883–1950)

The Englishman Lord Berners was born Gerald Hugh Tyrwhitt-Wilson and was that rare creature, a peer of the realm who achieved fame as a composer. He was also an excellent painter, a readable author and a confirmed eccentric. (He kept pigeons on his estate and dyed them all the colours of the rainbow, and he invariably carried a small clavichord in his Rolls Royce!) His early years were spent as a diplomat, mostly in Rome. But he turned increasingly to music and eventually had lessons from ▷Stravinsky among others. Stravinsky's influence can be heard in some of Berners's music, notably the *Fantaisie espagnole*. Mostly Berners wrote in an attractive and accessible style, often with considerable wit. His ballet *The Triumph of Neptune* (about a journalist's visit to fairyland) has a marvellous Scottish dance during which the orchestra players are called upon to shout 'Hooch!' and a hornpipe danced by Britannia. Another ballet, *A Wedding Bouquet*, with words by Gertrude Stein, is an amusing curio with some very catchy tunes. Berners contributed an excellent score to the film *Nicholas Nickleby*.

NOW LISTEN ▷

▷Constant Lambert, *Horoscope*; ▷Les Six, *Les mariés de la tour Eiffel*; ▷Igor Stravinsky, *The Rite of Spring*; ▷William Walton, *Façade*.

BERNSTEIN, Leonard (born 1918)

Leonard Bernstein could enter the Hall of Fame on the strength of one work, his Broadway musical *West Side Story*, a dazzling updating of Shakespeare's *Romeo and Juliet* in which the opposing sides are native New Yorkers and Puerto Rican immigrants. It boasts an impressive array of hit songs, including *Somewhere*, *I feel pretty*, *America* and *Something's Coming*. But this high-powered American, whose career as a conductor has probably overshadowed his activities as a composer, has written other works worthy of attention. Bernstein's musical version of the Voltaire classic *Candide* is consistently inventive; and his symphonies deserve a more permanent place in the repertory. The Second, sub-titled *'The Age of Anxiety'*, is an exciting work, with a vigorous and jazzy role for solo pianist. Bernstein's ballet *Fancy Free* is fresh and attractive, and the score he wrote for Elia Kazan's film *On the Waterfront* is a splendid example of the genre. Try to sample some of his many songs (especially the ones he wrote for a production of *Peter Pan*): they show a very different side of the composer. The *Songfest*, a large choral work with orchestra, is one of the composer's own favourites. The *Chichester Psalms* (written for Chichester Cathedral) and the theatrical *Mass* are typical of Bernstein.

BERWALD, Franz (1797–1868)

The Swedish composer Franz Berwald wrote a piano concerto, the thought of which must exhaust a soloist before he has played a note and sap the confidence of any orchestra assembled to play the accompaniment. The piano is not given a single bar's rest; and the composer remarks at the head of the score that the concerto can be played without the orchestra if desired! But Berwald was an extraordinary composer much given to the unexpected. One of his four symphonies, the *Sinfonie singulière*, is singular indeed. It was written in the 1840s but foreshadows not only the later works of ▷Brahms, but also the music of ▷Nielsen and even ▷Walton. It is a work like nothing else of its time. Another of his symphonies, the *Sinfonie serieuse*, is not so original but is striking and enjoyable nonetheless.

NOW LISTEN

▷Ernest Bloch, Sacred Service; ▷Aaron Copland, *El salón Mexico*; ▷George Gershwin, Piano Concerto; ▷Igor Stravinksy, *Ebony Concerto*; ▷Andrew Lloyd Webber, Requiem.

Some of Berwald's chamber music, notably a String Quartet in G minor and a Septet (for clarinet, bassoon, horn, violin, viola, cello and double bass, like ▷Beethoven's Septet), is delightfully refreshing.

BIRTWISTLE, Sir Harrison (born 1934)

Harrison Birtwistle writes music that has been described by at least one scholar as 'uncompromisingly tough'. His opera *Punch and Judy*, which takes a thoroughly unconventional view of the traditional children's entertainment, was hailed in 1968 as 'the first truly modern opera' written in Britain – a side-swipe, presumably, at ▷Britten and ▷Tippett.

Birtwistle studied at the Royal Manchester College of Music where he formed the New Music Manchester Group with ▷Goehr, ▷Maxwell Davies and John Ogdon.

BIZET, Georges (1838–1875)

The French composer Georges Bizet was a child prodigy who, by the time he was 19, had written a sparkling symphony (still often played) and won the Prix de Rome at the Paris Conservatoire. His career prospects were glittering, but in fact, things didn't work out well for him. He had little success with his operas *Les pêcheurs de perles* ('The Pearl Fishers'), a romantic adventure set in Ceylon and *La jolie fille de Perth*, ('The Fair Maid of Perth'), after Sir Walter Scott's novel and he abandoned *Ivan IV* (which told the story of Ivan the Terrible). Even the music he wrote for Alphonse Daudet's play *L'arlésienne*, now one of his most popular works, didn't receive its due attention because the play failed to run.

Carmen (1875) was Bizet's greatest achievement. Inexplicably, it had a disastrous reception and the failure hastened Bizet's sadly early death. There's a case to be made for it as the most 'complete' of all operas. It has a superb and totally believable story, which offers real scope for acting and production, and there is a hit tune every few minutes, among them the Toreador's Song, the Habañera, the Seguidilla, the Card Song, the Urchins' Chorus and the meltingly lovely Flower

NOW LISTEN ▷

▷Francesco Cilea, *L'arlesiana*; ▷Gaetano Donizetti, *Don Pasquale*; ▷Sergey Prokofiev, *Ivan the Terrible*, (film score); ▷Gioachino Rossini, *The Barber of Seville*.

Song. The music is vibrant: the orchestra is as important in the telling of the tale as the singers and the Spanish atmosphere is captured superbly. Carmen, the gypsy who loves men instantly and leaves them as suddenly, is a gift for a mezzo-soprano. But Don José, the soldier she cannot shake off, is no less impressive a role for a tenor if he has the intelligence to see its subtleties.

Other works by Bizet include the suite *Jeux d'enfants* ('Children's Games'), the colourful *Roma* symphony and two early operas which lean heavily on Rossini and other Italian composers, *Don Procopio* and *Le Doctor Miracle*.

- *Carmen Jones* was a Broadway musical version of the opera *Carmen*, using Bizet's score more or less as he wrote it but with words by Oscar Hammerstein; it was envisaged for a black cast.

BLACHER, Boris (1903–1975)
The composer Boris Blacher was born in China, of Baltic descent, but he studied and lived in Germany. He was much influenced by jazz in the early part of his career and went on to experiment with many new techniques of composition. His music, however, is fairly easily approached. The Variations on a Theme of ▷Paganini (the Caprice no. 2 for violin) is an exciting orchestral showpiece.

- Other works using the same Paganini caprice are ▷Brahms's Variations for solo piano, ▷Lloyd Webber's Variations for cello and jazz ensemble, ▷Lutoslawski's Variations for two pianos and ▷Rakhmaninov's Rhapsody for piano and orchestra.

BLISS, Sir Arthur (1891–1975)

Arthur Bliss started as an *enfant terrible*, writing works which alarmed his fellow Englishmen; but he ended as an establishment figure, as Master of the Queen's Music. His early style is quite tough, suggesting some of the experiments of ▷Stravinsky. But gradually he 'mellowed' and became unashamedly romantic. His splendid Piano Concerto is a follow-on from ▷Rakhmaninov (albeit with a bit of spice) and the *Colour Symphony* is a most approachable attempt to suggest in music various heraldic hues. The ballets contain some of the best of Bliss: *Miracle in the Gorbals*, a tale of street gangs and violent death in Glasgow, *Checkmate*, a game of life and death on a giant chess board, and *Adam Zero* which traces the life of an ordinary man from cradle to grave.

Morning Heroes (1930) is one of Bliss's most powerful and shamefully neglected works. He wrote it to rid himself of a deep depression that settled on him after the death of his brother in World War I. It is for a narrator, chorus and orchestra who muse on heroism and the pity of war with the help of words by Homer, Walt Whitman and Wilfred Owen. It's impossible, I believe, to listen to it unmoved. Other works by Bliss include Music for Strings, the incidental music for H.G. Wells's film *Things to Come* and the march *Welcome the Queen*, a fine example of his ceremonial style.

> **NOW LISTEN**
> ▷Benjamin Britten, *War Requiem*; ▷Edward Elgar, *Pomp and Circumstance Marches*; ▷Constant Lambert, Piano Concerto; ▷Francis Poulenc, *Aubade*; ▷Sergey Rakhmaninov, piano concertos.

BLOCH, Ernest (1880–1959)

The American composer Ernest Bloch wrote music whose every bar proclaims his deep involvement with the Jewish faith, speaking clearly of a genuine spiritual commitment springing from within. His most famous concert piece is *Schelemo* ('Solomon') for cello and orchestra, a moving and memorable rhapsody. But there is a good case for a revival of interest in the Violin Concerto, a strong, dramatic work championed for many years by Yehudi Menuhin, and the two Concerti grossi, inspired by Baroque models. The Sacred Service, for baritone, chorus and orchestra, is Bloch's most overtly 'religious' work. I recall hearing a performance of the *Concerto symphonique* for piano and orchestra in 1949, shortly after its composition, which

> **NOW LISTEN**
> ▷Leonard Bernstein, Symphony no. 3, 'Kaddish'; ▷Max Bruch, *Kol nidrei*; ▷Mario Castelnuovo-Tedesco, Violin Concerto no. 2, 'The Prophets'.

made a lasting impression – and I have not heard it since.

BOCCHERINI, Luigi (1743–1805)

The Italian Luigi Boccherini is famous for a tiny minuet which everyone has heard in some form or another: it has been arranged for just about every instrument known to man – and probably some not known to him! It comes from a String Quartet in E major (op. 13 no. 5) and, not surprisingly, sounds best in its original version. It shouldn't be forgotten, though, that Boccherini was a most adventurous and prolific composer. He wrote nearly 100 other string quartets, as well as more than 120 quintets, nearly 50 trios and much other music of all kinds. He settled in Spain, a move reflected in some of his works which include the guitar. He was a brilliant cellist, and wrote 11 cello concertos.

BOITO, Arrigo (1842–1918)

The Italian Arrigo Boito is best known today not as a composer but as the poet who wrote the libretto for ▷Verdi's last operas *Otello* and *Falstaff* (Boito based his librettos on Shakespeare's plays so successfully that in no way did he diminish the originals). But he was also able to write music of some interest. His opera *Mefistofele* has its origins in Goethe's poem *Faust*. Mephistopheles is the Devil who wins the soul of an aged philosopher in return for giving him back his youth. (When the Russian bass Feodor Chaliapin portrayed Mephistopheles on stage, he created much controversy by appearing almost naked and emitting ear-piercing whistles during one of the arias!) Since Boito lived very much in the shadow of the mighty Verdi, it is perhaps inevitable that his music owes something to the older master's. But it has enough touches of originality to catch the ear repeatedly. Boito was working on another opera when he died, *Nerone* ('Nero'), which calls for the city of Rome to be burnt on stage . . .

BORODIN, Alexander (1833–1887)

If the output of the Russian composer Alexander

> **NOW LISTEN**
>
> Richard Adler, *Damn Yankees*; ▷Hector Berlioz, *La damnation de Faust*; ▷Ferruccio Busoni, *Doktor Faust*; ▷Charles Gounod, *Faust*; ▷Richard Wagner, Overture to *Faust*.

Borodin is comparatively small that is because he was a part-time composer: most of his life was spent as a research chemist and lecturer. Indeed, he achieved so much as a scientist, including the founding of a School of Medicine for Women, that it's amazing he wrote as much as he did. His two completed symphonies are warm-hearted, very 'Russian' works whose tunes were eagerly seized by the creators of the Broadway musical *Kismet*, one of the more successful attempts to popularise a great composer. But don't ignore the Third Symphony, which was unfinished at Borodin's death (his colleague ▷Glazunov prepared it for publication); its two movements are delightful.

Prince Igor (1890) was also incomplete on Borodin's death. Glazunov and ▷Rimsky-Korsakov completed it, doing some orchestration and preparing it for the stage. It stands as one of the greatest Russian operas. A study in pride and nobility, it is the tale of a national hero who refuses to bow the knee to the enemy who has captured him. Borodin's music is by turns moving (the mighty aria in which Igor outlines his creed), exciting (the famous Polovtsian Dances staged to entertain the imprisoned Igor) and romantic (the love between Igor's son and his enemy's daughter). The opera's splendid overture was never written down by Borodin. It exists, it is said, because Glazunov remembered hearing Borodin play it on the piano, and was able to reconstruct it.

Other works by Borodin include two string quartets (the second of which has a succession of ravishing tunes and should be required listening for anyone suspicious of chamber music), a colourful orchestral piece *In the Steppes of Central Asia* and the *Petite suite* for piano, which also exists in an orchestral version by Glazunov. Borodin was a member of 'The Five', the group of Russian composers who wanted to create a distinctive national school of composition.

BOULEZ, Pierre (born 1925)
The Frenchman Pierre Boulez is both a celebrated conductor and a leading avant-garde composer. On the rostrum, he is renowned for his performances of the French impressionists (particularly ▷Debussy and

NOW LISTEN >
▷Mily Balakirev, *Tamar*;
▷Alexander Glazunov, Symphony no. 4;
▷Modest Musorgsky, *Boris Godunov*;
▷Nikolay Rimsky-Korsakov, *Antar*.

▷Ravel) and large-scale 20th-century works; at his work desk, he writes music stemming from the world inhabited by ▷Stockhausen and Bruno Maderna. In his compositions, Boulez uses all manner of instruments. You will find, for instance, prominent parts ascribed to the guitar and the vibraphone, as well as the ondes martenot – an electronic instrument invented in 1928 whose keyboard, oscillating valves, condensers and wires combine to make a strange and haunting sound. Boulez has also made a chorus speak instead of sing and called upon singers to whisper and to cry. He believes a composition is never finished, is always 'in progress', and constantly revises his works, frequently adding to them. He also likes to encourage spontaneity among performers; one of his compositions has five movements which need not be played in the printed order. Boulez dislikes tradition for its own sake, believing it can breed stuffiness and a stagnation of ideas: he once declared all opera houses should be blown up. You will not sing a Boulez tune in your bath. But if you take his music on board, you can expect to be astonished by sounds that are often magical and otherworldly. You should also be ready to respond to the aural equivalent of a sun-burst. Two of this challenging composer's most important early works are *Pli selon pli* ('Fold upon Fold') and *Le marteau sans maître* ('The Hammer without a Master').

● The music of ▷Messiaen can help the listener approach Boulez's works. Messiaen was Boulez's teacher, and his influence is marked. The massive *Turangalîla Symphony*, in which Messiaen uses the ondes martenot, is a good starting-point.

BRAHMS, Johannes (1833–1897)
Johannes Brahms was a musical architect, whose works are firmly constructed on the most solid, classical foundations. But this most German of composers was also a Romantic, and what he wrote endures as much for its heart as for its impeccable form. He was deeply in love with Clara, the wife of his friend and

NOW LISTEN ▷

▷Johann Sebastian Bach, Cantata no. 150;
▷Carl Nielsen, Symphony no. 1;

fellow musician ▷Robert Schumann. But when Schumann died, they did not marry and Brahms remained a bachelor. (I recall a frightful Hollywood film which had Robert Walker, a most unlikely Brahms, trying to persuade Katherine Hepburn's Clara to stop mourning her husband!) It is not fanciful to state that Brahms's unrequited passion left its mark on his music, particularly the later works which have a strong thread of melancholy running through them.

Many lovers of Brahms turn to his chamber music for the best of him: the three violin sonatas and the Piano Quartet in G minor are among my favourites. There are wonderful things, too, in the solo piano works: for a compendium of Brahms's virtues you need look no further than the intermezzos and the rhapsodies. But it's the large concert works which tend to be heard most often. The Violin Concerto, with its 'gypsy' finale (perhaps reflecting Brahms's early contact with Hungarian gypsies) and the more unusual Double Concerto for violin and cello are much-loved. Nor should you ignore the two orchestral serenades, especially no. 2 which banishes the violins from the platform; the jolly little Scherzo is a fine 'taster'. The symphonies, of course, are mainstays of the orchestral repertory: no. 1 a rugged outpouring, struggling upwards towards the sun of a marvellous tune in the last movement (a melody that bears a close resemblance to the 'Ode to Joy' in ▷Beethoven's Ninth Symphony). Nos. 2 and 3 are warmer, less stark. The Fourth must be regarded as crucial in any assessment of Brahms. It begins with a musical phrase which is almost a sigh of yearning and ends with a set of variations (on a theme from ▷J. S. Bach's Cantata no. 150) – summing up Brahms's entire orchestral achievement.

The *German Requiem* (which uses a text drawn from Luther's translation of the Bible) is for soprano, baritone, chorus and orchestra and is Brahms's largest work. He wrote many lovely songs and his vast output includes two splendid overtures, the *Tragic* and the *Academic Festival* (which quotes student songs), and 21 *Hungarian Dances*, originally for piano duet and later orchestrated (mostly by others, including ▷Dvořák.)

▷Hubert Parry, *Elegy for Brahms*; Wilhelm Stenhammar, Piano Concerto no. 1.

BRIAN, Havergal (1876–1972)

Havergal Brian composed 32 symphonies, but had reached the age of 78 before one of them was performed. The neglect of his music would undoubtedly have daunted, not to say destroyed, a lesser man. But Brian kept on writing almost until his death, and had the satisfaction of knowing that, at last, people were waking up to his existence. His music is 'British' in character but it cannot easily be compared with that of any of his contemporaries. It is at its most impressive when quiet and tranquil: pauses and silences are used frequently to telling effect. However, the symphonies, of which no. 2, the 'Gothic', is the most impressive, are an acquired taste. Brian usually used a very large orchestra and his scoring can sound thick and extravagant unless a conductor has a keen ear for balance. Those seeking a different experience, however, will find much to admire in Brian's music.

• Another British symphonist whose career blossomed late is George Lloyd (born 1913). World War II took its toll on Lloyd's health and for some years he wrote virtually nothing. Recently, however, he has become prolific and his symphonies have found a cult following. They have more immediate appeal than Brian's, being written in a more popular idiom.

BRIDGE, Frank (1879–1941)

Frank Bridge's name is rarely mentioned without the rider 'the teacher of ▷Britten'. But the fact that Bridge helped shape the talents of such a major figure shouldn't blur his own achievements as a composer. He began his musical career very much in the mould of his teacher, ▷Stanford, but soon changed his style, espousing some of the ideas of ▷Schoenberg and his 'school'. He has never been, and probably never will be, a popular composer, but those who take music seriously consider him to be among the more forward-looking composers of his day. His *Oration*, a substantial piece for cello and orchestra, has been compared with the Cello Concerto of ▷Elgar. The Second String Quartet is a particularly fine example of Bridge's chamber music.

• Britten paid eloquent tribute to his teacher in his marvellous Variations on a Theme of Frank Bridge for string orchestra; the theme comes from one of Bridge's *Three Idylls* for string quartet.

BRITTEN, Benjamin (1913–1976)
If ever a living composer were able to reach out and communicate with a wide audience, it was Benjamin Britten, who gave fresh impetus to British music in the years after World War II. His musical fingerprints are unmistakable. His idiom is modern and highly personal but he placed great emphasis on melody and his tunes are frequently beautiful, haunting and memorable. Britten's greatest success was in the theatre. His operas cover a wide variety of subject. The social comedy *Albert Herring* (about a village lad elected May King because no virtuous girls can be found to be May Queen), the Shakespeare opera *A Midsummer Night's Dream* and *Gloriana* (a study of Elizabeth Tudor composed for the coronation in 1953) show one aspect of Britten's art. The terrifying *The Turn of the Screw* and the underrated *Owen Wingrave* (both based on ghost stories by Henry James), *Billy Budd* (on Herman Melville's story of a young sailor falsely accused of treachery) and *Death in Venice* (after Thomas Mann's story) are darker and more introspective. Something close to classical restraint can be seen in *The Rape of Lucretia*.

Peter Grimes (1945) was Britten's first and, I believe, finest opera. It may even be his greatest work. With a libretto after Crabbe's poem, it explores a theme beloved of Britten: the outsider in society, persecuted by his fellows. It is the story of an enigmatic fisherman, Peter Grimes, whose actions give the inhabitants of his Suffolk village cause for suspicion and hatred. Ultimately, they hunt him down, believing him to have killed two apprentices. Grimes's reason snaps and he drowns himself. Britten's music is brilliant. The crowd

NOW LISTEN

▷Alban Berg, *Wozzeck*;
▷Frank Bridge, *Oration*;
▷Peter Maxwell Davies, *The Lighthouse*;
▷Henry Purcell, *Abdelazar*; ▷Dmitry Shostakovich, Symphony no. 14;
▷Michael Tippett, *A Midsummer Marriage*.

scenes, some of them violent, are hair-raising; the
character of Grimes is agonisingly drawn, the other
villagers sharply etched. The use of the orchestra is
masterly. Four 'Sea Interludes', played between key
scenes by the orchestra alone, vividly convey the story's
atmosphere and are often played as a group in concert
programmes. *Peter Grimes* is among the finest operas.

Britten was a natural composer for the voice, many
of his operatic roles and vocal works being conceived
for his companion, the tenor Peter Pears; among the
best known is the Serenade for tenor, horn and strings.
He wrote many splendid songs, notably the Thomas
Hardy cycle *Winter Words*, and made arrangements of
folksongs. His one ballet, The *Prince of the Pagodas*,
contains much colourful music and reflects Britten's
interest in Balinese music and instruments. His early
orchestral music includes the *Spring Symphony* (a joyous outpouring, with soloists and chorus), a lively Piano Concerto, a reflective Violin Concerto and *The
Young Person's Guide to the Orchestra*, written for a children's film (Britten wrote several pieces for children to
perform, too). His most famous contribution to the
cinema was the score for the Post Office documentary
Nightmail, which also included verses by W.H. Auden.
His large choral *War Requiem* (he was a pacifist), a
setting of the liturgical Latin text interleaved with
poems by Wilfred Owen, is extremely moving.

BRUCH, Max (1838–1920)
The fame of the German Max Bruch rests largely on a
single work, the Violin Concerto no. 1. Its popularity
with players and audience alike made him come to hate
it. He once wrote, wryly, that he would like to prohibit
its performance so that the public could hear some of
his other music. In fact, the concerto is probably his
finest composition. But there are felicities elsewhere
in his output. His other two violin concertos are far
from uninteresting: the *Scottish Fantasy* for violin and
orchestra contains some marvellous music, based on
traditional Scots airs (including 'Scots wha ha'e'), and
there's a fascinating Concerto for two pianos and
orchestra, fairly recently discovered, which should delight those who love romantic music (its main theme

NOW LISTEN

▷Johannes Brahms,
Piano Concerto no. 2;
▷Antonín Dvořák, Violin
Concerto; ▷Felix
Mendelssohn, Scottish
Symphony; ▷Charles
Villiers Stanford, *Irish
Symphony*.

was heard by Bruch on the island of Capri when he was watching a children's procession outside a church). Bruch's two symphonies are virtually ignored by concert planners, and that's a pity. They may reflect his admiration for ▷Brahms but are none the worse for that and are much too enjoyable to be gathering dust on library shelves. Cellists will always be grateful to Bruch for one work, the *Kol nidrei*, inspired by the opening prayer in the Jewish service marking the Day of Atonement (Yom Kippur).

BRUCKNER, Anton (1824–1896)
Anton Bruckner is frequently mentioned in the same breath as ▷Gustav Mahler, but the link is spurious. Bruckner and Mahler, it is true, each wrote nine numbered symphonies, all lengthy, substantial works. But where Mahler could be said to be concerned with Man and the human condition, Bruckner's music reflects his profound religious faith (he also wrote five masses and a *Te Deum*). Bruckner is not to everyone's taste: the symphonies, most important in his output, are unwieldy and, unless they are well conducted, can sound formless. But it's unfair to say (as some do) that a Bruckner symphony is simply a massive organ solo transferred to the orchestra; nor are the symphonies Wagner operas without the stage action. They belong to a great Austrian symphonic tradition and speak personally. Brucknerians have their favourite symphonies and may disagree when I recommend the third as the one with which to strike up an acquaintanceship with this somewhat misunderstood and misrepresented composer.

BUSONI, Ferruccio (1866–1924)
Ferruccio Busoni's music hasn't a very strong personality. At least, that is the reason usually given for its never having impinged greatly on the public's consciousness. But it has a devoted band of followers (to which I belong) that would probably be a lot bigger if it were played more frequently. Busoni's life was, to some extent, a tale of two nations: Italy, where he was born, and Germany where he lived and spent most of

NOW LISTEN
Franz Schmidt, Symphony no. 4; ▷Franz Schubert, Symphony no. 9; ▷Richard Wagner, *Parsifal*.

NOW LISTEN
▷Béla Bartók, Concerto for Orchestra; ▷Ludwig van Beethoven, Symphony no. 9, the 'Choral'; ▷Johannes Brahms, Piano Concerto no. 1; ▷Fryderyk

his life. His music reflects both. The opening movement of the gigantic Piano Concerto, for instance, sounds like what ▷Brahms might have written if he'd been sitting in the Mediterranean sun. (What a marvellous work this is: full of interest throughout its 70 minutes and culminating in a splendid finale which features a male chorus!) One of his most attractive compositions, the *Indian Fantasy*, uses Red Indian tunes and is scored for piano and orchestra (Busoni was fascinated by American Indian culture and there is an *Indian Diary* among his many works for solo piano). The opera *Arlecchino*, based on the exploits of Harlequin, Columbine and the other *commedia dell'arte* characters, is short and attractive. But it is Busoni's full-length opera *Doktor Faust* which is considered his masterpiece. Its treatment of the familiar Faust legend appeals to the head rather than to the heart but should not be ignored on that count. Another opera, *Turandot* (a reworking of Carlo Gozzi's play), contains a delightful musical 'clanger': just before a scene in the apartments of Turandot, the icy Chinese princess, the old English tune 'Greensleeves' appears; it seems Busoni found it in a book of lute music and thought it was a traditional Chinese air!

Chopin, 24 Preludes; ▷Giacomo Puccini, *Turandot*, ▷Peter Tchaikovsky, *Capriccio Italien*.

BYRD, William (1543–1623)
William Byrd was a survivor, in addition to being one of the foremost English composers of his time. He was a Roman Catholic at a time when that was not a good thing to be, and several times he was cited for failing to attend Anglican services. Moreover, Byrd was often in the law courts litigating over property. But he was liked by Queen Elizabeth and lived to old age. He wrote fine church music and many inventive pieces for the virginal (a small harpsichord with one keyboard), which are most enjoyable.

● The 20th-century British composer ▷Jacob wrote a *William Byrd Suite* for wind and brass instruments, based on several of Byrd's compositions for virginal.

CAGE, John (born 1912)

The works of the American composer John Cage are not for the faint-hearted. They're not even for people who have clear ideas about what music is. He is an experimenter. It was Cage who developed the 'prepared piano', a piano in which anything from rubber bands to carpenter's nails have been placed between the strings to alter the sound. It was Cage who offered the world the first piece of 'silent' music – *4'33"*, in which the performer makes no sound for that length of time and the 'music' is simply whatever sounds are provided by the environment. The titles of some of his other works suggest the diversity of his interests: *HPSCHD* for one to seven harpsichords and one to 51 tape machines; *Imaginary Landscape* no. 4 for 12 radios; *Speech* for five radios and newsreader; *0'00"* to be performed in any way by anyone. You may not enjoy Cage's music, but he cannot be ignored!

CANTELOUBE, Marie-Joseph (1879–1957)

Marie-Joseph Canteloube wrote several works, including an opera on the life of the Roman leader Vercingetorix. But today this French composer is remembered chiefly for his arrangement for voice and orchestra of songs from his native Auvergne. The singer is required to perform them in the original Auvergne dialect (which bears little resemblance to vernacular French!) Several, notably *Bailero* (which has been used for a television advertisement), have become very popular. Some may find Canteloube's orchestrations rich and fussy for such simple, peasant airs. But only a curmudgeon wouldn't sit back and surrender to their charm.

• Canteloube's teacher ▷d'Indy composed a *Symphony on a French Mountaineer's Song*, for piano and orchestra.

CARTER, Elliott (born 1908)
Elliott Carter, like ▷Copland, is both an American and an octogenarian, but their styles and contributions to music are quite dissimilar. Carter's music is grittier and more demanding than Copland's. Nor does he have the same compulsion to produce a recognisably 'American' sound. If you are prepared to get to grips with Carter's individual and powerful musical language, you will be rewarded. The ballet *The Minotaur* is the easiest of his scores to tackle: dramatic, dark music underlining the Greek myth of Theseus and his adventures in the labyrinth. His Variations for Orchestra, the Piano Concerto and the Double Concerto for harpsichord, piano and two chamber orchestras are contenders for the next stage. The string quartets, certainly among the finest since ▷Bartók's, are for those who have a firm hold of Carter's other pieces. But all ears and perceptions are different – maybe they're the works to start with . . .

CASTELNUOVO-TEDESCO, Mario (1895–1968)
The Italian Mario Castelnuovo-Tedesco is probably best known to guitarists and devotees of that instrument. His pieces for guitar are admirably suited to it and often performed by its leading practitioners. The enchanting Guitar Concerto, which he wrote in 1939, was first played by the great Segovia and popularised by him over the next 20 years. This most approachable composer wrote much other music, including operas based on Shakespeare's *All's Well that Ends Well* and *The Merchant of Venice* (he also wrote overtures to several of the Bard's other plays). His Second Violin Concerto was espoused by Heifetz, who made an exciting

recording of it; its sub-title is 'The Prophets' and it was composed in the USA shortly after Castelnuovo-Tedesco had settled there in 1939 after fleeing from persecution in Italy. The work proclaims his Jewish roots in a rather lush manner: those familiar with the music for Hollywood biblical epics will relish it.

---

* Other enjoyable guitar concertos have been written by ▷Arnold, ▷Dodgson, ▷Previn and Rodrigo.

CAVALLI, Pietro Francesco (1602–1676)
Pietro Francesco Cavalli wrote nearly 30 operas for opera houses in Venice. He also held appointments at St Mark's, Venice, composing much religious music for its singers. Cavalli didn't have the dramatic instincts or strengths of his near-contemporary, the great ▷Monteverdi. But his operas, usually about amorous intrigues and involving disguises and mistaken identities, are immensely enjoyable. The best of Cavalli's operas is probably *Calisto*, which tells how a princess becomes a star in the heavens. The scores of Cavalli's operas give the vocal line and only an outline of the accompaniment, and some of them have been 'fleshed out' by the conductor Raymond Leppard who has prepared performing versions; these have been criticised as over-elaborate, but the revival of interest in Cavalli's music is largely due to Leppard's advocacy.

NOW LISTEN ▷
▷Gaetano Donizetti, *L'élisir d'amore*; ▷Pietro Mascagni, *L'amico Fritz*; ▷Giacomo Puccini, *Gianni Schicchi*; ▷Gioachino Rossini, *Le comte Ory*; ▷Giuseppe Verdi, *Falstaff*.

CHABRIER, Emmanuel (1841–1894)
Not many composers have ever been as enthusiastically admired and loved by their fellows as Emmanuel Chabrier. ▷Debussy and ▷Ravel were only two who hailed him as a genius and the most imaginative talent in France for decades. Ironically, for much of his life he was a part-time composer. He was a civil servant with the French Ministry of the Interior, and only late in life devoted all his time to music. Today we know him best for two short orchestral pieces – *España*, ar-

NOW LISTEN ▷
▷Jean Françaix, Concertino for piano and orchestra; ▷André Messager, *Véronique*; ▷Francis Poulenc, *Le bestiaire*; ▷Maurice Ravel, *L'heure*

guably the best piece of Spanish music not from Spain, and the *Joyeuse Marche*, a brilliantly carefree showpiece. But Chabrier's finest music is in a pair of entertaining operas. *L'étoile* is about an eccentric monarch who likes to execute someone on his birthday, just to cheer up his court. *Le roi malgré lui* ('The King in spite of himself') is about another ruler who discovers a plot against him, disguises himself, mingles with the conspirators and beats them at their own game. Chabrier's music flows and sparkles like a stream in the sunlight. One marvellous tune follows another with apparent ease and the listener waits eagerly for the next one. (In fact, Chabrier confessed to finding composition a trial – 'like giving birth to an infant', was how he put it.) His compositions are full of a commodity rarely found in music: genuine, unforced wit. They are the work of a man in love with music and with life. His piano pieces, notably the charming *Pièces pittoresques* (of which four were orchestrated as Suite Pastorale), and his many songs, which include a charmer called *Villanelle des petits canards* ('Villanelle of the Little Ducks') should be sought out and devoured.

espagnole; ▷Nino Rota, *The Italian Straw Hat.*

CHARPENTIER, Gustave (1860–1956)

The French composer Gustave Charpentier brought the working class and its problems to opera, in a manner of speaking. The heroine of his opera *Louise* stays with her family in the poor quarter of Paris. She's in love with a poet, but her parents don't approve. When they forbid her to see him, she goes to live with him. The opera raised many eyebrows in 1900 because it was blatantly permissive and the first opera to concern itself with women's liberation. Nevertheless, *Louise* was a great success. It's still staged and in Paris alone it has notched up well over 1000 performances since its première. It was the opera, incidentally, that launched the career of the Scottish soprano Mary Garden. She took over the role of Louise midway through a performance, without rehearsal, and saved the show, becoming the toast of Paris and a star overnight. (▷Debussy later gave the role of Mélisande in his opera *Pelléas et Mélisande* to her.) Charpentier tried to emulate his success with a sequel to *Louise* called *Julien*, using some of the same characters, but if failed. Though he lived a very long life, he never achieved another winner. He did, however, busy himself with good works. Charpentier set up a conservatory where working girls could go for free tuition in singing, acting and dancing.

- Another French composer named Charpentier (Marc-Antoine, 1640s–1704) was no relation. He wrote 17 operas, all well received even at a time when the star of ▷Lully was in the ascendant. Charpentier worked for a time with Molière and his theatre company and became master of music to the Jesuits in Paris, for whom he wrote much distinguished church music.

CHAUSSON, Ernest (1855–99)

The French composer Ernest Chausson studied law but found the lure of music too strong. His talent as a composer was not enormous. But anyone who enjoys the music of ▷Franck, who taught Chausson, will enjoy the Symphony in B flat, Chausson's major achievement. Its last movement has a fine, big tune that stays in the memory (this part of the work also sees Chausson moving towards the sound-world of ▷Debussy). His *Poème de l'amour et de la mer* ('Poem of Love and the Sea') for voice and orchestra is worth its occasional airings, and lovers of musical curiosities will relish the Concerto for violin, piano and string quartet, which is quite beguiling. Chausson was once described as 'a man with iris eyes which do not smile'. That may hold good for the man, but not for his melodies, which smile very often.

CHÁVEZ, Carlos (1899–1978)

If any Mexican composer is known to the world at large, it is Carlos Chávez, whose music is strongly nationalistic, making great use of the characteristics of

Mexican Indian melodies, without actually quoting them. (An exception is the *Sinfonia india* which is a highly-coloured, immensely exciting score based on traditional tunes.) It's not hard to get on Chávez's musical wavelength. His scores are in a modern idiom but readily acceptable and often very sophisticated. The American composer ▷Copland said: 'There is nothing of the Mexican *peon* about Chavez. His music knows its own mind'.

The substantial Piano Concerto is one of Chávez's most inspired creations in which the piano and orchestra are equal partners. This is not a showpiece during which a star soloist can exhibit his brilliance at the keyboard. There are long stretches when he is silent. But the overall effect is compelling and almost hypnotic. The nocturne-like slow movement has great atmospheric beauty (and frequently suggests ▷Bartók's piano concertos). Chávez's Piano Concerto, like that of ▷Bliss, is a work that would make a welcome change from the staple fare that monopolises our concert-platforms. Chávez's six symphonies are all, in their different ways, typical of his style. There's a highly original ballet called *Horse Power* about the machines that surround us and threaten our peace of mind; and another called *The Daughter of Colchis* (that is, Medea) contains some memorable music, notably a sarabande for strings which has the beauty and tranquillity of ▷Bach.

> **NOW LISTEN** ▷
>
> ▷Aaron Copland, *El salón Mexico*; ▷Alberto Ginastera, Concertante Variations; ▷Constant Lambert, *The Rio Grande*; ▷Darius Milhaud, *Saudades do Brasil*; Silvestre Reveultas, *Sensemaya*; ▷Heitor Villa-Lobos, Harp Concerto.

CHERUBINI, Luigi (1760–1842)

It's one of the twists of musical fate that we don't often get the chance to see the operas of Luigi Cherubini. In his day, the appearance of a new one was a major event. Perhaps the finest of them is *Medea*, which takes a powerful hold on the old Greek tale of jealousy and matricide. But the one that encouraged ▷Beethoven to compose his only opera was *Les deux journées* (known in English as 'The Water Carrier'). It has a dramatic 'rescue' plot not unlike that of Beethoven's *Fidelio*. Cherubini, who was born in Italy and lived most of his life in Paris, wrote a single symphony. It looks back to the style of ▷Haydn, though it nods a few times in the direction of newer ideas, and is utterly delightful.

CHILDREN'S CORNER
▷Béla Bartók, *For Children*
▷Benjamin Britten, *The Young Person's Guide to the Orchestra*
▷Claude Debussy, *Children's Corner*
▷Gabriel Fauré, *Dolly*
▷Francis Poulenc, *Story of Babar, the Little Elephant*
▷Sergey Prokofiev, *Peter and the Wolf*
▷John Rutter, *Brother Heinrich's Christmas*.

CHOPIN, Fryderyk (1810–1849)
The Victorians didn't do much for Fryderyk Chopin. They fostered the idea that he was a pallid poet of the keyboard, dying of consumption and languishing in drawing-rooms, with ladies dancing attendance. The image persisted into this century, not helped by Hollywood. (You may recall that luckless actor Cornel Wilde coughing blood on to a snow-white keyboard!) In fact, Chopin was much more the innovator, the intrepid seeker, unafraid to go where none had gone before in music. His works were ahead of their time, baffling to some of his contemporaries, and explored the piano in new ways. The music is intensely personal, sometimes almost painfully so. But it communicates readily and retains its freshness even after years of familiarity.

Chopin's two piano concertos are heard in the concert hall regularly. These are not mere showpieces – their content is substantial – and the orchestral writing is more interesting than many writers would have us believe. The last two of the three piano sonatas are strong, exciting statements. (The B flat minor contains

NOW LISTEN ▷
▷Johann Sebastian Bach, *The Well-tempered Clavier*, or '48'; ▷Vincenzo Bellini, *La sonnambula*; ▷John Field, nocturnes; ▷Johann Nepomuk Hummel, piano sonatas; ▷Felix Mendelssohn, Piano Concerto no. 1; ▷Wolfgang Amadeus Mozart, *Don Giovanni*.

the celebrated funeral march and a finale that lasts just over a minute which could have been written this century. (▷Schumann, normally an admirer of Chopin, declared: 'This isn't music!') The waltzes contain some of Chopin's most popular music (including the so-called 'Minute Waltz' which can scarcely be played in 60 seconds). The études conjure up a wide variety of moods; among them is the 'Revolutionary Study' said to be Chopin's reaction to Polish persecution by the Russians. Only two of the polonaises are well known: the other eight are worth investigating. Perhaps the best of Chopin is to be found in the mazurkas, based on a Polish dance-form; some are reflective and very moving. The nocturnes contain many of Chopin's most arresting and overtly beautiful ideas; the four scherzos, sardonic and adventurous, carry on from ▷Beethoven: the ballades are simply poems in music. The little *Berceuse*, or cradle song, is among Chopin's most enchanting creations.

The 24 Preludes (1839), one in each key and composed as a tribute to ▷Bach, make up a single work typical of Chopin. They are, by turns, bright and brilliant, dark and haunting, poetic and dramatic, and charming. The most substantial, nicknamed the 'Raindrop' comes midway through the set and is said to have been suggested by rain dripping through the roof of the house in Majorca in which Chopin and George Sand, with whom he was allegedly having an affair, were staying. The final prelude is positively cataclysmic, leaving a disturbing impression.

Two ballets have been created using Chopin's music, *Les sylphides* (1907) and *A Month in the Country*, based on Turgenev's play (1976).

CHRISTMAS MUSIC

Christmas has always been a time for music – from the earliest days when carols were danced rather than sung. The felicities of Yuletide have encouraged composers to write many splendid hymns – notably ▷Mendelssohn's 'Hark, the herald angels sing'. Some of the loveliest Christmas music is to be found in ▷Johann Sebastian Bach's *Christmas Oratorio* and in ▷Handel's *Messiah* (whose purely orchestral 'Pastoral' is said to have been inspired by a movement in ▷Corelli's '*Christmas Concerto*'). In more recent times, ▷Messiaen has contributed an organ masterpiece for Christmas, *La Nativité du Seigneur* ('The Birth of Our Lord'), and ▷Benjamin Britten's *Ceremony of Carols* has become popular. Several operas have Christmas backgrounds: ▷Puccini's *La bohème* begins on Christmas Eve – and *Christmas Eve* is the title of a fairy-tale opera by ▷Rimsky-Korsakov. ▷Menotti's *Amahl and the Night Visitors* revolves around the Three Kings on their way to the stable at Bethlehem. Tchaikovsky's ballet *The Nutcracker* takes place during a Christmas party at which an unruly mob of boys and girls turns a family household upside-down. The commercialisation of Christmas over the years has led to a rash of pretty appalling songs – of which 'Rudolph the Red-nosed Reindeer' is probably the best, and 'I saw Mummy kissing Santa Claus' the worst.

CILEA, Francesco (1866–1950)

The Italian composer Francesco Cilea had the misfortune to be writing his operas at the same time as ▷Puccini was producing his very successful ones. Nevertheless, two of Cilea's works for the theatre are highly enjoyable and full of the kind of melodies in which people love to wallow. *Adriana Lecouvreur* is the story of a great actress who dies after inhaling poison from a bouquet sent to her by a rival in love (Agatha Christie would have loved such a plot!). *L'arlesiana* is based on the same play for which ▷Bizet wrote incidental music: a young man is torn between his childhood sweetheart and a *femme fatale* and chooses suicide. Anyone who isn't familiar with Cilea's music should try Adriana Lecouvreur's marvellous Act 1 aria, in which she outlines what it means to be an actress. Cilea stopped writing music halfway through his life and devoted himself to teaching.

CIMAROSA, Domenico (1749–1801)

The Italian Domenico Cimarosa wrote more than 60 operas and in his day was often compared with ▷Mozart. Some of the lighter elements in his writing,

NOW LISTEN ▷

Some operas by other composers who came under Puccini's shadow: ▷Umberto Giordano, *Andrea Chenier*; ▷Ruggero Leoncavallo, *Pagliacci*, ▷Pietro Mascagni, *L'amico Fritz*; ▷Riccardo Zandonai, *Francesca da Rimini*.

notably in *Il matrimonio segreto*, ('The Secret Marriage'), his masterpiece, make the comparison understandable. But Cimarosa never aspired to the emotional depths of Mozart. Only in the non-operatic Requiem do we find a tougher, more serious composer capable of plumbing a few depths. Cimarosa, like ▷Verdi, was a political animal, and his republican sympathies caused him to be arrested and sentenced to death. But he was reprieved and died in Venice soon afterwards.

● Other comic operas by Italians include ▷Donizetti's *Don Pasquale*, ▷Rossini's *La Cenerentola* ('Cinderella') and ▷Verdi's *Un giorno di regno* ('King for a Day').

CLARINET
The clarinet is the mellowest of the woodwind instruments, capable of long, sustained and sinuous phrases or highly effective, lively leaps (jazz musicians have exploited both qualities in their improvisations). The one most commonly used is pitched in B flat. Some fine concertos have been composed for the clarinet – by ▷Copland, ▷Finzi, ▷Mozart, ▷Nielsen and ▷Weber among others. ▷Stravinsky's *Ebony Concerto* takes its name from the clarinet's nickname in the jazz world, 'ebony stick'. ▷Brahms composed a beautiful quintet for clarinet and strings. One of the longest (and loveliest) solos written for the instrument in the orchestral repertory is at the start of the slow movement of ▷Rakhmaninov's Second Symphony.

The E flat clarinet is smaller and higher in pitch and capable of sounding piercing and hysterical as it does in ▷Richard Strauss's tone poem *Till Eulenspiegel* (where it represents the luckless Till pleading with his captors not to be led to the scaffold). The bass clarinet, much bigger and deeper in pitch than its fellows, may be heard bubbling away in Stravinsky's *The Rite of Spring* and ▷Gershwin's *Rhapsody in Blue*.

CLEMENTI, Muzio (1752–1832)

Muzio Clementi was an Italian virtuoso pianist and composer roundly criticised by ▷Mozart and much admired by ▷Beethoven. He made many concert tours and it was on one of these that he took part in a famous contest with Mozart, to determine who was better at improvising and sight-reading at the piano. Clementi wrote many sonatas which became models for several composers (including Beethoven) and he did more than anyone else to develop the possibilities of the piano, still a relatively new instrument, becoming a piano manufacturer. Clementi's collection of 100 pieces for the piano, *Gradus ad Parnassum*, remains a foundation-stone for piano technique. His most distinguished pupil was the Irishman John Field, who first used the term 'nocturne' for a particular kind of reflective piano piece. Clementi's music makes good listening, not merely for its own sake but also because of the influences it exerted on others.

COATES, Eric (1886–1957)

The Englishman Eric Coates considered he was paid his finest compliment by the formidable woman composer Dame Ethel Smyth. When she was introduced to him, she said: 'Ah yes. The man who writes tunes!'. Coates did, indeed, write tunes, for more than half a century. Good ones, which caused him to be respected as the father of British light music. No less a person than ▷Elgar wore out a record of Coates's concert suite *Summer Days*. His early years as a viola player in Sir Henry Wood's orchestra gave him a useful insight into writing for the different orchestral instruments and his scoring is often described as 'exemplary'. Because most of Coates's melodies are instantly memorable and can be readily whistled, the BBC used some as signature tunes for radio programmes during and after World War II. The march 'Knightsbridge' from the suite *London* introduced the popular programme 'In Town Tonight', *Calling all Workers* was played every morning before 'Music While You Work', and *By a Sleepy Lagoon* is still the prelude to 'Desert Island Discs'. When the BBC wanted a piece to mark the opening of television in Britain, it was to Coates they turned. His march for the 1954 film *The Dam Busters* is probably his most popular piece today. His most ambitious work was the *Saxo-Rhapsody*, written in 1937 for the distinguished saxophonist Sigurd Rascher (who recorded it with Coates conducting). It conveys the nature of the instrument well and makes absorbing listening.

● Some of ▷Elgar's lighter pieces (such as the *Chanson de matin*) influenced Coates. Other light-music composers include Robert Farnon, Ron Goodwin and ▷Ketelbey.

COLERIDGE-TAYLOR, Samuel (1875–1912)

Samuel Coleridge-Taylor was the first black composer to attain international eminence. He was the son of a doctor from Sierra Leone and an English woman, and showed promise as a musician from early boyhood. Before he was 20, he was attracting the attention of celebrated British composers like ▷Elgar, ▷Sullivan and ▷Parry. One of his earliest successes is also the work by which he is best remembered – *Hiawatha's Wedding Feast*, based on the verses by Henry Longfellow describing the life and times of an American Red Indian. In the years before World War II, it was performed more often in Britain than any other choral work apart from ▷Handel's *Messiah*. Since then, its star has faded. But the occasional recent performance has shown it to have lost none of the freshness and spontaneity for which it was welcomed in 1898. The tenor aria 'Onaway! Awake, beloved' is as affecting as it is beautifully conceived.

Coleridge-Taylor went on to set more of Longfellow's verses in *The Death of Minnehaha* and *Hiawatha's Departure*, but they failed to make an impact. His purely orchestral music includes the *Petite suite de concert* which has always been a favourite and has assumed the status of a light music 'classic'. *The Bamboula*, based on a West Indian dance, and the Symphonic Variations on an African Air reflect his black heritage.

CONTRALTO

The contralto voice is the lowest female voice. Many singers who call themselves contraltos are, in fact, mezzo-sopranos. The black American Marian Anderson was a genuine contralto. So were the British singers Dame Clara Butt, Kathleen Ferrier, and Gladys Ripley. The male countertenor voice has some of the same qualities as the contralto. The British countertenor James Bowman is one of the finest today. ▷Britten uses a countertenor for the role of Oberon in his opera *A Midsummer Night's Dream* to give the character an other-wordly quality. Countertenors now often sing the operatic roles that in ▷Handel's time and earlier were written for castrati, whose high vocal ranges had been preserved through surgical intervention.

COPLAND, Aaron (born 1900)

When Aaron Copland introduced his Organ Symphony to the American people, a famous conductor of the day declared: 'If he can write like that at 23, in five years he'll be ready to commit murder!' Another critic talked of it 'screaming like a banshee'. Since then, of course, Copland has become the Grand Old Man of music in the USA and people have become attuned to his own highly original style. Even so, the Organ Symphony is still not the best work with which to approach Copland: one should start with the ballets. *Appalachian Spring* with its homely, folksy atmosphere; *Billy the Kid* with an orchestral representation of a gun-fight, as well as of a Wild West town having a ghastly shindig to celebrate the death of a wretched boy; and *Rodeo* in which a cowgirl invades a male sport and beats the boys at their own game. *El salón Mexico*, too, is very approachable, being a tourist's eye-view of a dance-hall in Mexico City; and the Clarinet Concerto, written for and marvellously recorded by the jazzman Benny Goodman, is inspiring. Copland's invigorating film music is at its most attractive in *The Red Pony*, a gentle tale of a boy growing up.

The Symphony no. 3 (1946) is arguably Copland's most impressive work which the composer hoped would stop him being labelled 'folk-inspired' or 'jazz-based'. It was written for the great conductor Serge

NOW LISTEN ▷

Other works commissioned or first performed by the conductor Serge Koussevitzky: ▷Samuel Barber, Cello Concerto; ▷Béla Bartók, Concerto for Orchestra; ▷Benjamin Britten, *Peter Grimes*; ▷Roy Harris, Symphony no. 3.

Koussevitzky and the Boston Symphony Orchestra
and reflects a time of war. As Copland has pointed out,
it was not intended to be a description of the conflicts
of World War II but rather an expression of 'general
sentiments'. The most unusual feature of this strong
work is in the last movement which incorporates a
complete statement of one of Copland's most popular
works, the *Fanfare for the Common Man*. For some, this
smacks rather too much of the grand gesture. But
Copland has never been afraid of such gestures and
they are a part of his musical make-up. The Symphony
no. 3 sees him in full flight and unstoppable.

Copland has also written some memorable chamber
music (notably a tough but interesting Piano Quartet),
works for solo piano (the Variations are typical), ten
Old American Songs and settings of 12 Poems of Emily Dickinson, and an opera *The Tender Land*. (This
unpretentious tale of love on the range was once dis-
paragingly described as an up-market *Oklahoma*.)

COR ANGLAIS
The cor anglais, or English horn, is a woodwind in-
strument, larger than the oboe but of the same type. Its
sound is deeper and richer. Many composers have
used it to create an atmosphere of longing or nostalgia.
It plays the big tune in the slow movement of
▷Dvořák's 'New World' Symphony and represents
the swan in the tone poem *The Swan of Tuonela* by
▷Sibelius (a swan sings only once, just before it dies).
▷Franck exploited the colour of the cor anglais most
effectively in the second movement of his Symphony.
There is a lovely Chamber Concerto by ▷Honegger
for cor anglais, flute and strings.

CORELLI, Arcangelo (1653–1713)
The three-score years of the Italian Arcangelo Corelli
knew no hardship. He was born into an affluent family,
had a spectacularly successful career as a violinist and
composer and died a wealthy man with an unusually
fine art collection. In many ways, his music reflects his
life: it is able to touch the emotions but does not suggest any agony of body or soul. The so-called 'Christ-

mas Concerto' is among his most attractively memorable works; its Pastorale section is thought to have provided ▷Handel with the inspiration for the Pastoral Symphony in his oratorio *Messiah*. ▷Bach's famous Brandenburg Concertos were influenced by Corelli's concerti grossi, 12 masterpieces that helped shape the future of orchestral music.

COUPERIN, François (1668–1733)

François Couperin came from a family of distinguished French musicians and because he was its most successful member, he became known as 'Couperin le Grand'. He held a special position at the court of Louis XIV and had to provide new music for the monarch every Sunday. Not surprisingly, he was a prolific composer. Couperin's greatest contribution to posterity was his harpsichord music and his treatise on playing the instrument. The pieces are well worth investigating, as are his organ solos. Couperin's church music is immensely dignified and enjoyable. Don't ignore, either, the small number of chamber works he composed. His sense of humour is often revealed in his music, but nowhere more effectively than in pieces he composed in the style of ▷Corelli and ▷Lully.

- In the 20th century ▷Ravel demonstrated his admiration of Couperin in his piano suite *Le tombeau de Couperin* and ▷Richard Strauss orchestrated some of Couperin's harpsichord pieces in his *Dance Suite*.

COWARD, Sir Noel (1899–1973)

Noel Coward could almost be described as the Oscar Wilde of the musical theatre: a brilliant wit who wrote shows and revues, fitting his own usually acerbic words to catchy tunes. His finest achievement, the musical *Bittersweet*, is an unashamed tear-jerker tracing the life of a young girl who runs away with her singing teacher. Its many hits include 'I'll see you again', 'Tokay', 'Zigeuner', 'If love were all' and 'Dear little café'.

Many of Coward's cabaret songs have become classics, notably *Mad Dogs and Englishmen* and *Don't put
your daughter on the stage, Mrs Worthington* (no-one can
sing these ditties with quite the same dry malice as
Coward himself. Happily, his performances are on
record).

- In present times, the most successful composer
  for the musical theatre who also writes his own
  lyrics is ▷Sondheim.

DALLAPICCOLA, Luigi (1904–1975)

Luigi Dallapiccola was the first Italian to use the 12-note method of composition devised by ▷Schoenberg. Yet the heritage of his native land (which had given us ▷Verdi and ▷Puccini) can be traced in his writing, which is often lyrical. His operas contain some of his best music, notably *Volo di notte* ('Night Flight'), about the tensions and anxieties in an airport control room when a plane is badly overdue. *Il prigioniero* ('The Prisoner') underlines Dallapiccola's hatred of fascism and constant striving for political freedom. The opera revolves round a prisoner who manages to break out of his cell only to discover his 'escape' has been arranged by his captors. He has been submitted to the torture of hope.

NOW LISTEN ▷

▷Ludwig van Beethoven, *Fidelio*; ▷Alban Berg, *Lulu Suite*; ▷Arnold Schoenberg, Variations op.31; ▷Anton Webern, Concerto op.24.

DEBUSSY, Claude (1862–1918)

Whenever the term 'French impressionism' is used of music, the name that comes immediately to mind is that of Claude Debussy. In a sense it describes what he was trying to create: 'a halo of sound' were his own words. The term, however, shouldn't obscure the fact that Debussy composed precisely and calculated his effects carefully. His music is not, or should not be, a wash of sound, hazy and blurred. It benefits from being played luminously, but clearly and accurately. The *Prélude à l'après-midi d'un faune* is one of his most frequently played orchestral works, a shimmering, languorous piece with a long opening flute

NOW LISTEN ▷

▷Manuel de Falla, *Homage to Debussy*; ▷Olivier Messiaen, *Les offrandes oubliées*; ▷Giacomo Puccini, *La Fanciulla del West* ('The Girl of the Golden West'); ▷Igor Stravinsky, *The Firebird*.

solo of exquisite line. *La Mer*, a sound picture of the sea in all its moods, captivates audiences with its electrifying scoring; the *Nocturnes*, representing clouds, a bustling festival and sirens luring sailors to their doom, are heavily atmospheric. The *Images* include a long musical portrait of Spain and a piece based on the old Northumbrian song *The Keel Row*.

Debussy's considerable body of fine piano music includes two of his most popular pieces, *Clair de lune*, a limpid evocation of moonlight, and *The Golliwog's Cakewalk* (part of the *Children's Corner* Suite written for his daughter). The two books of preludes contain a wide variety of pieces; best known are the exquisite little *La fille aux cheveux de lin* ('The Girl with the Flaxen Hair') and *La cathédrale engloutie*, the description of a church, now underwater, whose bells still sound as the waves disturb them.

The opera *Pelléas et Mélisande* (1902) is considered Debussy's greatest achievement. It takes a story similar to ▷Wagner's *Tristan und Isolde*, which he loved, but uses musical techniques quite unlike Wagner's. It is based on a play by Maurice Maeterlinck which has a plot as enigmatic and strange as any that has been given musical treatment. The prince Golaud marries Mélisande without knowing anything about her. Soon she becomes attracted to his half-brother, Pelléas. The succeeding events are the result of Golaud's fearsome jealousy (there is a chilling sequence in which he uses his child by a former marriage to spy on Mélisande). Debussy's music is superbly, magically coloured. But it is always subtle and restrained. He does not offer the singers 'arias' as such: the vocal writing is declamatory, after the manner of speech, yet it always sounds lyrical. *Pelléas* is unforgettable even on disc but especially in a good production in the opera house.

Other interesting works by Debussy include the String Quartet, a number of songs and a Rhapsody for saxophone and orchestra. The ballet *Jeux* ('Games'), a mysteriously attractive and forward-looking score, is concerned with a love match (in the romantic sense) during a tennis game. The early *Petite suite* for piano duet, later orchestrated by Henri Büsser, is perhaps Debussy's most approachable work.

• Other music inspired by Maeterlinck's *Pelléas et Mélisande* is by ▷Fauré, ▷Schoenberg and ▷Sibelius.

DELIBES, Léo (1836–1891)
Ballet-lovers have reason to be grateful to the Frenchman Léo Delibes: he composed *Coppélia*, a guaranteed success for any dance company. It's the story of a village girl who plays a trick on an old doll maker, and the music helps greatly in the telling of it. The Mazurka is the best-known tune from the score, but it's only one of many. Especially appealing is the amusing and imaginative music which accompanies the automatons when they are activated in the toyshop. Delibes wrote another ballet, *Sylvia*, which is peopled by gods and goddesses, nymphs and shepherds. The score (which includes the famous 'pizzicato' dance, ridiculed by generations of comedians) is strong and parts of it are regularly heard in a concert suite.

In my view, however, Delibes surpassed both these with his opera *Lakmé* (1883). It's set in India and concerns the love of a priestess for a British soldier; she saves his life but he leaves her and she commits suicide by eating the leaf of a poisonous plant. Not for nothing has the piece been described as an Indian *Madam Butterfly*. The music is meltingly lovely, full of melodies which should be heard as often as those in ▷Bizet's *Carmen*. The heroine's celebrated Bell Song, which includes several stratospheric notes, is exciting but not typical of the score; try, instead, the love-duet from Act 1.

DELIUS, Frederick (1862–1934)
Frederick Delius might have been a businessman in the wool trade in Yorkshire. His German father wanted that. Instead, he became a remarkable composer. People tend either to love or to loathe his music. It is sometimes criticised for having no shape or form. It has both, but its shapes and forms are unlike anyone else's. While others tend to make strong gestures in

NOW LISTEN ▷

Other operas in which the heroine takes her own life: ▷Leos Janáček, *Katya Kabanova*; ▷Amilcare Ponchielli, *La Gioconda*; ▷Giacomo Puccini, *Tosca* and *Madame Butterfly*; ▷Henry Purcell, *Dido and Aeneas*; ▷Giuseppe Verdi, *Il trovatore*; ▷Richard Wagner, *Der Fliegende Holländer* ('The Flying Dutchman').

NOW LISTEN ▷

▷Percy Grainger, *Two Hill Songs*; ▷Edvard Grieg, Norwegian Folk Tunes; ▷Richard Strauss, *Also sprach*

their scores, Delius preferred to rhapsodise. It is the sheer beauty of the sound he creates that has won him his followers. The gateway to his music is provided by such orchestral pieces as *On Hearing the First Cuckoo in Spring*, *In a Summer Garden*, and *Brigg Fair*. The Piano Concerto and the elusive but lovely Violin Concerto are less easily assimilated. His biggest concert work, *A Mass of Life* (with a text drawn from Nietzsche's *Also sprach Zarathustra*), is to be tackled only when a sympathy for the Delian style has been established.

Delius wrote several operas, the best of which is *A Village Romeo and Juliet* (1901). Here, the 'star-crossed lovers' are Sali and Vreli, whose fathers fight over a strip of farm land. The ensuing court action ruins both men but their children continue to see each other. Eventually, Sali and Vreli decide that life holds nothing for them; they make a suicide pact and drown themselves. The opera is difficult (but not impossible) to stage: it calls for the two fathers to be ploughing in the opening scene and a barge must sink in view of the audience in the final scene. But the glorious music makes the effort of solving such problems well worthwhile. The most famous sequence from the score is the orchestral 'Walk to the Paradise Garden', during which Sali and Vreli, hand in hand, stroll through the woods and fields to an old inn. It represents Delius, a poet of the orchestra, at his most eloquent.

Other works by Delius include *Paris: The Song of a Great City*, *Appalachia* (a product of a spell the composer spent growing oranges in Florida), *A Song of Summer* and the wistful little dance *La Calinda*. Some incidental music that Delius wrote for a production of Flecker's drama *Hassan* is colourful and atmospheric, and the songs and chamber music provide a fascinating contrast to his orchestral fare.

Zarathustra; ▷Peter Warlock, Serenade for Delius on his 60th Birthday.

- Sir Thomas Beecham, who was Delius's most vigorous champion, made many records of his music and they are still to be preferred to any others.

DOHNÁNYI, Ernö (1877–1960)

The Hungarian composer Ernö Dohnányi used the tune we sing to the children's rhyme *Twinkle, Twinkle, Little Star* as the basis of his Variations on a Nursery Song, which is among the wittiest and most attractive of 20th-century works for piano and orchestra. In the silence that follows a long and portentous orchestral introduction, the piano suddenly introduces the simple melody and the stage is set for a delicious sequence of fun and games. Dohnányi's friends and contemporaries were ▷Bartók and ▷Kodály, but his own style is much less advanced and certainly less nationalistic. Dohnányi reminds us more of ▷Brahms or ▷Liszt, or even ▷Wagner, but creates his own distinctive sound.

Dohnányi was a brilliant pianist. Unfortunately his large-scale Piano Concert no. 1 is a sadly neglected work. It is an unmistakable manifestation of his respect for Brahms – an admiration that was mutual. When Brahms first heard Dohnányi's Piano Quintet, he declared: 'I could not have composed it better myself'. The Suite in F sharp minor used to be played much more often that it is now: I recall hearing it in the concert hall several times as a boy. It is worth reviving. So is the suite *Ruralia hungarica*, which suggests more of Dohnányi's native land than any of his other pieces. The ballet *The Veil of Pierrette* contains a Viennese waltz which is among the best of light music. Dohnányi's piano pieces include some especially fine rhapsodies.

NOW LISTEN ⟩

Johann Sebastian Bach, Passacaglia and Fugue in C minor for organ; ▷Johannes Brahms, Piano Concerto no. 2; ▷Antontin Dvořák, *Scherzo capriccioso*; ▷Ferenc Liszt, Piano Concerto no. 2.

DOUBLE BASS

The double bass is the largest of the string instruments used in the orchestra today. Its deep and sometimes gruff sound can be used for comic effect: it represents the elephant in the *The Carnival of the Animals* by ▷Saint-Saëns. But its powerful qualities are exploited by ▷Beethoven in the Scherzo of his Symphony no. 5 and ▷Mahler used it to create a strangely bleak picture at the start of the slow movement of his Symphony no. 1. The instrument's many facets can be heard in a particularly entertaining Double Bass Concerto by the 18th-century German composer Karl Ditters von Dittersdorf.

DONIZETTI, Gaetano (1797–1848)
Because the Italian composer Gaetano Donizetti composed numerous operas – around 70 – most of them at great speed, he had for many years a reputation for superficiality. Some of the operas are, indeed, lightweight and rely on a star soprano to give them any real credibility. But in recent years there has been a reappraisal of Donizetti's achievements and he has come to be recognised as a leading opera composer – as, indeed, he was in his own day. His Walter Scott-inspired tragedy *Lucia di Lammermoor* (with its virtuoso Mad Scene for the heroine and a memorable sextet) and *Maria Stuarda* point the way to ▷ Verdi (who, in his early days, was not averse to borrowing musical ideas from Donizetti). *La favorite*, too, is strong stuff, about a novice monk's disastrous love for a noblewoman. It's Donizetti's gift for comedy, though, that endears him to us most. *L'elisir d'amore* ('The Love Potion') is the deliciously funny tale of a simple-minded youth who enlists the help of a quack doctor to win the heart of a village maiden. *Don Pasquale* revolves round an ageing Lothario who marries a pert young thing and lives to regret it. The music for these operas ranges from the ear-tickling, in the comic patter-songs, to the warmly lyrical in the love-songs. The chorus is used with point and economy.

- Two stage works which also involve the disastrous effects of a love potion are ▷Britten's *A Midsummer Night's Dream* and ▷Sullivan's *The Sorcerer*.

DUKAS, Paul (1865–1935)
It would be easy to dismiss the Frenchman Paul Dukas as a single-work composer. The only one heard with any regularity is the masterly orchestral scherzo *L'apprenti sorcier* ('The Sorcerer's Apprentice'), the amusing tale of a trainee magician who creates havoc when he uses spells to help him with the housework. The chuckling bassoon tune which runs through the work will be familiar to most listeners. (The score provided Walt Disney with some of his best material for

NOW LISTEN ▷

Works which also explore, in different ways, the Bluebeard legend: ▷Béla Bartók, *Duke Bluebeard's Castle*; ▷Jacques Offenbach, *Barbe-bleue*;

the classic animated film *Fantasia*; Mickey Mouse portrayed the apprentice.) Dukas, however, composed other music which shouldn't be missed. The ballet *La péri*, for instance, contains many magical, mystical moments; so does his one symphony. The massive Piano Sonata was an ambitious and adventurous work that is still challenging. ▷Debussy was an obvious influence on Dukas. But his own music had an effect on that of young composers still to make their mark, such as ▷Poulenc, ▷Françaix and ▷Ibert. Perhaps Dukas's finest music is in his opera *Ariane et Barbe-bleue*, a reworking of the grisly tale of the woman who opens a forbidden door and finds the bodies of several murdered wives. Dukas looked beyond the *grand guignol* aspect of the story and his music reaches emotional depths.

Emil Rezniček, *Bluebeard the Knight*.

DURUFLÉ, Maurice (born 1902)

In spite of his great age, the French composer Maurice Duruflé has written very little: barely a dozen works, most of them for the organ, which he himself plays. He must, however, be included here because of his one large composition, a Requiem (1947). It is a strangely muted, hauntingly beautiful creation which looks back to the era (and indeed the Requiem) of ▷Fauré. A fellow student of Duruflé's at the Paris Conservatoire was ▷Messiaen, whose musical language is quite different.

DVOŘÁK, Antonín (1841–1904)

Antonín Dvořák's music is capable of arousing profound happiness. From humble origins, he was deeply committed to his Czech heritage, and many of his works use the tunes and dance rhythms of his native country's folk music, creating a spirit of warm spontaneity. But Dvořák was also an eminent international figure, travelling to Britain, where he was enthusiastically received, and to the USA, where for three years he was director of the National Conservatory in New York.

Dvořák's two sets of *Slavonic Dances*, originally for piano duet and later orchestrated, are varied and col-

NOW LISTEN

▷Johannes Brahms, Violin Concerto; ▷Edward MacDowell, *Indian Suite*; ▷Vitežslav Novák, *Slovak Suite*; ▷Bedřich Smetana, *Ma vlast* ('My Country'); ▷Arthur Sullivan, *Iolanthe*.

ourful and they soon made his name abroad. He wrote
nine symphonies which, though of different character,
are all rich in melody. The best known is the Ninth,
'From the New World', written when Dvořák was in
America and incorporating references to negro tunes.
(His string quartet in F, also written during those
years, is known as the 'American' for the same reason.)
Dvořák's shorter orchestral works are lively and appealing; as well as symphonic poems he wrote overtures, including the rumbustious *Carnival*, the dazzling showpiece *Scherzo capriccioso* and the richly
inventive Symphonic Variations. His Violin Concerto
is splendid, with a jolly gypsy finale; his Piano Concerto is less memorable.

But it is Dvořák's Cello Concerto (1895) which, for
me, is his most arresting piece. From its hushed opening – a clarinet gently murmuring the theme that is to
dominate the first movement – to its scintillating finale, this is one of the greatest works written for the
cello, a difficult instrument to pit effectively against an
orchestra. Dvořák composed it in American after
hearing ▷Herbert's Cello Concerto.

Dvořák was attracted to opera but his gifts really lay
elsewhere. However, *Rusalka*, about a water-sprite's
ill-fated love for a mortal, is still performed; *The Devil
and Kate*, for long ignored, has recently been revived
and deserves to be better known. It's the very funny
story of a girl who climbs on the back of the devil and
won't get off until he has taken her on a visit to Hell!

E

ELGAR, Sir Edward (1857–1934)

There were two sides to the musical character of Edward Elgar, one that led him to compose light salon pieces of a warm and genial nature, like the *Chanson de matin* or the *Salut d'amour* and the other that produced introspective, deeply moving works such as *The Dream of Gerontius* with its disturbing vision of what happens to a soul after death. One of his best known works is the *Pomp and Circumstance* march no. 1, the central tune of which became a second national anthem in Britain when it acquired the words 'Land of Hope and Glory'. Its popularity has led to an undervaluing of the other four *Pomp and Circumstance* marches, which are worth anyone's attention.

Elgar's two symphonies are among the finest produced in Britain this century, full of rich melodies and orchestrated with great flair and sense of purpose. His marvellous Violin Concerto and the Cello Concerto (even more impressive, perhaps) are – like the symphonies – central to his work. Those who know Elgar's music well regard his symphonic study *Falstaff* in a special light; it is an entertaining look at Shakespeare's fat knight, a well-judged mixture of comedy and pathos. The concert overture *Cockaigne*, the word from which 'Cockney' derives, is a picture of London town, full of whistling urchins, brass bands and lovers in the park. (It is said that an American concert programme once described it as 'Cocaine – a musical study of drug abusers in London'!)

The Enigma Variations (1899) will always be Elgar's most-played work. In it, he draws musical sketches of some of his best friends, identified in the score only by

NOW LISTEN ▷

▷Johannes Brahms, *German Requiem*;
▷Arthur Bliss, *Welcome the Queen*, march;
▷Fryderyk Chopin, Piano Sonata in B flat minor; ▷Eric Coates, *London Suite*; ▷Ralph Vaughan Williams, Symphony no. 6;
▷William Walton, Cello Concerto.

initials or by nicknames. With affectionate if merciless skill he focuses on their mannerisms or traits and exposes them. One tune, for instance, features little jerky hesitations: the lady it describes had a slight stammer. Another sequence is a headlong musical rush, culminating in a gigantic splash: the man it represents had a big dog which loved bounding down riverbanks. The best loved variation is 'Nimrod' which is used at all solemn state occasions in Britain, even though it was conceived merely as an expression of lasting friendship for Elgar's publisher. It is typical of the composer's very 'British' sense of humour that the huge, grand finale of the work represents himself.

Other works by Elgar include the delectable *Sea Pictures* for mezzo-soprano and orchestra, *From the Bavarian Highlands* for chorus and orchestra, the *Wand of Youth* suites (based on music Elgar wrote as a boy) and *The Starlight Express* (no relation to ▷Lloyd Webber's musical but a children's entertainment containing much charming music). Elgar was a good conductor and made many records which, not surprisingly, give insight into his music. His speeds are often a good deal brisker than is fashionable today.

ENESCO, Georges (1881–1955)

The Romanian Georges Enesco was a great violinist and an inspired teacher; his pupils include Yehudi Menuhin and Arthur Grumiaux. His career as a composer was less impressive. Enesco's music is somewhat characterless and tends to overstay its welcome. Two Romanian Rhapsodies, however, have earned their place in the repertory. They are firmly based on folk-tunes and are lively and brilliantly scored, rather in the manner of ▷Liszt's *Hungarian Rhapsodies*.

F

FALLA, Manuel de (1876–1946)

One of the greatest Spanish composers is Manuel de Falla. But because he was relentlessly self-critical, he didn't publish very many works. He was taught early in life that a country's music should be rooted in folksong. It was a view he respected, but in his music he followed it in spirit rather than to the letter. Folktunes, as such, play little part; Spanish rhythms, on the other hand, are vital. His opera *La vida breve* ('Life is Short') established him and is still one of his strongest works; it is the story of a woman who dies of a broken heart when the man she loves marries someone else. His two ballets, *The Three-Cornered Hat* and *Love the Magician*, however, are by far Falla's most popular scores. They are brilliantly conceived with the most exciting orchestration, and it's quite possible to enjoy them without knowing anything about the stage action. *The Three-Cornered Hat* concerns the downfall of a pompous civic dignitary who tries to seduce the wife of a local miller; the glorious Miller's Dance is popular as a concert item. *Love the Magician* shows what happens when a girl's new affair keeps being interrupted by the ghost of her dead lover. Here, the hit number is the thrilling Ritual Fire Dance. Falla's *Nights in the Gardens of Spain* for piano and orchestra is an evocative, sensitive work, not a concerto-type showpiece, and his solo piano pieces are highly and attractively individual. The Harpsichord Concerto is delightfully unusual in that the solo instrument is accompanied by an ensemble of only five players. His Seven Popular Spanish Songs are a gift for a soprano looking for a recital attraction.

NOW LISTEN

▷Claude Debussy, *La soirée dans Grenade*; ▷Roberto Gerhard, *Don Quixote*; Walter Leigh, Concertino for harpsichord and strings; ▷Maurice Ravel, Rapsodie espagnole.

FAURÉ, Gabriel (1845–1924)

The French composer Gabriel Fauré served God and man most effectively. His compositions include, at one end, the superb Requiem; at the other, music to accompany a play about the evil Roman emperor, Caligula. The theatre, indeed, played a prominent part in Fauré's life. The score he wrote for the first London performances of Maeterlinck's play *Pelléas et Mélisande* is among the finest examples of his translucent style. So, too, is the *Shylock* music, composed for an adaptation of Shakespeare's *The Merchant of Venice*. Possibly his most popular short work is the *Dolly* Suite, whose opening movement was the signature tune for the BBC Radio programme 'Listen with Mother' for many years. The tiny *Pavane* for chorus and orchestra, with its haunting flute melody, is also familiar to many. Two less-often played works for piano and orchestra are undemonstrative but appealing, the *Ballade* and the *Fantaisie*, and the all-too-short *Berceuse* for violin and orchestra is magical. Anyone seeking the key to Fauré's musical personality, of course, must turn to his numerous songs (a medium in which he was an undisputed master) and to his piano music. It lies somewhere between ▷Chopin and ▷Debussy, without sounding like either. The nocturnes and barcarolles are especially lovely.

The Requiem (1887) was probably never surpassed by its composer. Fauré's God is not angry or vengeful. If there is a Day of Judgment, then it is a muted affair (unlike ▷Verdi's). In Heaven, a warm and gentle welcome awaits. The final 'In paradisum' is a promise of eternal bliss, if ever there was one. The work was written with boys' voices in mind and there's little doubt that they are superior in effect to women's, especially if they are French boys with their characteristically 'open' sound. Fauré's *Messe basse* (or 'Low Mass') for trebles and organ is a charming little work which sounds almost like a rehearsal for the Requiem. Seek it out. Some of Fauré's chamber music, particularly the violin sonatas, is most rewarding, though it does require a particular sympathy on the part of its performers. The opera *Pénélope*, about the wife of the Greek adventurer Odysseus, is sombre but effective and affecting. Fauré's music, often understated but always

> **NOW LISTEN** ▷
>
> ▷Claude Debussy, *Children's Corner*; ▷Maurice Duruflé, Requiem; ▷Maurice Ravel, *Le tombeau de Couperin*; ▷Andrew Lloyd Webber, Requiem.

poetic and warm, made a profound impression on many later French composers. ▷Ravel's music often betrays similar, if more vivid, colouring.

FEATHERED FRIENDS
▷Emmanuel Chabrier, *Villanelle of the Little Ducks*
▷Louis-Claude Daquin, *Le Coucou*
▷Edvard Grieg, *The Little Bird*
▷Olivier Messiaen, *Oiseaux exotiques*
▷Jean-Philippe Rameau, *The Hen*
▷Nikolay Rimsky-Korsakov, *The Golden Cockerel*
▷Ralph Vaughan Williams, *The Lark Ascending*.

FILM MUSIC
Film music began in a modest way. A pianist sat in the cinema and played something appropriate to what was happening in the silent movie being shown on the flickering screen. Roistering stuff for the chases and fights, 'hearts and flowers' for the romantic scenes and so on. Later, in more luxurious cinemas, orchestras and theatre organs were used. When the movies became 'talkies', film makers began to commission scores specially from composers. Many musical figures from other countries, some of them fleeing from Nazism in Europe, found their way to Hollywood and became the core of a mighty musical industry. ▷Korngold (*Robin Hood*, *The Sea Hawk*) was one; Miklós Rózsa (*Ben Hur*, *Julius Caesar*) was another. Names like Dimitri Tiomkin (*The Lost Horizon*) and Max Steiner (*Gone with the Wind*) began to appear on the credits, with such Americans as ▷Herrmann (*Citizen Kane*, *Psycho*), Alfred Newman (*The Robe*) and Alex North (*Spartacus*). ▷John Williams is one of the best known living Hollywood composers *Star Wars*, *E.T.*, *Close Encounters*, *Superman*).

But 'serious' composers in the USA also became

involved in writing for films, notably ▷Copland (*Our Town, The Heiress, The Red Pony*), ▷Thomson (*The Plough that Broke the Plains*) and ▷Bernstein (*On the Waterfront*). In Britain, many leading composers have written film music with varying success: ▷Vaughan Williams (*Scott of the Antarctic*), ▷Walton (*Henry V, Hamlet, Richard III*), ▷Bliss (*Things to Come*), ▷Bax (*Oliver Twist*), ▷Arnold (*The Bridge on the River Kwai*), William Alwyn (*The Way Ahead*) and ▷Bennett (*Murder on the Orient Express*). The Russian film industry has received much support from composers of the calibre of ▷Prokofiev (*Alexander Nevsky, Lieutenant Kijé*) and ▷Shostakovich (*The Gadfly, Hamlet*).

Great composers have had their music 'raided' by the cinema industry, including ▷Bach (*The Silence*), ▷Mahler (*Death in Venice*), ▷Mozart (*Elvira Madigan*) and ▷Rakhmaninov (*Brief Encounter*).

- The first piece of 'original' film music, written in 1908 for a silent film, was by ▷Saint-Saëns. ▷Richard Strauss adapted his score for the opera *Der Rosenkavalier* to accompany a silent version. ▷Schoenberg composed *Accompaniment to a Film Scene* with no film or scene in mind.

FINZI, Gerald (1901–1956)

The English composer Gerald Finzi is known by only a few works. These are beautifully crafted and will appeal to anyone who enjoys the English school of composition. Sometimes Finzi's music suggests ▷Vaughan Williams, at others ▷Ireland or ▷Walton. Yet it is very personal. The Cello Concerto, the last work Finzi completed, is probably his most satisfying and certainly his most ambitious. It has a slow movement of Elgarian solemnity and nobility and the work has been compared favourably with ▷Elgar's Cello Concerto. The Clarinet Concerto is a memorable work, one of the best for the instrument, and the Grand Fantasia and Toccata for piano and orchestra is much undervalued. It moves from a ▷Bach-like beginning to a conclusion reminiscent of ▷Prokofiev,

NOW LISTEN ▷

▷John Ireland, *These Things shall Be*; ▷Sergey Prokofiev, Piano Concerto no. 3; ▷Ralph Vaughan Williams, *Norfolk Rhapsody*; ▷William Walton, *Sinfonia concertante*.

and is thoroughly rewarding. Finzi is at his best writing for the voice: the song cycles and *Dies natalis* for soprano or tenor and orchestra are full of imaginative ideas.

FLOTOW, Friedrich von (1812–1883)

The German composer Friedrich von Flotow composed 18 operas, only one of which endures today. *Martha* is the charming tale of two high-born ladies who, for a joke, offer themselves as servants during a village hiring fair. The joke misfires when they find themselves legally bound to a couple of rough-and-ready farmers who inevitably fall in love with them. Flotow's music is light and beautifully fashioned, and is often memorable. A gem in the score is the famous tenor aria known always by its Italian title 'M'appari'; another is the quartet in which the men teach the women how to spin. Flotow makes frequent use of the old Irish air 'The Last Rose of Summer' during his opera – so frequent that the work is greatly improved if some of the roses are pruned!

FLUTE

The flute and its smaller brother the piccolo are the highest of the woodwind instruments (in fact, today they are usually made of metal). The player blows across an open mouthpiece and holds the instrument at right angles to his body. The sound of the flute, which can be penetrating, silvery, full-toned or mellow, is well displayed in the concertos by ▷Mozart and the Danish composer ▷Nielsen. There are memorable solos for it in ▷Debussy's *Prélude à L'aprés-midi d'un faune*, where it conjures up a shimmering summer day, the nocturnal Prelude to Act 3 of ▷Bizet's *Carmen*, and the *Pavane* by ▷Fauré. The piccolo screams defiance in the Scherzo of the Fourth Symphony of ▷Tchaikovsky and adds piquancy to the overture to ▷Rossini's opera *Semiramide*.

FOSTER, Stephen (1826–1864)

The American Stephen Foster taught himself to write music and left a rich legacy of songs, some 200 of them. Many have been popular for so long that they are believed to be folksongs. *Camptown Races, Old Folks at Home* (better known as *Way down upon the Swanee River*), *Jeanie with the Light Brown Hair, My Old Kentucky Home*, and *Beautiful Dreamer* (written a few days before Foster's death) are only a few. He was the first of the great American songwriters and paved the way for ▷Gershwin, ▷Kern and ▷Porter.

FRANÇAIX, Jean (born 1912)
The Frenchman Jean Françaix has composed operas, ballets, a symphony and many substantial works. Today he is best known for a little Concertino for piano and orchestra which is the epitome of Gallic elegance and wit. It was so successful on its first appearance that Françaix's publishers asked him for something similar; he obliged with a longer Piano Concerto which is enjoyable if less spontaneous. It is, however, worth finding on disc. So is *L'horloge de flore* ('The Floral Clock'), an unusual suite for oboe and orchestra which is less flippant than some of his pieces; each of its seven movements represents a flower. The music of Françaix belongs in the realm of ▷Ibert, ▷Poulenc, ▷Milhaud and ▷Sauguet.

FRANCK, César (1822–1890)
César Franck spent so many years in Paris playing and teaching the organ that he is often thought to be a French composer. In fact, he was Belgian and, like Agatha Christie's Hercule Poirot, proud of it. His music is often said to have suffered from his long spells in the organ loft: the mighty Symphony in D minor has been described as an organ solo arranged for orchestra. There are times when the colour of the music changes dramatically and we can almost imagine Franck pulling out some new stops. But that's an oversimplification, for Franck's orchestral sound is very much his own and the symphony, with its fine big tunes (one of which is particularly effectively played on the cor anglais), occupies a distinguished place in the repertory. The Symphonic Variations for piano and orchestra is a work whose brevity militates against its

NOW LISTEN ⟩

▷Ernest Chausson, Symphony; ▷Vincent d'Indy, *The Enchanted Forest*; ▷Oliver Messiaen, *La nativité du Seigneur*; Charles Widor, organ symphonies.

being performed more regularly at concerts; managements are unwilling to engage a star soloist for rather less than 20 minutes. Franck's symphonic poems are more rarely heard, though one, *Le chasseur maudit* ('The Accursed Huntsman'), is a rollicking success, full of whooping horns and pounding hooves. Three operas are never performed. Franck's organ pieces (notably the Three Chorales), some chamber music and a handful of oratorios complete the output of a man whose music may not be spectacular yet whose influence on Gallic culture was considerable.

FRIML, Rudolf (1879–1972)

Rudolf Friml started his musical life as a 'serious' composer. He played his Piano Concerto in New York shortly after arriving there as an immigrant from Czechoslovakia. It didn't take long for him to discover that the American people liked musicals, and he began composing them. His most successful are *Rose Marie*, a tale of the Canadian Rockies and the Mounted Police who 'always get their man', and *The Vagabond King*, a romance about the French poet François Villon who supposedly became king for a day. The 'Indian Love Call' from the former and the duet 'Only a Rose' from the latter are typical of Friml's melodic writing.

FUČIK, Julius (1872–1916)

The Czech Julius Fučik wrote what has become one of the best-known marches in the world, thanks to generations of circus bands. *The Entry of the Gladiators* is now exclusively associated with the Big Top, though it was intended to describe activities in a very different kind of sawdust ring! (Curiously, in the USA it is known as *Thunder and Blazes*). Fučik, a pupil of ▷Dvořák, composed much other music, including the splendid *Florentine* march, a charming Romance for bassoon and orchestra and the waltz *Winter Storms*. In his native land, he is considered to rank alongside ▷Johann Strauss as a purveyor of popular fare.

NOW LISTEN ⟩

Other works which have circus or fairground associations: Louis Ganne, *Les saltimbanques* ('The Entertainers'); ▷Imre Kálmán, *The Circus Princess*; ▷Henri Sauguet, *Les forains* ('The Show People'); ▷Igor Stravinsky, *Circus Polka*.

G

GABRIELI, Giovanni (1557–1612)

It was once said of Giovanni Gabrieli that he anticipated stereophony. The remark was flippant, but this adventurous Italian experimented with sound and musical colours, and many of his works benefit from modern recording techniques. Gabrieli was organist at St Mark's, Venice, for many years and wrote much music for voices and brass. He exploited the architecture of St Mark's by placing his musicians in separate groups so that they sang and played to each other across the building, creating 'echo' effects. Gabrieli composed organ works which are of more than passing interest. His style is fresh, colourful and forward-looking – some of it sounds as if it were written much nearer our own time.

● One of Gabrieli's star pupils was Heinrich Schütz, whose Passions and oratorios led him to be considered among the greatest of ▷Bach's predecessors.

GADE, Niels (1817–1890)

Niels Gade could almost have found himself arrested for being under the influence of ▷Mendelssohn. This Danish composer's music shows countless signs of his admiration for his German friend and colleague. His music is frequently charming and very skilfully put together. The eight symphonies are the pillars of his output, the last perhaps the most impressive, and his violin sonatas have much of interest (nearly 40 years separate the first from the third, yet Gade's style changed little). *The Fairy Spell*, described as an opera-ballet, makes pleasant listening with lovely choruses and orchestral interludes. It begins with a phrase remarkably similar to the main theme of Mendelssohn's overture *The Fair Melusine*. But it's nevertheless a delightful melody.

GAY, John (1685–1732)

John Gay wasn't a composer but a poet, playwright and theatre manager. But it was he who put together and first staged *The Beggar's Opera* in London in 1728, and it is his name that is always attached to it. The music for this ballad opera was arranged by a German composer, Johann Pepusch. He made extensive use of folktunes and other popular tunes, including some by ▷Purcell and ▷Handel. *The Beggar's Opera* tells of the adventures of the swashbuckling highwayman Macheath and his desperate attempts to please both his mistresses – the sweet Polly Peachum and the volatile Lucy Lockit. In the process, the piece parodies the style of some of the well known operas of the day.

● In 1928, Berlin audiences were treated to a modern interpretation of *The Beggar's Opera* by Bertolt Brecht and ▷Kurt Weill. It was called *The Threepenny Opera*; Macheath becomes Mack the Knife, a small-time crook operating in Soho, London.

GERHARD, Roberto (1896–1970)

The Spanish-born British composer Roberto Gerhard was always reassessing his ideas and using new techniques. Some of his music is easily assimilated on first hearing; the ballet *Don Quixote*, for instance, is melodic, attractive and very 'Spanish'. His melodrama for speaker, chorus and orchestra based on Camus' *The Plague*, on the other hand, is not fully appreciated without repeated hearing. The Concerto for Orchestra is a striking and original showpiece and the Violin Concerto is considered by many Gerhard devotees as among his finest works. The third of his four symphonies, sub-titled 'Collage', begins electronically with an evocation of a transatlantic flight.

● Don Quixote was the subject of a theatre piece by ▷Falla (*Master Peter's Puppet Show*), a ballet by Leon Minkus, a song cycle by ▷Ravel (*Don Quichotte à Dulcinée*) and a symphonic poem by ▷Strauss. ▷Massenet wrote a Don Quixote opera for the great Russian bass Chaliapin.

GERMAN, Sir Edward (1862–1936)
Edward German was the composer of the comic opera *Merrie England*, which kept the Savoy Theatre in London going after the Gilbert and Sullivan operas had ceased to flow. Its tale of love and intrigue at the court of Elizabeth Tudor involves such real characters as Sir Walter Raleigh and the Earl of Essex and it was considered good enough to be given a revival in the 1960s by Sadler's Wells Opera. Even better is German's other operetta *Tom Jones*, decorously based on Fielding's bawdy novel. It includes a gavotte for a crowd of snobbish gentry which anticipates ▷Loewe's *My Fair Lady* with its 'Ascot opening day'. German also wrote incidental music to several Shakespeare plays, a splendid *Welsh Rhapsody* and two symphonies, now never played.

● Musicals, operas and operettas about historical figures include ▷Berlin's *Annie Get Your Gun* (sharp-shooter Annie Oakley), ▷Donizetti's *Maria Stuarda* (Mary Queen of Scots), Leo Fall's *Madame Pompadour* (the mistress of Louis XV of France), Lehár's *Friederike* (Goethe) and ▷Suppé's *Boccaccio* (the Italian writer).

GERSHWIN, George (1898–1937)
The songs of the American George Gershwin are among the finest written in the 20th century. Most have scintillating lyrics by George's brother, Ira, and range from the wit of *By Strauss* (in which the singer extols the waltzes of the great Johann) to the pathos of *But not for me* and the rich warmth of *Our love is here to stay*. In between are such all-time greats as *Embraceable You*, *I got rhythm*, *The Man I Love*, *Fascinating Rhythm* and *Love Walked In*, most of them composed for films or Broadway stage shows. One of his theatre pieces, *Of Thee I Sing*, is a satire on the American presidential elections; its libretto won a coveted Pulitzer Prize. Gershwin said the show was an attempt to write a 1930s-style Gilbert and Sullivan operetta. Gershwin's fount of melody was patently inexhaustible: he was still at the height of his creative powers when he died of a brain tumour. Yet the songs are only a part of his legacy. *Rhapsody in Blue* is among the most popular works for piano and orchestra and is one of the few concert pieces to use elements of jazz successfully. His later Piano Concerto, a direct descendant of the *Rhapsody*, is to many ears even better (with a marvellously jazzy trumpet solo in the slow movement). The purely orchestral *An American in Paris* is vintage Gershwin – he uses tuned motor-horns to create the city's atmosphere – and the *Cuban Overture* deserves to be much better known: it's an exciting piece of Caribbean froth.

The opera *Porgy and Bess* (1935) contains the cream of Gershwin. It was written for a predominantly black cast. Gershwin lived in a black community while he worked on the score, in which he captured the spirit of the people and their music in a way that has yet to be equalled by a white composer. Porgy is a legless cripple who forms a relationship with Bess, a goodtime girl. Under his loving influence, she changes her ways and takes to domesticity. But in the end she succumbs to temptation and leaves him. The story introduces one of the most odious villains in opera, the drug-pusher and pimp Sporting Life. *Porgy and Bess* contains many wonderful songs, including 'Summertime', 'I got plenty of nothing', 'Bess, you is my woman now'. The orchestral writing is highly charged and atmospheric and the chorus frequently contributes to the dramatic

NOW LISTEN
▷Leonard Bernstein, *On the Town*; ▷Aaron Copland, Three Latin American Sketches; Ferde Grofe, Piano Concerto; ▷Scott Joplin, *Treemonisha*; ▷Jerome Kern, songs.

action. Gershwin uses an interesting device: the white people in the cast speak, the black people sing.

GINASTERA, Alberto (1916–1983)

The Argentinian Alberto Ginastera is one of the most distinguished South American composers, but his considerable output is virtually unknown in Europe. His *Variaciones concertantes* are played occasionally – and an exciting 'older person's guide to the orchestra' they make, scored with great brilliance and flair. The atmospheric, compelling Harp Concerto should be sampled, and the opera *Bomarzo* (about the trials and tribulations of an Italian hunchback) is much admired whenever it is performed. The rhythmically ebullient music from the cowboy ballet *Estancia* has always struck me as being a potential audience winner in the concert hall: it is perhaps what ▷Khachaturian might have written if he had been South American not Armenian.

GIORDANO, Umberto (1867–1948)

It has often been suggested that the Italian opera composer Umberto Giordano made clever use of a somewhat threadbare talent. It is true that of his ten operas, only two are now heard, but in my view they make good listening. *Fedora*, set in Russia, is a tale of ill-fated love; *Andrea Chenier* is about a real poet who became a victim of the French Revolution because he loved the wrong woman. Giordano's music is full-blooded and easy to absorb. It is in the style of ▷Puccini but his melodies are not so memorable or plentiful. *Fedora* and *Andrea Chenier*, however, would make a pleasant change from *Tosca* and *La bohème*.

- Another opera set against the French Revolution is ▷Benjamin's *A Tale of Two Cities*, after Dickens's novel.

> **NOW LISTEN**

▷Benjamin Britten, *The Young Person's Guide to the Orchestra*; ▷Carlos Chávez, Piano Concerto; ▷Aram Khachaturian, *Gayane*; ▷Giuseppe Verdi, *Rigoletto*.

GLAZUNOV, Alexander (1865–1936)
When the First Symphony of the Russian composer Alexander Glazunov was first played, people found it hard to believe that a work with such style, authority and originality could have been written by a 16-year-old. Glazunov's talent was prodigious from the beginning, and he went on to produce one warm, colourful work after another – rich in melody if not too adventurous. He resisted experiment and his attractive style changed little in 40 years. Glazunov nevertheless encouraged his forward-looking pupils, among them ▷Stravinsky and ▷Shostakovich.

The Violin Concerto is among the best of Glazunov's works, its finale including a melody which, once heard, is never forgotten. Two piano concertos are pleasant but less original. The Saxophone Concerto is a splendid piece, admirably written for this rarely heard instrument. Glazunov's eight symphonies have a great deal of distinctive character; the Fifth is arguably the most concise and memorable. The Eight has a sweep and dignity that may remind you of ▷Elgar. The symphonic poem *Stenka Razin* (which uses the Russian 'Song of the Volga Boatmen' with its chorus of 'Yo-heave-ho!') and two seductive concert waltzes always make attractive concert items. Glazunov's two ballets show his gifts most clearly. *The Seasons* is a most tuneful score: the Waltz of the Cornflowers and Poppies and the Autumn Bacchanale are show-stoppers. *Raymonda*, a longer work with an absurd story set in the days when knights were bold, is marvellously put together and contains numerous ear-tickling dances.

GLIER, Reyngol'd (1875–1956)
Reyngol'd Glier was much better known in the USSR than in the West. He was for many years highly respected as a teacher as well as a composer and numbered among his pupils ▷Prokofiev and ▷Khachaturian. The two works of his which have gained currency outside his native land are colourful, and appealing in the line of ▷Rimsky-Korsakov. The ballet *The Red Poppy* (one of the earliest to promote Communist ideals) is set in the docklands of Shanghai and shows how some Russian sailors help the oppressed

> **NOW LISTEN**
>
> ▷Alexander Borodin, *Prince Igor* and *Petite suite*; ▷Eric Coates, *Saxo-Rhapsody*; ▷Reyngol'd Glier, *The Bronze Horseman*; Dmitry Shostakovich, *The Age of Gold*; Sergey Taneyev, Symphony no. 5; ▷Peter Tchaikovsky, *The Seasons*.

> **NOW LISTEN**
>
> ▷Anton Arensky, Two Orchestral Suites; ▷Alexander Borodin, Symphony no. 1; ▷Alexander Glazunov, *Stenka Razin*; ▷Mikhail Ippolitov-Ivanov, *Caucasian Sketches*; ▷Sergey Taneyev,

coolies to overcome their cruel capitalist bosses; the
Russian Sailors' Dance is often performed as a concert
item. Glier's Symphony no. 3, sub-titled 'Il'ya
Muromets', charts the adventures of a Russian
dragon-slayer. Glier's handling of the orchestra is
masterly.

Symphony no. 2.

GLINKA, Mikhail (1804–1857)

Mikhail Glinka is generally considered to be the 'Father of Russian music', though, ironically, two of his
most impressive orchestral works are decidedly Spanish in character. The *Jota aragonesa* and *Memories of a
Night in Madrid* date from three years he spent in the
Spanish capital. Glinka was an inveterate traveller, living in Paris, Milan, Berlin and Warsaw before returning to settle in his native land. His first opera, *A
Life for the Tsar*, tells of a peasant who gives up his life to
save his country's leader. But, while the subject is
strongly nationalistic, the music is only slightly so. It
wasn't until his second opera, *Ruslan and Lyudmila*,
that genuine Russian characteristics shone through
the music. *Ruslan* has aspects of ▷Mozart's *Magic
Flute* and ▷Wagner's *Ring* in its plot, about a prince's
search for a beautiful princess who has been abducted
and imprisoned by a wicked dwarf. Magic swords and
an enchanted golden ring are involved in the successful outcome. Glinka's music is bold, romantic and red-
olent of his country's folk traditions (the overture is a
concert favourite) and it was on this work that later
Russian composers modelled a 'national' style. Some
of the music Glinka wrote to accompany a play called
Prince Kholmsky might have been composed many
years later by ▷Tchaikovsky.

- Glinka began his working life in the Ministry of
  Communications. Other composers who started
  different careers include ▷Berlioz (medical student), ▷Borodin (scientist), ▷Bruckner (schoolteacher), ▷Chabrier (civil servant), ▷Khachaturian
  (biologist), ▷Musorgsky (soldier),

▷Rimsky-Korsakov (sailor), ▷Tchaikovsky (law student).

GLUCK, Christoph Willibald von (1714–1787)
The Bohemian-German composer Christoph Willibald von Gluck introduced new ideas and ideals into opera. He wanted to make the music serve the story, mirroring its emotions; he felt the flow of the music should not be interrupted to allow singers the opportunity for florid displays. His masterpiece, *Orfeo ed Euridice*, is performed regularly all over the world and can be a moving, memorable experience. The aria 'Che faro senza Euridice?', which Orpheus sings on losing his wife, exemplifies Gluck's ideals about simplicity and purity of line. His use of the chorus to underline the tragedy is telling, and the ballet is an integral part of the work; 'The Dance of the Blessed Spirits', with its mellifluous flute solo, is often heard as a concert item. Gluck wrote many other operas, including *Alceste* which is considered in some ways to anticipate the music dramas of ▷Wagner. With reference to the spare, uncluttered and ultimately beautiful nature of Gluck's operas, ▷Berlioz enthused: 'Nudity merely enhances goddesses'.

NOW LISTEN ▷

▷Ludwig van Beethoven, *Fidelio*; ▷Hector Berlioz *The Trojans*; ▷Wolfgang Amadeus Mozart, *Idomeneo*; Gasparo Spontini, *La vestale*.

GOEHR, Alexander (born 1932)
It would be idle to pretend that the music of Alexander Goehr is always immediately accessible. He studied at the Royal Manchester College of Music at the same time as ▷Birtwistle and ▷Maxwell Davies, and does not compromise in his writing. Goehr was influenced early by ▷Schoenberg and the Second Viennese School of composers, and his style has developed from there. It is worth persevering with Goehr's music. The Little Symphony, written in memory of his father, the conductor Walter Goehr, is a fine work. So is the *Romanza* for cello and orchestra composed for Jacqueline du Pré. The *Metamorphosis Dance* is a striking and original 'imaginary ballet', of which its title is the most daunting aspect.

GOLDMARK, Carl (1830–1915)

The talents of the Hungarian Carl Goldmark were not sufficient to entitle him to be in the same league as contemporaries such as ▷Brahms, ▷Bruckner or ▷Dvořák. The skill with which he presents his material sometimes disguises the fact that it is a trifle thin. Nevertheless, Goldmark could produce good tunes and it is not dismissive to say that several of his works make a pleasant change from the staple fare we tend to be offered at concerts. The Rustic Wedding Symphony contains a good deal of attractive music, as does the Violin Concerto in A minor (which has a short slow movement of grave beauty). The opera *The Queen of Sheba* was popular for many years until it became unfashionable; perhaps a revival would give it a new lease of life.

GOTTSCHALK, Louis Moreau (1829–1869)

It would be a mistake to dismiss the music of the American Louis Moreau Gottschalk as merely showy or spicy. Some of it is, and deliberately so, for Gottschalk was not only a composer but a virtuoso concert pianist who knew the kind of thing that went down well with his audiences. But a good deal of Gottschalk's music has something to say, and says it with simplicity and refreshing directness. His frequent stays in the Caribbean led him to attempt to capture the spirit and flavour of West Indian music in his compositions. His flippant side is to be found in such piano pieces as *The Banjo* (in which there's a cheeky snatch of ▷Foster's *Camptown Races*) and the *Tournament Galop*, in which the pianist appears to require four hands. The other side is typified by *The Dying Poet*, a study of Schumann-like beauty. *Le bananier* describes an oppressed black worker and his ceaseless toil; the basic melody anticipates that of the Polish ox wagon in ▷Musorgsky's *Pictures at an Exhibition*.

Gottschalk's orchestral and vocal music is fascinating in an unexpected way. The finale of the First Symphony is nothing less than a samba – and a catchy one. His miniature opera *Country Scenes* might have been written much later by a composer of Spanish zarzuelas or operettas. Gottschalk's love of big orchestras,

NOW LISTEN ▷

▷Arthur Benjamin, *Jamaican Rumba*; ▷Hector Berlioz, *Symphonie funèbre et triomphale*; Federico Chueca, *La gran via*, ▷Scott Joplin, piano rags; ▷Darius Milhaud, *Le boeuf sur le toit*.

sometimes augmented by brass bands, reminds us that he worked for a time in Paris under ▷Berlioz. He is a composer to liven up the most jaded of palates.

GOUNOD, Charles (1818–1893)

The Frenchman Charles Gounod is best remembered today for one work, his opera *Faust*, which is loosely (and rather simplistically) based on Goethe's great poem. For many years it was one of the most frequently performed French operas but it gradually fell out of fashion: performances are comparatively rare today. The story of the old philosopher who sells his soul to the Devil in return for his lost youth inspired Gounod to compose sufficient tunes for three operas: the Jewel Song, Valentine's Farewell, the Calf of Gold and the Soldiers' Chorus are only a handful. The music for the ballet (danced as Faust is tempted by celebrated beauties from the past) has become popular in the concert hall in its own right. Gounod wrote other operas of which two are worth noting. *Roméo et Juliette* after Shakespeare and *Mireille*, a saga of love and jealousy in a French village. Each has a good deal to commend it and, thanks to recordings, we can appreciate that Gounod's gifts did not stop at *Faust*.

His two symphonies are not very memorable. But the *Petite symphonie* for wind instruments has a youthful charm and vigour which belie the fact that Gounod wrote it at the age of 70. His sense of humour can be detected swiftly in the *Funeral March of a Marionette*, a cheeky piece composed for a puppet show, later adopted by the film director Alfred Hitchcock to introduce his regular television thrillers.

- Other works suggested by the story of Romeo and Juliet are by ▷Bellini (opera, *I Capuletti ed i Montecchi*), ▷Berlioz (dramatic symphony), ▷Bernstein (musical, *West Side Story*), ▷Tchaikovsky (fantasy overture).

GRAINGER, Percy (1882–1961)

Quite early in his long career, Percy Grainger made an orchestral work out of an English morris dance tune called *Country Gardens*. The public adored it and the composer made a fortune out of it. But it tended to make people overlook his other works and even today it is still Grainger's best-known work. Grainger, an Australian who lived for a time in Britain and later settled in the USA, was a brilliant pianist who was also eccentric (he used to jog through the streets of Edwardian London in the small hours of the morning wearing a woollen track-suit he had knitted himself). His music is also eccentric. It is highly original, unorthodox and progressive for its day. At one point, long before others, Grainger experimented with rudimentary electronic equipment. He spent much time collecting folktunes, from England, Scotland, Ireland and the Antipodes, which provide a basis for many of his works.

At one end of the Grainger spectrum are lighter pieces like *Molly on the Shore*, *Shepherd's Hey*, *Handel in the Strand* and the *Irish Tune from County Derry* (which we know better as the 'Londonderry Air' *or* 'Danny Boy'; at the other are such masterly settings as the sea shanty *Shallow Brown* for solo voice, chorus and orchestra, the two *Hill-songs* and the affecting *Colonial Song*. The work Grainger himself liked best, the 'imaginary ballet' *The Warriors*, contains remarkable music of the wild, free sort that made the American ▷Ives celebrated. Grainger's musical voice is among the most fascinating and rewarding of the 20th century and his importance goes far beyond the *Country Gardens* of which he once said: 'Think of turnips when I play it!'.

NOW LISTEN ▷

▷Benjamin Britten, *A Time there was*; ▷Frederick Delius, *Brigg Fair*; ▷George Gershwin, *Porgy and Bess*; ▷Edvard Grieg, Piano Concerto; Ronald Stevenson, *Jamboree for Grainger*.

GRANADOS, Enrique (1867–1916)

The crew of a German submarine were responsible for ending the career of the Spaniard Enrique Granados. He had been in the USA to supervise a production of his opera *Goyescas*, a tale of jealousy and sudden death under the Iberian sun. The liner in which he and his wife were returning home was torpedoed and they drowned. Granados's orchestral music is seldom

NOW LISTEN ▷

▷Isaac Albéniz, *Iberia*; ▷Manuel de Falla, *La vida breve*; ▷Federico Mompou, *Cançons i dansas*; ▷Joaquin Turina, *Canto a Sevilla*;

played today, though he wrote a number of colourful scores, including an Arab Suite. His piano music, however, is deservedly popular with pianists the world over. It has a distinctly Spanish flavour without sounding 'folky' and is lyrical. Granados wrote a number of pieces inspired by the paintings of Goya, and these are among his finest compositions: one of them, *The Maiden and the Nightingale*, is especially memorable. In lighter vein, he composed three *Marches militaires*, perhaps a Spaniard's tribute to ▷Schubert.

▷Robert Schumann, *Kinderszenen*.

GRIEG, Edvard (1843–1906)

The Norwegian composer Edvard Grieg was a miniaturist at heart and was not comfortable writing large-scale music (he suppressed a youthful symphony which wasn't performed until more than half a century after his death). Not surprisingly, his piano works and his many songs display his gifts most effectively. The *Lyric Pieces* for piano are endlessly enjoyable: some are light and charming, others deeply affecting. Late in life, Grieg experimented at the keyboard and produced music that seems to anticipate ▷Bartók. The best known of Grieg's vocal pieces is the song usually sung in German and known as *Ich liebe Dich* ('I love you'). His orchestral works are few but warmly attractive. The incidental music he composed for the first production of Ibsen's drama *Peer Gynt* has deservedly achieved a life of its own; the concert suite usually played consists of only four of the pieces from this score but there are in fact eight times that number, and investigation of them is well worth while. Grieg's Four Norwegian Dances are delightful little 'lollipops'. So are his *Symphonic Dances*, which are longer but are neither 'symphonic' nor really dances. *From Holberg's Time*, a suite for strings, has an abundance of charm and skilfully suggests the atmosphere of the 18th century without resorting to pastiche.

Grieg's Piano Concerto (1868) is one of his few essays into 'bigger' music and is among the best-loved concertos ever written. It's not especially well constructed but it has, quite rightly, won its place in everyone's heart through its many lovely melodies. ▷Liszt

NOW LISTEN ⟩

▷Béla Bartók, *For Children*; ▷Frederick Delius, *On Hearing the First Cuckoo in Spring*; ▷Percy Grainger, Suite of Danish Folk Tunes; ▷Ferenc Liszt, Piano Concerto no. 1.

played it and enjoyed it; as did ▷Grainger. It is sometimes said, mischievously, that Grieg is Scotland's
greatest composer: his great-grandfather was a Scot
named Greig!

H

HAHN, Reynaldo (1875–1947)

Reynaldo Hahn was born in Venezuela but spent his life in Paris and is regarded as a French composer. He had written a successful song by the time he was 16, *Si mes vers avaient des ailes* ('If my verses had wings'), and carried on producing songs almost until his death, many of them very fine. One of his song cycles, *Venise*, was given its première in Venice under unusual circumstances: the composer, a good baritone, accompanied himself on the piano from a gondola in the middle of the Grand Canal; the audience stood on bridges and on the banks, applauding. Hahn's operetta *Ciboulette* is regarded as the best example of the genre in France from the 1920s; it's set in Les Halles, once the huge, fruit and vegetable market in Paris, and revolves round the love-life of Ciboulette (the French word for 'chives'). His Piano Concerto is short but packed with elegant melodies; the little suite from his ballet *Le bal de Béatrice d'Este* is delightful and scored for the unusual combination of wind instruments, two harps and piano, conjuring up a 16th-century atmosphere with deceptive simplicity.

- Other operettas which visit the Parisian market of Les Halles are Charles Lecocq's *La fille de Madame Angot*, ▷Messager's *Les p'tites Michu*, and ▷Offenbach's *Mesdames de La Halle*.

HALVORSEN, Johen (1864–1935)
Johen Halvorsen suffered more than a little from composing in his native Norway at the same time as the more talented ▷Grieg. Indeed, the eclipse was so complete for a time that some leading reference books don't mention him. Yet he wrote music in the best Scandinavian tradition which is very enjoyable. He was originally a violin virtuoso and much of his music is written for that instrument with piano or orchestral accompaniment, most notably a tuneful and attractive concerto and a set of memorable *Norwegian Dances*. Halvorsen later became musical director of the National Theatre in Oslo and wrote much music for plays there, including Ludvig Holberg's *Maskarade* and Sigurd Eldegard's *Fossegrimen* (water sprites who play the fiddle). The latter was the first orchestral score to include the Hardanger fiddle (a Norwegian folk instrument with four or five extra wire strings which vibrate in sympathy with those being played). His most popular concert work is a flamboyant march, *The Entry of the Boyars*. Halvorsen married one of Grieg's nieces.

● ▷Nielsen composed an opera after Holberg's *Maskarade*. ▷Grieg wrote a piece for strings to mark the 200th anniversary of Holberg's birth.

HAMILTON, Iain (born 1922)
The early works of the Scottish composer Iain Hamilton pose few problems to the listener. The overture *Bartholomew Fair*, for instance, is a splendidly lively and approachable piece, and his *Scottish Dances* outdo ▷Arnold's for wit and charm. But by the late 1950s his style had changed, becoming tough and uncompromising. His Sinfonia for two orchestras caused a stir at the 1959 Edinburgh Festival when scores of people filed silently out of the hall. His opera *The Catiline Conspiracy*, first performed in Scotland in 1974, had a similarly mixed reception. I found it very effective theatre, cogently argued and with music that suited the stark tale of dark deeds in ancient Rome. More recently, Hamilton's approach has changed again. His

opera *Anna Karenina* (1980) was described by many as 'lyrical'; other recent works have suggested the music of ▷Ravel to some critics.

HANDEL, George Frideric (1685–1759)

The name of Handel conjures up one work to the vast majority of people. In spite of the fact that he wrote nearly 50 operas and more than 30 oratorios (which contain a wealth of material, representing some of the composer's best music), Handel is known primarily for *Messiah* (1742). In Britain, it is still performed more regularly than any other major choral work: many cities and towns have traditional performances every Christmas and Easter. It is easy to understand why. Handel, a German who became a British citizen, wrote it after recovering from a stroke. He was not a devout man like his exact contemporary ▷J.S. Bach, but this is an inspired work. Its many solos, such as 'Every valley', 'Rejoice greatly', and 'I know that my Redeemer liveth', help tell the story of Christ's birth and death with unquenchable strength. The choruses add weight and excitement as well as emotional depth, the famous Hallelujah Chorus remaining a marvellous Handelian utterance. The orchestra, too, plays its part. The little Pastoral Symphony that precedes the Nativity portrays the shepherds with magical clarity.

Handel, indeed, was a masterly orchestral composer. His *Water Music* (played on a barge to entertain King George I during a party on the River Thames) is admirably rich and varied, both melodically and rhythmically, and the *Music for the Royal Fireworks*, written for another special occasion, is even grander if less immediately memorable. The concerti grossi are immensely attractive (they inspired such composers as ▷Bloch to write works in a similar vein in the 20th century); the organ concertos are gems and the many harpsichord pieces – especially the so-called 'Harmonious Blacksmith' – are worth investigating. But the operas (such as *Alcina* and *Serse*) and the oratorios (like *Samson, Semele, Judas Maccabaeus*, and *Solomon* probably yield the finest prizes.

There's much discussion about how to perform Handel's music. The present trend is to give small-

NOW LISTEN ▷

Other great choral works regularly performed today: ▷Johann Sebastian Bach, *St Matthew Passion*; ▷Edward Elgar, *The Dream of Gerontius*; ▷Wolfgang Amadeus Mozart, Requiem; ▷Carl Orff, *Carmina burana*; Giuseppe Verdi, Requiem; ▷William Walton, *Belshazzar's Feast*.

scale performances, using period instruments, to create the kind of sound Handel would have had in mind. Speeds can be more fleet (especially with a small choir). But in the case of *Messiah* many still enjoy the more operatic performances, using large forces, that they grew up with. (▷Mozart made an orchestration of it, as did Eugene Goossens for Sir Thomas Beecham.)

HARP

The harp may be the instrument of the angels, but with its rows of strings and seven pedals it is the very devil to play. It is so difficult to tune, and keep in tune, that the harpist in an orchestra can always be seen on the platform long before the other instrumentalists have arrived. There is a lovely harp concerto by the Frenchman François Boieldieu (1775–1834) and others by ▷Ginastera and Germaine Tailleferre. ▷Mozart composed a Concerto for flute and harp, and ▷Rodrigo a serenade. ▷Tchaikovsky's ballets feature the harp prominently (before the Waltz of the Flowers in *Nutcracker* for instance) and it can be heard to great effect in many of the scores of ▷Debussy. There is a magical harp part in ▷Ravel's Introduction and Allegro.

HARRIS, Roy (1898–1979)

Roy Harris is best known outside his native America by one work, the Symphony no. 3. But what a work it is! In one continuous movement, it lasts barely 20 minutes and is probably the finest symphony to be written in the USA. It begins with a bold, striding melody in the strings and simply grows, becoming livelier and more intensely coloured until it reaches a huge climax; it then returns inexorably to its beginnings. There are no tricks, no playing to the gallery. The argument is direct and straightforward as befits the man who once said: 'The shadow of Abe Lincoln has hovered over my life from childhood'. Harris wrote 12 symphonies, but with the possible exception of no. 7 none has approached the Third for sheer power, cogency and excitement.

> **NOW LISTEN** ⟩
>
> Some other symphonies by 20th-century Americans: ▷Leonard Bernstein, Symphony no. 2, 'Age of Anxiety'; ▷Aaron Copland, Symphony no. 3; Paul Creston, Symphony no. 2; Howard Hanson, Symphony no. 2, 'Romantic'; ▷Walter Piston, Symphony no. 4.

HARTY, Sir Hamilton (1871–1971)

Sir Hamilton Harty was the Irish conductor who for
more than ten years held the reins of the Hallé
Orchestra and turned it into a great European institution. His work on the rostrum took precedence over his
activities as a composer. But what he wrote is melodious, attractive and beautifully scored. His concertos
for piano and – especially – for violin are warm, lyrical
outpourings, posing no difficulties for the anxious.
The *Irish Symphony*, full of Celtic tunes and conjuring
up the lush greenery of Erin's Isle, is splendidly refreshing and deserves more hearings. Harty was a fine
arranger and his orchestrations of ▷Handel's *Water
Music* and *Music for the Royal Fireworks* were for many
years the only ones performed in the concert hall. His
John Field Suite, based on the music of his fellow
Irishman, is charmingly unpretentious.

- Other conductors also known as composers include ▷Mahler, ▷Bernstein, Wilhelm Furtwän-
  gler, Otto Klemperer, ▷Lambert and ▷Previn.

HAYDN, Joseph (1732–1809)

Joseph Haydn was a happy, contented man with a
warm sense of humour – easy to believe if you listen to
his music. Much of it is traditional and cheerful; he
was not an innovator but he brought to all he wrote
great skill, ingenuity and wit. He was also capable,
however, of expressing in his music strong emotions
and sadness. For most of his life Haydn was in the
service of a famous Hungarian family who lived near
Vienna. But latterly Haydn became an international
figure, and the opportunity to travel abroad – to Paris
and London – stimulated him to write orchestral music of great brilliance and inventiveness. To say that he
was prolific is an understatement: he wrote 104 symphonies, more than 80 string quartets and over 50 piano sonatas, not to mention 20 operas and numerous
choral and chamber works, concertos and arrangements.

Haydn's symphonies are wonderful and listening to

:hem in sequence allows you to trace his development as a composer. The last 12, written for London, are the best known and include no. 94, 'The Surprise', so called because of a loud drumbeat following a passage of quiet music; no. 96, 'The Miracle', is so nicknamed because it was said that at its first performance the audience rushed forward to congratulate Haydn and so miraculously escaped being crushed by a chandelier that fell on to their vacated seats (the incident was in fact in 1795 after a performance of the Symphony no. 102); no. 100, 'The Military', whose second movement has a rallying trumpet-call; and no. 101, 'The Clock', which includes a tick-tocking slow movement. In one of his earlier symphonies, no. 45, 'The Farewell', Haydn tried to convey a message to his employer through his music: in the final extra movement, the number of players is gradually reduced until only two violinists remain – a broad hint to the prince that his musicians were tired of being at his country palace and wanted to return to their families.

Haydn composed a number of fine masses. But his greatest choral works are arguably *The Creation* and *The Seasons*. The first contains the famous aria 'With verdure clad' and the great chorus 'The Heavens are telling'; the second has been called 'a work effervescent with the optimism of old age'. With the exception of the popular Trumpet Concerto, Haydn's compositions for solo instruments and orchestra are less enduring; his operas are less assured but they are being reassessed.

● Other works involving creation (in some form) and the seasons: ▷Beethoven's *The Creatures of Prometheus*, ▷Bliss's *Adam Zero*, ▷Glazunov's *The Seasons*, ▷Loewe's *My Fair Lady*, ▷Milhaud's *La création du mond*, ▷Suppé's *Beautiful Galathea*, and ▷Vivaldi's *The Four Seasons*.

HENZE, Hans Werner (born 1926)

The listener dipping for the first time into the work of the leading German composer Hans Werner Henze

cannot be sure what kind of music he will hear. It may
be spare and stark; it may be sensuous and warm. The
sound may be delicate to the point of transparency, or
simply massive. It may recall ▷Schoenberg or
▷Stravinsky, or even ▷Weill. It's just as likely to suggest the French or the Italian musical worlds. Yet such
is Henze's immense talent and imagination that he
stamps his own personality on everything he writes.
The symphonies are a good demonstration of his gifts.
Their moods are totally different, one from the next.
Each is full of atmosphere. Nor are they as 'difficult' as
many contemporary works, though they do require to
be heard often before they make their full impact.
Henze's Piano Concerto no. 2 is an impressive work
which one critic has called the only truly successful
large-scale piano concerto since ▷Brahms. The Violin Concerto no. 2 is possibly unique in having a part
for a speaker. Henze's chamber works, which include
some variations for harpsichord and a striking sonata
for solo violin, are challenging. His choral music
reveals a strong understanding of the potentialities of
the human voice, even more clearly shown in his
operas.

Henze's first opera, *Boulevard Solitude*, is a modern
version of the Abbé Prevost story *Manon Lescaut* and it
was an instant success in 1952. Later operas include
Der junge Lord ('The Young Lord'), a merciless indict-
ment of the German bourgeoisie, and *The Bassarids*, a
massive work based on *The Bacchae* and calling for the
kind of choral and orchestral forces not easy to come
by in the average opera house today. For many,
Henze's finest opera is *Elegy for Young Lovers*, a study of
a successful poet who feeds on those around him and
ultimately sucks them emotionally dry. In recent years,
Henze has become increasingly involved in international socialism, and that is reflected in his music. *Das
Ploss der 'Medusa'* ('The Raft of the "Medusa"') is a
requiem for Che Guevara; its première in Hamburg
(1968) was disrupted after a red flag had been draped
on the stage.

● Abbé Prevost's tale of *Manon Lescaut* has attracted

other composers besides Henze, including Daniel Auber, Richard Kleinmichel, ▷Massenet and ▷Puccini.

HERBERT, Victor (1859–1924)
Victor Herbert was the father of American operetta. He was born in Ireland and trained in Germany, but his music is very much of the 'New World' and it was on his theatrical shows that ▷George Gershwin, ▷Richard Rodgers and the others built. Herbert's most successful 'musicals' were *Naughty Marietta*, *Sweethearts*, and *Babes in Toyland* – all of which were filmed, the first two with Nelson Eddy and Jeanette Macdonald and the third with Laurel and Hardy. Earlier in his career Herbert was a distinguished conductor and was in charge of the Pittsburgh Symphony Orchestra for a number of years. (Once, when giving a concert in aid of the American Anti-Vivisection League, he informed the audience, with a straight face, that he was performing the music 'without cuts'.) His Cello Concerto No. 2 (written for his own considerable gifts as a soloist) was the work which inspired ▷Antonín Dvořák to compose *his* concerto for that instrument.

HERRMANN, Bernard (1911–1975)
It is for his film music that the American composer Bernard Herrmann is best known. He provided the scores for the great Orson Welles film *Citizen Kane* and for the amusing update of the Faust legend, *The Devil and Daniel Webster* (for which he won an Oscar). He also worked on several of Alfred Hitchcock's finest films, including *Vertigo*, *North by Northwest* and *Psycho* (in which the murder of Janet Leigh in a motel shower was made almost unbearably terrifying by Herrmann's screeching strings, slashing and thrusting with the killer's blade). But Herrmann also wrote works unconnected with the cinema industry. His symphony uses an unadventurous musical vocabulary but has plenty of vigour and a slow movement of some beauty. The opera *Wuthering Heights* captures much of the spirit of

Emily Brontë's novel and is often extremely lyrical. Edgar's aria in Act 3, 'Now art thou, dear, my golden June', could well become popular in its own right if the work were performed. Herrmann's mastery of the orchestra is always apparent, possibly because among his teachers was ▷Grainger, whose innovatory ideas still fascinate.

HEROES AND HEROINES
▷Vincenzo Bellini, *Norma*
▷Alexander Borodin, *Prince Igor*
▷Arthur Honegger, *Jeanne d'Arc au bûcher* ('Joan of Arc at the Stake')
▷Aram Khachaturian, *Spartacus*
▷Giacomo Puccini, *La Fanciulla del West* ('The Girl of the Golden West')
▷Richard Strauss, *Don Quixote*
▷Richard Wagner, *Lohengrin*

HINDEMITH, Paul (1895–1963)
The German composer Paul Hindemith was a leading figure in German musical life, whose views, expressed through his music, made him fall foul of the Nazis. His opera *Mathis der Maler*, about Matthias Grünewald, the 16th-century German painter who sided with the peasants against the authorities, conveyed a clear message. Hindemith was denounced in his native land: his works were banned and no mention of him was permitted in the press. He finally fled to Switzerland, then to the USA where he flourished and continued to compose prolifically.

Mathis der Maler (from which he made a 'symphony' for orchestra) is undoubtedly Hindemith's masterpiece. But his highly individual musical style is heard to excellent effect in another opera, *Cardillac*, about a maker of jewellery who prefers to murder his customers rather than have them take away his creations. It

> **NOW LISTEN**
>
> ▷Leonard Bernstein, *Serenade after Plato's Symposium*; Arnold Cooke, Clarinet Concerto; Lukas Foss, Baroque Variations; ▷George Frideric Handel, *Semele*; Walter Leigh, Concertino for harpsichord; ▷William Walton, Viola Concerto.

was an attempt to compose a neo-classical opera. Hindemith's output (which includes a vast amount of chamber music, most of it striking) rests on a number of colourful and exciting orchestral compositions. One of the best is the *Symphonic Metamorphosis on Themes by Carl Maria von Weber* whose forbidding and unwieldy title cloaks a marvellously engaging and easily enjoyed work. The *Konzertmusik* for strings and brass brilliantly contrasts the two sections of the orchestra. The music for the ballet *Nobilissima visione* , is arguably the most lyrical and beautiful Hindemith wrote. His shamefully neglected Violin Concerto is memorable, as is the Clarinet Concerto which exploits the instrument's colours and versatility to the full. Hindemith was a fine viola player and wrote several works for the instrument, including *Der Schwanendreher* in which the viola plays the role of minstrel, singing old German folktunes to the orchestra which represents 'a merry company'. He was also a distinguished teacher whose pupils included ▷Bernstein, Arnold Cooke, Lukas Foss and Walter Leigh.

HODDINOTT, Alun (born 1929)

The Welsh composer Alun Hoddinott writes music which is strongly constructed and mostly serious. He occasionally uses the 12-note technique, codified by Schoenberg, but is not a slave to it. Two works will show the listener whether Hoddinott's is the kind of music likely to intrigue: the *Sinfonia fidei*, which is economical in its gestures and whose reasoning is not hard to grasp, and the Variants for Orchestra, a slow and complex piece which can be rewarding. That Hoddinott is far from lacking in wit may be seen from his *Welsh Dances*, which are in the tuneful, charming vein of ▷Arnold.

HOLST, Gustav (1874–1934)

Gustav Holst belies more effectively than most the old image of the composer as a straggle-haired Bohemian, living in poverty in a garret. He spent nearly 30 years teaching music in a London girls' school: a respected bespectacled figure with a mild and charming manner.

NOW LISTEN ▷

Some music inspired by astrology or space: Karl-Birger Blomdahl, *Aniara*; ▷Emmanuel Chabrier,

He evidently enjoyed the job and devoted himself to it wholeheartedly, never allowing his composing to impinge on his duties. Holst is often, very properly, linked to ▷Vaughan Williams, the pair being regarded as pillars of English music. They were both deeply interested in folksong; both wrote music that shares a certain visionary quality. But Holst's style, besides being more austere, is also more imaginative and more inclined to stretch the intellect. It was a work of his, the opera *Sāvitri*, that paved the way for the church parables of ▷Britten. Holst's many fine concert works include the First Choral Symphony, which sets poems of John Keats, the enigmatic *Egdon Heath*, the lovely *Hymn of Jesus* and a couple of oriental works that repay attention, *Beni Mora* and the *Japanese Suite*.

But it is *The Planets* (1916) for which Holst will be remembered, a work enjoyed by everyone, irrespective of musical knowledge or experience. There are seven movements, nearly all concerned with the astrological influence supposedly exerted on Earth by the planets: Mars (war), Venus (peace), Jupiter (jollity), Uranus (magic), Saturn (old age) and Neptune (mysticism). Mercury, the winged messenger of the gods, also has a place. Mars, with its relentless, rhythmic menace, is said to have terrified the composer himself. The other planets are no less brilliantly characterized, with the dazzling effervescence of Mercury and Saturn's chilling progress to death seeing Holst's command of the huge orchestra at its most impressive. Jupiter is the one that contains the big, broad 'English' tune sometimes sung to the words 'I vow to thee, my country'.

Holst was always fascinated by military bands and the possibilities they offered to a composer. He wrote several superb pieces in this genre, none more remarkable than the Prelude and Scherzo *Hammersmith*. This haunting, elusive music is not what most people will expect from a band.

L'étoile; ▷Leoš Janáček, *The Excursions of Mr Brouček*; ▷Constant Lambert, *Horoscope*; ▷Josef Strauss, *Music of the Spheres*; ▷John Williams, *Star Wars*.

HONEGGER, Arthur (1892–1955)

It was a railway engine that first brought international fame to the French composer Arthur Honegger: he wrote a short orchestral piece intended to describe the locomotive known as Pacific 231. It starts with much

hissing and clanking, goes clickety-clack along the
track for a while, then pulls up at the next station
amidst more steam and squealing of brakes. The public loved it, and still do. It's good fun. With the exception of another hectic piece, *Rugby*, the rest of Honegger's output is fairly serious and includes a biblical
opera *Judith*, a dramatic psalm *King David*, and a stage
oratorio *Jeanne d'Arc au bûcher* ('Joan of Arc at the
Stake'). The five symphonies are much underrated
and underplayed. They are fresh, invigorating and
striking and have something individual to say (no. 4
makes considerable use of Swiss folktunes). Some of
Honegger's shorter concert works, notably a charming
Chamber Concerto for flute, cor anglais and strings
and a peaceful little essay called *Pastorale d'été*, are very
attractive. The three string quartets and some violin
sonatas show another side of this interesting composer.

- Honegger's taut Symphony no. 1 was commissioned by the conductor Serge Koussevitzky to
  mark the 50th anniversary of the Boston Symphony Orchestra. Other symphonies he commissioned for the occasion were ▷Prokofiev's
  Fourth, ▷Roussel's Third and ▷Stravinsky's
  Symphony of Psalms.

HORN
The horn is one of the most temperamental instruments in the orchestra. It is extremely difficult to play
and exponents are liable to 'split' notes or create 'bubbles' at embarrassing moments during solos. Nevertheless, the sound of the horn is one of music's great
glories and it has been used by countless composers to
create all kinds of mood – romantic melancholy
(▷Tchaikovsky's Fifth Symphony), impertinence
(▷Richard Strauss's *Till Eulenspiegel*), excitement
(▷Delibes' *Sylvia*), heroism (▷Wagner's *Siegfried*),
humour (▷Arnold's *Tam O'Shanter*). There are some
fine concertos, notably by ▷Mozart (four), ▷Richard
Strauss (two) and ▷Musgrave (one). Dennis Brain,

who died tragically young in 1957, was considered the greatest horn player of his time: indeed, some would say his uncanny brilliance has not been equalled since.

HOVHANESS, Alan (born 1911)

Alan Hovhaness is an American composer of Armenian and Scottish descent who has the distinction of having written a work for humpbacked whale and orchestra – *And God Created Great Whales*. The whale, to be sure, is on tape: performances would otherwise be hard to arrange. But, far from being a gimmick, the piece makes a profound impact. The almost human 'singing' of the highly intelligent mammal, interspersed with dramatic orchestral passages, must do more towards conservation of the species than any amount of banner-waving. Hovhaness has written a vast number of works, including 20 symphonies of which no. 4 is for wind and percussion and influenced by 7th-century Armenian church music and ▷Handel, among other composers. It is most enjoyable.

• Whales are depicted (instrumentally) in the *Sinfonia antarctica* by ▷Vaughan Williams.

HUMMEL, Johann Nepomuk (1778–1838)

One of ▷Mozart's pupils, Johann Nepomuk Hummel enjoyed success as a composer in his own time. Unluckily for him, he lived at the same time as ▷Beethoven, who overshadowed him. He wrote some attractive works. The Trumpet Concerto is a great favourite with players (the finale is enormous fun) and the Mandolin Concerto gives lots of opportunities to exponents of a somewhat neglected member of the lute family. Hummel's *Military Septet* is not especially military, but it is highly enjoyable. His seven piano concertos are rarely heard today but are known to have influenced ▷Chopin.

- Other composers who have used the mandolin in-
  clude ▷Mahler (Symphony no. 7), ▷Mozart (*Don
  Giovanni*), ▷Prokofiev (*Romeo and Juliet*), ▷Verdi
  (*Otello*) and ▷Webern (Five Orchestral Pieces).

HUMPERDINCK, Engelbert (1854–1921)
The German composer Engelbert Humperdinck
should not be confused with the English singer who
adopted the name in the 1960s to further his career in
the pop world. The real Humperdinck worked with
▷Wagner on the opera *Parsifal* (and, indeed, wrote a
few bars of music for its first performance which were
later dropped). His own operatic success was *Hänsel
und Gretel*, which has held its place in the repertory
since 1893, when its première was conducted by
▷Richard Strauss. Its style nods in the direction of
Wagner – not surprisingly, perhaps. But its melodies
have the direct simplicity and charm of nursery songs.
The famous duet 'Brother, come and dance with me' is
one of the most delightful in late 19th-century opera;
the Children's Prayer and the Sandman's Song are
meltingly lovely and the Witch's Ride is splendidly
rumbustious. The Grimm story of the youngsters who
find something nasty in the gingerbread house in the
woods could not have found a more sympathetic musical interpretation. None of Humperdinck's other
works (many of which were directed at children)
achieved comparable success and have largely been
forgotten.

I

IBERT, Jacques (1890–1962)

Jacques Ibert made his name outside his native France with a deliciously crazy piece for chamber orchestra called *Divertissement*, based on music he had written for the Labiche farce *An Italian Straw Hat*. It has everything from distorted versions of ▷Johann Strauss the younger's waltz *Blue Danube* and ▷Mendelssohn's 'Wedding March' to a cops-and-robbers finale featuring police whistles and a pianist who appears to take leave of his senses! Ibert is also known for a large-scale orchestral work, *Escales* ('Ports of Call'), which takes us on a musical tour of the Mediterranean – and splendidly exotic it is. He also wrote the popular little piano piece known as 'The Little White Donkey'. These works apart, little is heard of Ibert's output. If the opportunity arises, hear his scintillating Flute Concerto (which has been espoused by James Galway), the atmospheric *Symphonie marine*, depicting the sea in all its moods, and a riotously dishevelled *Bachannale* – written for, of all things, the tenth anniversary of the BBC Third Programme (now Radio 3).

INCIDENTALLY...

Music written to accompany stage productions includes:

▷Georges Bizet, *L'arlésienne* (Daudet)
▷Edvard Grieg, *Peer Gynt* (Ibsen)
▷Aram Khachaturian, *Masquerade* (Lermontov)
▷Dmitry Shostakovich, *Rule, Britannia* (Pyotrovsky)

▷Jean Sibelius, *Pelleas and Melisande* (Maeterlinck)
▷Arthur Sullivan, *The Merchant of Venice* (Shakespeare)

INDY, Vincent d' (1851–1931)

The opportunity to hear the music of the Frenchman Vincent d'Indy comes but seldom – a pity, for it is easy to become fond of this neglected composer. He was a disciple of ▷Wagner and a pupil of ▷Franck and there is something of both these men in his works. There is also a quality that takes us on to the French music of this century – and d'Indy was not averse to flouting conventions. His orchestral variations *Istar* are constructed the wrong way round. The ravishing tune on which the work is based doesn't appear until the last few moments; until then only tantalising hints of it have been given. D'Indy composed a fair number of other works, the best being the *Symphony on a French Mountaineer's Song* for piano and orchestra. It's a warmly tuneful work which could be used to enliven many a flagging concert season.

NOW LISTEN ▷

Some works by pupils of Vincent d'Indy: Georges Auric, *Phèdre*; ▷Joseph Canteloube, *Songs of the Auvergne*; ▷Albert Roussel, *Bacchus et Ariane*; ▷Erik Satie, *Parade*; ▷Joaquin Turina, *Canto a Sevilla*.

IPPOLITOV-IVANOV, Mikhail (1859–1935)

Mikhail Ippolitov-Ivanov was a Russian academic and conductor who left behind a handful of attractive works. He was a pupil of ▷Rimsky-Korsakov and his music progressed little from the older composer's style, being melodic and accessible. Ippolitov-Ivanov's best-known compositions are the *Caucasian Sketches*, of which the last 'The Procession of the Sardar', enjoys a life of its own as a concert encore. The Symphony in E minor is pleasant, with a succession of attractive tunes (▷Borodin, ▷Glazunov, or even ▷Tchaikovsky might have had a hand in some of them). *The Turkish Fragments*, dating from a visit to that country, are delightfully exotic.

IRELAND, John (1879–1962)
John Ireland, the English composer, wrote no operas or symphonies and few large-scale concert works. His was not that area of expertise. Ireland's talents are at their best in his piano music; many isolated pieces like the atmospheric *April* and the Nativity study *The Holy Boy* are exquisite while the collections (such as the 'island sequence' called *Sarnia*, about Guernsey) yield endless pleasure. Ireland's songs, too, are mostly splendid examples of a great English tradition. The cycle *The Land of Lost Content* is most beautiful. Such individual songs as *Sea Fever* and *I have twelve oxen* have rightly earned their place in recitals. There are many treasures to be unearthed among the chamber works, including a wonderful Cello Sonata and the Phantasie Trio for violin, cello and piano. The music Ireland wrote for orchestra is backward-looking in the best sense: it is melodic and romantic but in no way imitative. Ireland was very much his own man.

His Piano Concerto, with its ravishing slow movement and unexpectedly jazzy finale, is one of the finest works of its kind written in Britain this century. The orchestral pieces *Mai-Dun* and *The Forgotten Rite* are typical of this engaging composer and *A London Overture* (with its suggestion of a bus conductor calling out 'Piccadilly!') is a delight. *These Things shall Be* is a cantata written when war clouds were gathering over Europe in 1937; it is extraordinarily naive in its optimism but very enjoyable. Ireland was unhappy composing for the cinema. But his one film score, for *The Overlanders*, an Australian epic about cattle drovers, has some successful moments.

• Some other important 20th-century British piano concertos are by ▷Bliss, ▷Britten, ▷Delius, ▷Rawsthorne, ▷Rubbra, Cyril Scott and ▷Vaughan Williams.

IVES, Charles (1874–1954)
There has been nobody in musical history quite like

NOW LISTEN ▷

the American Charles Ives. He was a successful insurance man by trade, but his experiments as a composer produced music which was ahead of its time. In some cases, it is still puzzling. It was once said that no matter what ▷Schoenberg or ▷Stravinsky did, Ives had done it first. His musical attitudes were formed by his father who was a bandmaster and liked studying the effects of listening to four bands playing different tunes, in different keys at the same time. He encouraged Charles to whistle a melody in one key while he played the piano accompaniment in another – 'Just to stretch your ears', was how he put it. Ives grew up questioning musical conventions and seeking to expand them in all directions; and this he proceeded to do. Some of his music is as horrendously difficult to perform as it is to grasp: the Symphony no. 4, for instance, can need as many as four conductors just to hold it together. Even the 'simpler' pieces are demanding. *Putnam's Camp*, the second of the *Three Places in New England*, offers the listener several tunes played simultaneously in different keys. His most enigmatic and haunting work is *The Unanswered Question*, in which a solo trumpet discusses the problems of existence against a background of muted strings: but it still requires to be heard by ears sympathetic to the Ives world.

How does one enter that world? There are a great many works to try: orchestral and choral compositions, over 100 songs, piano pieces, chamber music and organ works, including a set of variations on the tune America which we know as 'God Save the Queen'. (This also exists in a version orchestrated by the American composer William Schuman). Ives's Third Symphony is straightforward and melodic and doesn't set your head spinning. So have a shot at it – then, when you've dipped a toe in the water, you can try experimenting with the great experimenter. Believe it or not, it's fun!

▷Percy Grainger, *The Warriors*; ▷Thea Musgrave, Chamber Concerto no. 2; ▷Charles Ruggles, *Suntreader*; ▷Edgard Varèse, *Arcana*.

J

JANÁČEK, Leoš (1854–1928)

The Czech composer Leoš Janáček was over 50 before he tasted real success, but having done so he never looked back, and in his last 25 years was powerfully creative. Somebody once described Janáček as 'the thinking man's ▷Puccini', no doubt intending a mild insult to both. Janáček certainly had the same feeling for the theatre as Puccini and the same ability to exploit the medium of opera to the full. His operas are tightly constructed, full of dramatic intensity. They also respond to human emotions with the most wonderful melody of a highly personal kind. Janáček was fascinated with the rhythms and colours of speech; he is known to have written down the 'notes' used by a hotel page-boy calling for a guest. Not surprisingly, his music moves – like speech – in short but telling bursts. His writing for the instruments of the orchestra often favours the high registers: even the timpani sometimes sound stratospheric.

Janáček's best-known operas cover a wide range of subjects. *Katya Kabanova* has an eternal triangle at its centre from which suicide is the only escape; *The Excursions of Mr Brouček* lampoons its hero's bourgeois weaknesses; *The Makropoulos Case* tells us that death is not to be feared but gives a meaning to life; *The Cunning Little Vixen* is about the cruelties and wonders of nature and features animals as well as humans; and *From the House of the Dead* (an adaptation of Dostoyevsky) extends pity to all prisoners but in particular to those incarcerated for their beliefs.

Jenůfa (1904) was Janáček's first major opera and his first success. In many ways it is also his finest. It is

NOW LISTEN ⟩

Other operas with folk themes: ▷Zoltán Kodály, *The Spinning Room*; ▷Bohuslav Martinů, *The Greek Passion*; Aarre Merikanto, *Juha*; Eugen Suchoň, *The Whirlpool*.

the harrowing tale of a village girl who has a child by an unscrupulous ne'er-do-well. She keeps the baby hidden from her neighbours until her mother takes it from the house and drowns it in the river, putting it under the ice. Later, in a horrifying climax, the ice melts and the tiny body is found. The drama moves at the pace of a play, the music mirroring perfectly its shifting moods: the long, claustrophobic scene in which mother, daughter and baby are cooped up in the darkened house, is almost unbearably tense.

Janáček's concert works are impressive. The substantial and strongly written *Glagolitic Mass*, designed to be sung in the open air but rarely enjoying that luxury, is a fine creation. The Sinfonietta, with its huge array of brass and percussion, is a thrilling experience; and so is *Taras Bulba*, a brilliant evocation of the Cossack hero. The *Lachian Dances* and the *Moravian Dances* are Janáček's equivalents of ▷Brahms's *Hungarian Dances* and ▷Dvořák's *Slavonic Dances*: lightweight pieces of great charm.

There is a small but interesting store of chamber music which includes a wind sextet called *Mlada* ('Youth') and a Concertino for piano and small ensemble. Two string quartets of a very personal nature were inspired by the young married woman with whom Janáček was deeply in love for the last years of his life. He wrote her more than 600 letters.

JOPLIN, Scott (1868–1917)

The black American composer Scott Joplin learnt his craft the hard way. From an early age he played the piano in brothels (so did ▷Brahms and ▷Puccini!). He soon became known as the 'King of Ragtime' and became famous when his *Maple Leaf Rag* was published in 1899. His rags are little piano pieces of a jazzy nature, mostly cheerful; the tunes are highly distinctive and cannot be confused with anyone else's. Joplin tried to write more extended pieces and craved the 'respectability' that might come if he composed an opera. *Treemonisha* received only one, woefully inadequate performance during his lifetime; its failure contributed greatly to the mental and physical collapse of Joplin, who died in an institution. Sadly, a recent per-

NOW LISTEN ▷

▷George Gershwin, Three Piano Preludes; Billy Mayerl, *Marigold* and other piano pieces; ▷Darius Milhaud, *La création du monde*; ▷Igor Stravinsky, *Ragtime*.

formance of the work reminds us that his skills lay elsewhere. The popularity of Joplin is due to the revival of ragtime in the early 1970s and to the film *The Sting*, which used his music, especially the rag *The Entertainer*. Two ballets, *Elite Syncopations* and *The Prodigal Son*, have been devised using the tunes of this most endearing composer.

K

KABALEVSKY, Dmitry (1904–1987)

Unlike some of his colleagues in the USSR, Dmitry Kabalevsky always followed party policy in relation to the business of composing. Where ▷Khachaturian, ▷Prokofiev and ▷Shostakovich among others found themselves in the musical wilderness for writing music that was 'unacceptable' to the authorities, Kabalevsky had no such problems. His list of works is vast but outside his native land he is known only for two: the overture to his opera *Colas Breugnon* (a sparkling showpiece) and some of the music he wrote for a children's play called *The Comedians*. The frenetic *Galop* is often used by acrobats and jugglers to whip up excitement and is almost as well known as Khachaturian's *Sabre Dance*, if not quite so noisy. Kabalevsky's three piano concertos are worth hearing if the chance arises. So is the Symphony no. 2 (of which there used to be a recording). It contains some high-spirited music which is appealing if undemanding.

KÁLMÁN, Imre (1882–1953)

The Hungarian Imre Kálmán began his musical career as a pianist and by all accounts would have become internationally famous. He had to change his plans, however, when he found he was suffering from neuritis. 'All that was left to me', he declared, 'was to write.' And write he did – to great effect. Kálmán quickly became one of Europe's most popular operetta composers – the best of his output being *The Gipsy Princess*, *Countess Maritza* and *The Circus Princess*. All had much the same story but Kálmán's invention never flagged

NOW LISTEN ▷

Some other examples of popular Viennese operetta: Ralph Benatzky, *White Horse Inn*; Eduard Künneke, *The Cousin from Nowhere*; ▷Franz Lehár, *Frasquita*; Robert

and each had a freshness that can still be enjoyed. His musical style belongs to what might be called the ▷Lehár school. But Kálmán is not so 'operatic' and is more inclined towards Hungarian melodies and rhythms. Towards the end of his life, he settled in the USA, where he continued to write for the theatre but without his earlier success.

Stolz, *Wild Violets*; ▷Johann Strauss the younger, *The Gipsy Baron*.

KERN, Jerome (1885–1945)

Jerome Kern was one of the great American songwriters of the 20th century, sharing the hall of fame with ▷Berlin, ▷Gershwin and ▷Porter. He successfully bridged the gap between the old-style Broadway shows of the early 1900s and the 'new' American musicals of the 20s and 30s. Kern's songs, simple yet infinitely refined, are still much performed: *Look for the silver lining*, *The way you look tonight*, *All the things you are*, and *Long ago and far away* are only a few. His big success in the theatre was the musical *Show Boat*, the tale of a Mississippi gambler's love for a young girl aboard a floating theatre in the days of slavery. The song *Ol' man river* was a personal success for the great bass Paul Robeson; other numbers from the show are *Only make believe*, *Why do I love you*, *Can't help loving that man* and the incomparable *Bill*. Another of Kern's musicals, *Roberta*, includes the imperishable *Smoke gets in your eyes*.

KETÈLBEY, Albert W. (1875–1959)

If ▷Coates ruled for many years as king of British light music, then Albert W. Ketèlbey was undoubtedly his crown prince. His talent was not of the sort that moves mountains but it was sufficient to give people the sort of tune they can whistle or sing in the bath. His greatest successes were *In a monastery garden* (complete with monks' chorus), *In a Persian market* (with the street cries of beggars), *Sanctuary of the heart* and *Bells across the meadows*. But Ketèlbey devotees will know *The Clock and the Dresden Figures* (in which the clock gets over-wound and the spring bursts with a twang at the end) and *'Appy 'Ampstead* (which quotes from ▷Verdi,

▷Rossini and *The Policeman's Holiday*). Ketèlbey composed purely to entertain – and succeeded.

KHACHATURIAN, Aram (1903–1978)
The Armenian composer Aram Khachaturian burst on the ears of the Western world through his rumbustious *Sabre Dance*, part of his ballet *Gayane*. In fact, this piece is representative neither of the composer at his best nor of the ballet. The rest of *Gayane*, a tale of love blossoming on a collective farm, shows more imagination and contains dances that are far more inventive. It leans heavily, as does all Khachaturian's music, on Armenian folk melodies and is attractively exotic. Another ballet, *Spartacus* (about the slave who led a revolt against the Romans) features the marvellous, sweeping melody that for years introduced the television series 'The Onedin Line'. The music Khachaturian wrote for a production of Lermontov's play *Masquerade* is popular in the concert hall, particularly its relentless waltz. His First Symphony is excellent in every way, highly atmospheric and striking in its orchestration and construction. Two other symphonies are considerably less good. The Violin Concerto is an exciting work which should be in every soloist's repertory but isn't: its breath-taking virtuosity is nicely contrasted with passages of lyrical poetry.

But his Piano Concerto (1936) is probably the work for which Khachaturian will be remembered. I recall a performance in the 1940s by Moura Lympany (who introduced the piece to Britain) which was quite hair-raising in its impact. The work is convincingly argued and full of contrasts – now electrifying, now languorous and sensuous. The first movement's opening, heavy-footed melody remains obstinately in the mind; the slow movement uses the eerie flexatone (an instrument which sounds rather like a musical saw) and the finale is launched by a tune which has more than a suggestion of saucy ragtime about it. Some of Khachaturian's chamber music is arresting (especially the highly original Trio for piano, violin and clarinet) and there is no shortage of interesting piano pieces (the *Album of Children's Pieces* is delightful).

NOW LISTEN ▷

▷Anton Arensky, Waltz from Suite no. 1 for two pianos; ▷Dmitry Kabalevsky, *The Comedians* suite; ▷Sergey Prokofiev, Piano Concerto no. 3; ▷Rodion Shchedrin, *The Little Humpbacked Horse*; ▷Dmitry Shostakovich, Symphony no. 1; Richard Yardumian, *Armenian Suite.*

KHRENNIKOV, Tikhon (born 1913)

Tikhon Khrennikov was the man who, as secretary-general of the Union of Soviet Composers, denounced such great composers as ▷Prokofiev and ▷Shostakovich for 'formalism': putting too much intellectual emphasis on the construction of their works at the expense of their content. In other words, for being too 'modern' and 'difficult' and not immediately appealing, in the spirit of socialist realism. Khrennikov's music is seldom played outside the USSR. What little has been heard, notably concertos for piano and for cello, is what one might expect: well fashioned and not unattractive, but empty and undemanding. He is worth remembering as a monument to a shameful period in Soviet musical history.

KODÁLY, Zoltán (1882–1967)

It was once said that to listen to Zoltán Kodály's music is to listen to the music of ▷Bartók without the problems and without the pain. The statement is, of course, a gross over-simplification, an insult to two great Hungarian composers, and it was intended to be flippant. There is, nevertheless, a tiny grain of truth in it. The two men were friends as well as colleagues and both worked diligently at collecting and transcribing the folk music of their native Hungary; and that folk music is at the root of everything they themselves wrote. Inevitably, a phrase here, a rhythm there, will be common to both. The difference between them lies in their musical language. Kodály's is more direct, less imaginative than Bartók's, perhaps. But it is equally significant in its own way.

Kodály's Concerto for Orchestra is a wonderfully vigorous, ear-catching work (astonishingly undervalued outside Hungary). The *Dances of Galanta* are a show-stopping experience with their dazzling colours, though Kodály buffs may prefer the less-often played *Peacock Variations*. The big choral work *Psalmus hungaricus* shows a deeper and more introspective side of Kodály: it is a significant and rewarding masterpiece. His opera *The Spinning-Room* is a village romance about a boy who has to lie low because he's accused of a crime he didn't do; his loved one helps to prove his

NOW LISTEN ▷

Some music by other Hungarian composers: ▷Béla Bartók, *Dance Suite*; ▷Ernö Dohnányi, *Ruralia hungarica*; Ferenc Erkel, *Bánk bán*; ▷György Ligeti, Six Bagatelles for wind quintet.

innocence. It's full of splendid folky tunes and dances and is told with a fine sense of theatre.

But it is the concert suite from another opera, *Háry János* (1926), that is Kodály's best-loved piece. Háry is an old Hungarian soldier who tells blatant lies about his prowess on the battlefield (he would have us believe that he defeated Napoleon's army single-handed). The score makes much use of the cimbalom, a Hungarian zither whose strings are struck with padded sticks. The Viennese musical clock movement is a marvellous confection using all manner of percussion effects; the Defeat of Napoleon features a hilariously doleful saxophone; and the Intermezzo has a catchy tune (which I recall being played on numerous radio request programmes in the 1950s). Kodály's genius is evident from the first bar (an orchestral sneeze) to the last (a massive thump on a solo bass drum). Much of his vocal music was written for amateur choral societies who enjoy its style, and his chamber music exerts a strong appeal. The Sonata for solo cello is a tour de force attempted only by the bold or the foolhardy!

KOECHLIN, Charles (1867–1950)
The French composer Charles Koechlin was very much his own man. It's possible to find all sorts of influences in his music, from the music of medieval monks to ▷Stravinsky and beyond. But a Koechlin score sounds like nobody else's. Unfortunately, for he is a composer of great fascination, performances of his works are rare. But don't miss any, and search for recordings, especially of the symphonic poem *Les bandar-log* (they, you will recall, were the monkeys in Rudyard Kipling's *Jungle Book*, a literary work of which Koechlin was extremely fond). The piece is a stunning musical depiction of the dark, green jungle. The monkeys chatter and screech with nerve-tingling abandon. (The opening pages recall ▷Stravinsky's *The Rite of Spring*, but with added warmth.) The Ballade for piano and orchestra sometimes reminds us that Koechlin was a pupil of the elegant ▷Fauré; sometimes we could be in the realm of ▷Bartók. But the whole splendid piece is organised by a highly original mind. The Seven Stars' Symphony is not really a

symphony, more a series of musical sketches written in homage to some of the leading figures in Hollywood at the time, including Douglas Fairbanks, Greta Garbo, Marlene Dietrich and Charlie Chaplin. Don't expect anything resembling film music: the piece is strange and mystical but very haunting.

KORNGOLD, Erich Wolfgang (1897–1957)
Film buffs know and love Erich Wolfgang Korngold for the wonderful scores he wrote for such films as *The Adventures of Robin Hood* (the Errol Flynn version) and *The Sea Hawk*, not to mention *Captain Blood*. They may not be so familiar with the music he wrote outside Hollywood. In his early days in Europe, before the Nazis forced him to flee to the USA, Korngold was considered one of the most important rising composers. His youthful talents were even likened to those of ▷Mozart and his achievements put on a par with those of ▷Schoenberg; ▷Puccini admired his work, ▷Richard Strauss was 'filled with awe' and ▷Mahler described him as a genius. He wrote many works between 1920 and 1935, including a Piano Concerto for the left hand, a delightful Sinfonietta and the opera *Die tote Stadt* ('The Dead City'), a slightly unhealthy fantasy about a husband who thinks his dead wife has been reincarnated in the form of another girl. The music is, notwithstanding, beautifully lush. Until the end of World War II, he devoted his energies to composing some of Hollywood's best film music. In 1945, however, he wrote his Violin Concerto. One critic said it was 'more Korn than Gold'; another described it as 'this most lovable of concertos'. Make up your own mind. The Symphony, which followed a few years later, is a striking work, harking back to Richard Strauss rather than attempting to cut new paths.

KREISLER, Fritz (1875–1962)
Fritz Kreisler was one of the greatest violinists of the 20th century, possessing a warm, sweet tone to which no other player has aspired. He also found time to compose operettas and salon pieces which have stood the test of time: *Liebesfreud, Liebesleid, Tambourin chi-*

NOW LISTEN ⟩
▷Franz Lehár, *Guiditta*; ▷Giacomo Puccini, *La rondine* ('The Swallow'); ▷Richard Strauss, *Alpine Symphony*; ▷William Walton, *Violin Concerto*; ▷Alexander Zemlinsky, *A Florentine Tragedy*.

nois, Schön Rosmarin and many others are in the reper-
tories of nearly all leading violinists today. Kreisler's
mischievous sense of humour got him into trouble with
some critics after he fooled them by playing pieces
which he claimed were by 17th- and 18th-century
composers but which were actually his own. His friend
▷Rakhmaninov made brilliant piano transcriptions of
some of Kreisler's music.

L

LALO, Edouard (1823–1892)
The French composer Edouard Lalo is one of those composers whose works are waiting to be discovered by many music-lovers who would enjoy them enormously if they knew them. The *Symphonie espagnole* for violin and orchestra is his only piece performed regularly in the concert hall and, delightful though it is, it's not his best. The splendid Cello Concerto is much more imaginative and better constructed (it has a deliciously cheeky sequence in its second movement which is utterly irresistible). The almost forgotten Piano Concerto is likewise effective with a particularly lovely slow movement. The Symphony in G minor, championed and conducted by Sir Thomas Beecham for many years, doesn't deserve its neglect, even if it does offer the odd whiff of ▷Brahms and ▷Schumann. Anyone seeking a quick idea of Lalo's engaging style can do no better than try some of the music he wrote for the ballet *Namouna*, which is set in Cyprus and revolves round a gypsy girl who fascinates two young men. (She enjoys smoking and the score contains a Cigarette Waltz, banned from some theatres because of fire risk.) The short Scherzo for orchestra is a powerful piece. The *Norwegian Rhapsody* is what ▷Grieg might well have written had he lived in France. Lalo's one successful opera, *Le roi d'Ys*, is attractive and offers many lovely melodies, including the tenor Aubade (morning song) which remains in the memory after one hearing. The story is about a woman, jealous of her happily betrothed sister, who floods the town in a fit of pique!

NOW LISTEN ⟩
▷Georges Bizet, *The Pearl Fishers*; ▷Jules Massenet, Piano Concerto; ▷Camille Saint-Saëns, Cello Concerto no. 1; Pablo Sarasate, *Zigeunerweise*.

LAMBERT, Constant (1905–1951)

The Englishman Constant Lambert made his name as a brilliant conductor of ballet. He never permitted performances in the pit to become sloppy, and dancers revered him. But he was also a gifted composer, as we are discovering thanks to the record industry. Not surprisingly, several of his scores were for dancing: *Romeo and Juliet* was commissioned by Diaghilev and is a brilliantly successful piece, dazzlingly orchestrated and ear-tickling. *Pomona* is nothing more than a diversion – nymphs and shepherds in ancient Rome – but the music is skilfully written and attractive. Lambert's love of jazz comes to the fore in his best ballet, *Horoscope*, which has an astrological story about two lovers. Jazz is also an element in the Concerto for piano and nine players, a surprisingly cerebral work which can sound dry unless idiomatically played. Lambert's finest achievement is *The Rio Grande* for piano, contralto chorus and orchestra. Its bouncing rhythms and sensuous interludes are effective and immensely enjoyable.

LANGLAIS, Jean (born 1907)

The blind French organist and composer Jean Langlais has made some fine contributions to organ literature. His French, American and Baroque suites are all popular with recitalists, as are his *Trois poèmes évangéliques*. His Mass 'Salve regina' is for three solo voices, choir, two organs and two brass ensembles and is highly effective, even if it is a clever pastiche of Renaissance French music.

LANNER, Josef (1801–1843)

Josef Lanner was the first composer to write a large quantity of Viennese dance music. For a time, he directed an ensemble with ▷Johann Strauss the elder (father of the 'Waltz King'). Later, they became rivals, vying with each other to play at leading ballrooms. One critic summed up their styles: 'With Lanner, it is: "Pray dance, I beg you!". With Strauss, it is: "You must dance, I command you!"'. Lanner's music is most attractive, well structured and the model for

NOW LISTEN

▷Arthur Bliss, *Rout*; Duke Ellington, *Hot and Bothered*; ▷Erik Satie, *Parade*; ▷Maurice Ravel, Piano Concerto in G; ▷William Walton, *Façade*.

many composers who followed in his footsteps. His finest works include the waltz *Die Werber* ('The Suitors'), which shows Hungarian influence, and the so-called *Steam Waltz and Galop*, written to mark the placing of a railway engine in a Vienna park for public inspection in 1834.

LEHÁR, Franz (1870–1948)

In the post-▷Johann Strauss era, Franz Lehár was the king of operetta in Vienna – and beyond. He had a string of successes, begun by the incomparable *Merry Widow*, which is probably the most popular musical ever written (and that includes Strauss's *Die Fledermaus*). Its story is every bit as flimsy as such stories invariably are: a wealthy woman is persuaded by a plausible playboy to keep her millions in her homeland. The tunes, however, are far from flimsy and include the perennial 'Vilja' (every soprano's dream), 'Maxim's' and the Merry Widow Waltz which must be familiar to everyone. Lehár never quite equalled its success. But many enthusiasts prefer the music of some of his other operettas, notably *The Land of Smiles* (a tear-jerker about a Chinese prince and his ill-fated love for a Viennese socialite), *The Count of Luxembourg* (revolving round an impoverished but charming nobleman) and *Paganini* (which romanticises the life of the great Italian violinist who was supposed to be in league with the Devil). *Friederike* is a pleasing piece about the poet Goethe; *Giuditta*, the most operatic of Lehár's theatre pieces, was not liked by Mussolini because it's about an Italian soldier who deserts the army for love. In many of his operettas, Lehár was writing for the great tenor Richard Tauber, who became strongly associated with the song 'You are my heart's delight' from *The Land of Smiles*. Lehár also wrote fine waltzes for the ballroom and concert hall, notably *Gold and Silver*. But a violin concerto and some symphonic poems seem to have vanished without trace. In 1975 the conductor John Lanchbery concocted a danced version of *The Merry Widow* for the Australian Ballet.

NOW LISTEN ▷

Lehár lived in what became known as the 'Golden Age of Viennese Operetta'; composers of the so-called 'Silver Age' that followed included: ▷Leo Fall, *The Dollar Princess*; ▷Imre Kálmán, *Countess Maritza*; ▷Fritz Kreisler, *Apple Blossoms*; Oskar Nedbal, *Polish Blood*; ▷Oscar Straus, *A Waltz Dream*.

LEONCAVALLO, Ruggero (1857–1919)
Fate dealt a poor hand to the Italian composer Ruggero Leoncavallo. He had high hopes for an opera he was writing called *La bohème*, based on a story by the French novelist Henri Murger. But ▷Puccini's opera on the same story, now among the most popular pieces in the repertory, was staged first and when the two were compared, Leoncavallo's came off worst. In fact, it is by no means bad and would probably have done well in other circumstances. (In Puccini's opera, the poet Rodolfo is the main character; in Leoncavallo's, the leading man is Marcello the painter.) The one great success of Leoncavallo's was the opera *Pagliacci* ('Clowns'), a wonderful piece of melodrama about the leader of a troupe of strolling players who discovers his wife is being unfaithful. In the final moments, he kills her in a jealous rage, in front of a horrified audience of villagers. The opera contains one of the most popular tenor arias ever written, 'Vesti la giubba' (or 'On with the motley' as it's known in English), sung by the wretched actor as he puts on his clown's make-up. The show must go on, despite his breaking heart.

• For many years *Pagliacci*, a short opera, has been paired in the theatre with ▷Mascagni's *Cavalleria rusticana* which is equally short and also based on the ravages of jealousy. The duo are affectionately known in the musical world as '*Cav* and *Pag*' or, more mischievously, 'The Terrible Two'.

LIGETI, György (born 1923)
Many people have been exposed to the music of György Ligeti and not realised it. Three of his works, the choral Requiem and *Lux aeterna* and the orchestral *Atmosphères*, were used in Stanley Kubrick's film *2001–A Space Odyssey*. They were selected by the director for their 'other worldly' effects, which are entirely suitable to scenes in outer space. But the ideas of this Hungarian leader of the avant garde are not always easy to take. Some of the 'clouds of sound' Ligeti conjures up are fascinating (one critic wrote 'they will in-

NOW LISTEN >
Other works selected by Stanley Kubrick for *2001*: ▷Aram Khachaturian, *Gayane*; ▷Johann Strauss the younger, *Blue Danube*; ▷Richard Strauss, *Also sprach Zarathustra*.

terest or exasperate the listener'). But on other occasions, when he requires singers to grunt and howl, the music actually sounds unpleasant. His early String Quartet no. 2 is in a very modern idiom but is not beyond the reach of anyone keen to 'stretch his ears', as ▷Ives might have said. If you can hear the Six Bagatelles for wind quintet, do so. They are splendid. Ligeti withdrew them from circulation for a while.

LISZT, Ferenc (1811–1886)

The Hungarian Ferenc Liszt (often known as Franz) has been called many things: genius, charlatan, virtuoso, showman, entrepreneur, libertine, innovator are only some. His personal life was certainly racy, to say the least. He was a brilliant and flamboyant pianist whose public appearances attracted the kind of wild following enjoyed by the ▷Beatles in the 1960s. He lived with, but never married, a countess for many years; one of their children, Cosima, married ▷Wagner. But tales of his love-affairs all over Europe were rife. Even after he took minor holy orders late in life, rumours of his sexual athleticism continued. Not surprisingly, this side of his life was exploited fully in Ken Russell's appalling film *Lisztomania*. But beneath all this frenzied, almost manic, activity there lay a sensitive, imaginative and extremely forward-looking composer whose music provided a spur to many who followed him, including ▷Debussy, ▷Richard Strauss and ▷Wagner.

Since Liszt had a phenomenal understanding of the piano and its capabilities, it is his piano music that brings out the best in him. The three books of pieces called *Années de pèlerinage* ('Years of Pilgrimage') contain many marvellous ideas and fresh use of old techniques; the celebrated *Hungarian Rhapsodies* are deliberately more popular in style but no less interesting and frequently exciting. The Sonata, a massive conception, is a pillar of the piano repertory and highly demanding of any pianist in its technique and interpretation. The *Transcendental Studies* explore aspects of pianism in the most testing but diverting of ways.

Unlike ▷Chopin, Liszt was at home writing for the orchestra, and his *Faust* and *Dante* symphonies are

NOW LISTEN ▷

Liszt transcribed for the piano several orchestral or vocal masterpieces by other composers, including: ▷Ludwig van Beethoven, Symphony no. 7; ▷Hector Berlioz, *Harold in Italy*; ▷Fryderyk Chopin, *Six Polish Songs*; ▷Gioachino Rossini, *William Tell* overture; ▷Franz Schubert, many songs (including *Erlkönig*); ▷Carl Maria von Weber, *Der Freischutz* overture.

wonderfully entertaining, as are the pioneering symphonic poems, particularly *Les préludes* and *Mazeppa*. He wrote several works for piano and orchestra. The *Hungarian Fantasia* and the *Totentanz* ('Dance of Death') are not as frequently played as they should be.

Liszt's two piano concertos (1855 and 1857) are deservedly popular. The First opens with a striding, energetic melody which becomes increasingly important as the work progresses, and actually ends it. In between are a nocturnal sequence of great beauty and a lively scherzo, pointed up by the triangle (Liszt's detractors still refer to this work as 'the Triangle Concerto'). The Second Concerto begins on a note of quiet mystery and only gradually builds to the power and intensity of its predecessor (the veiled beginning led it to be described as 'The Arabian Nights Concerto'). Liszt's songs should not be overlooked. They are a good deal more interesting and enjoyable than their comparative neglect would seem to suggest.

LITOLFF, Henry (1818–1891)

Henry Litolff was an Anglo-French composer and music publisher who wrote a large number of operas, operettas and chamber works. He also composed five substantial 'symphonic concertos' for piano and orchestra. All we know of his music today is the Scherzo from no. 4, a sparkling little piece based on two splendid tunes, often played at concerts of lighter fare. It can also be found as a 'fill-up' on many recordings of other people's music. Litolff has thus become one of the most famous of 'one-work' composers; but it's a work many would have been pleased to write.

LLOYD WEBBER, Andrew (born 1948)

The English composer Andrew Lloyd Webber has won awards for many of his musicals, including *Jesus Christ Superstar*, *Evita* (with its successful song 'Don't Cry for me Argentina'), *Cats*, *Starlight Express* and *The Phantom of the Opera*, as well as the most charming of them, *Joseph and the Amazing Technicolor Dreamcoat*. The best known of his non-theatre pieces are *Variations*, written for his cellist brother Julian and based on

▷Paganini's Caprice no. 2, and the Requiem, which has been recorded by a stellar assemblage including the tenor Placido Domingo and the conductor Lorin Maazel. Its 'Pie Jesu', strongly suggestive of the corresponding passage in ▷Fauré's Requiem, was a hit for a time. Some may find Lloyd Webber's musicals somewhat short in really memorable tunes but there is no denying their appeal.

LOESSER, Frank (1910–1969)

Frank Loesser composed American musicals. *Guys and Dolls* is based on stories by Damon Runyon and shows how a New York gambler sets out to dupe a Salvation Army girl, but has the tables turned on him. Its wonderful songs include 'Luck be a lady tonight' and 'If I were a bell' (the opening sequence includes a fugue sung by gamblers poring over the racing pages of their newspapers). Another, *Most Happy Fella*, is more operatic and has a less satisfactory plot about an aging man who resorts to trickery to win a young girl's hand. But the story is handled with great skill and taste. Its hit number is 'Standing on the corner, watching all the girls go by' and it requires a bass of opera-house quality to sing the leading role.

LOEWE, Frederick (1901–1988)

In collaboration with the writer Alan Jay Lerner, the American composer Frederick Loewe wrote five hit musicals before heart trouble forced him to retire. The inspired tunes of this Austrian-born composer enlivened *Brigadoon, Paint your Wagon, My Fair Lady, Camelot* and *Gigi*. *My Fair Lady*, a musical version of George Bernard Shaw's play *Pygmalion*, had the blessing of the crusty old dramatist himself and contains such numbers as 'I've grown accustomed to her face', 'Get me to the church on time', 'Wouldn't it be lovely?', 'I'm getting married in the morning' and 'The rain in Spain'. It is one of the all-time greats in the world of musical theatre.

• Another Shaw play was the basis of a musical,

NOW LISTEN ⟩

Other great Broadway musicals written since 1945: ▷Irving Berlin, *Annie get your Gun*; ▷Frederick Loewe, *My Fair Lady*; ▷Cole Porter, *Kiss me Kate*; ▷Richard Rodgers, *South Pacific*; ▷Stephen Sondheim, *Follies*; Jule Styne, *Gipsy*.

again with the playwright's approval: *Arms and the Man* became ▷Straus's *The Chocolate Soldier*, the nickname of the hero who prefers to carry a bar of chocolate rather than a gun.

LORTZING, Albert (1801–1851)

The German composer Albert Lortzing must be the only internationally known composer who began his musical career as the leading tenor in an opera company. It is not known what his voice was like, but his stage experience equipped him well for writing operas. His best are still performed regularly on the Continent and are delightfully tuneful in a thoroughly traditional way, in the line from ▷Weber on the German side and ▷Donizetti on the Italian. Lortzing's masterpiece is *Zar und Zimmermann* ('Tsar and Carpenter'), which has an amusing romantic plot built round the Russian ruler Peter the Great's stay in the Netherlands, where he learnt the trade of ship's carpenter. *Der Wildschütz* ('The Poacher') is probably his most popular work, despite a highly improbable plot. Opera students find it fascinating that Lortzing wrote an opera that anticipates one of ▷Wagner's: *Hans Sachs* is about the philosophical cobbler who was to become the central character of *Die Meistersinger*. There are certain similarities which suggest that Wagner knew the earlier work well.

● Many composers used Peter the Great's visit to the Netherlands as an opera subject; the best known are ▷Donizetti's *The Burgomaster of Saardam*, ▷Flotow's *Peter and Catherine*, Andre Grétry's *Peter the Great* and ▷Meyerbeer's *L'étoile du nord* ('The North Star').

LULLY, Jean-Baptiste (1632–1687)

Jean-Baptiste Lully began life as a servant but his musical talents were recognised and he quickly progressed, becoming a court dancer, a leading violinist and finally composer to the French king Louis XIV.

His music is not as imaginative as that of some of his contemporaries, but his works are fresh and attractive and often broke new ground. It was Lully who developed a style of writing particularly suited to the French language; he also introduced more ballet into the world of opera (employing professional female dancers for the first time) and recognised the dramatic use to which a chorus can be put in opera. Lully enjoyed a long association with the great French dramatist Molière, composing music for many of his plays, notably *Le bourgeois gentilhomme* (Lully appeared in the première of that comedy as an actor and dancer). While he was conducting a performance of his *Te Deum* with a large stick, he struck his foot; the foot became infected and Lully died.

• Some 20th-century composers who have based works on Molière's plays include ▷Benjamin (*Tartuffe*), ▷Martin (*M de Porceaugnac*), ▷Richard Strauss (*Le bourgeois gentilhomme*), ▷Wolf-Ferrari, (*L'amour médécin*) and ▷Walton (*Les fourberies de Scapin*).

LUMBYE, Hans Christian (1810–1874)
Hans Christian Lumbye was known as 'the Scandinavian Strauss' because for years he entertained the people of Copenhagen with concerts of his music at the Tivoli Gardens. His waltzes, polkas and especially galops are still played in Denmark with as much affection as the music of the ▷Strauss family is in Vienna. Some of Lumbye's music found its way into the repertory of the Royal Danish Ballet, though he could never be described as a ballet composer. He shared with Johann Strauss the ability to conjure up a dance at a moment's notice – and for practically any occasion. His most popular galop was inspired by the opening of a railway line into Copenhagen.

LUTOSŁAWSKI, Witold (born 1913)
The sound-world created by the Polish composer Witold Lutosławski is fascinating. Early in his career, between 1940 and 1960, his music followed traditional paths and is often beguiling: the Symphonic Variations, the Concerto for Orchestra and the Variations on a Theme of Paganini for two pianos date from this period and are recommended to questing listeners without reservation. Lutosławski's later compositions, however, are rather more uncompromising. His idiom changed radically. His Symphony no. 2, *Mi-parti* for orchestra and the String Quartet are examples of this later style. But give his *Livre* for orchestra of 1968 a try. If its sighs, stabs, snarls, sunshine and shadows appeal to you – as well they may, for it is a compelling piece – then this remarkable man's music is probably for you. As a conductor Lutosławski is a persuasive interpreter of his own music.

• Other composers noted for the perceptive conducting of their own scores are ▷Bliss, ▷Britten, ▷Copland, ▷Elgar, ▷Henze, ▷Khachaturian and ▷Walton.

LYADOV, Anatol (1855–1914)
If he hadn't been so lazy and self-critical, the Russian composer Anatol Lyadov might have occupied a more important place in musical history. He was commissioned to write the score for Diaghilev's ballet *The Firebird* but he failed to produce it and the task was handed to ▷Stravinsky. Lyadov composed little of substance, though his works are excellent, especially the three tone poems *Baba-Yaga*, *Kikimora* and *The Enchanted Lake* (all based on Russian folktales). Lyadov did much research into Russian folksongs and orchestrated eight of them to attractive effect. His piano music, notably a tiny novelty called *A Musical Snuffbox*, is enjoyable and plainly has ▷Chopin as its distant model.

MACDOWELL, Edward (1860–1908)

Edward MacDowell is often called 'the father of American music' yet is remembered today mainly by one tiny piano piece, *To a Wild Rose*. Exquisite though it is, he wrote much better and more significant piano music. The *Sonata eroica*, for example, is a splendidly powerful work of ▷Lisztian proportions, inspired by the Arthurian legend. The strength and dignity of Arthur himself are memorably depicted as are the forest of Camelot, the love of Guinevere for Lancelot and the final battle between the king and the evil Modred. The Piano Concerto no. 2 is a particularly enjoyable example of MacDowell's style (it's plain that he had heard ▷Tchaikovsky's famous B flat minor Concerto) and the *Indian Suite* for orchestra is as fascinating as it is unusual, using melodies the composer heard when he was among the Iroquois Indians. MacDowell became mentally ill towards the end of his life and died at the age of 47. In Peterborough, New Hampshire, MacDowell Colony still exists where musicians and artists can study and work.

NOW LISTEN ▷

Other works inspired by the Arthurian legend: ▷Arnold Bax, *Tintagel*; ▷Edward Elgar, *King Arthur*; ▷Frederick Loewe, *Camelot*; ▷Henry Purcell, *King Arthur*; ▷Richard Wagner, *Tristan und Isolde*.

MAGNARD, Albéric (1865–1914)

The death of Albéric Magnard was a good deal more dramatic than his life. He perished at his home outside Paris while trying to keep out invading German soldiers; he killed one before he himself was fatally injured. The Germans then burnt his house, destroying some of his music. Magnard was a quiet, dignified academic and some of his music is rather austere. But the third of his four symphonies is warmly romantic ınd exciting, and the fourth is strongly structured and richly rewarding. None of his three operas is performed today, though Magnard experts declare that *Bérénice* (based on Racine's great work) is well worth reviving. Magnard's music has touches of his friend >Franck about it; hints, too, of his teacher ▷d'Indy and even of ▷Bruckner. But it has a firm stamp of originality and occasionally looks ahead to the world of >Ravel. He is a composer not well represented by recordings, but what there are will not disappoint a listener seeking something different.

MAHLER, Gustav (1860–1911)

It took a long time for the music of Gustav Mahler to 'arrive'. But having done so, it established itself with the utmost rapidity. Mahler's music is romantic, eloquent and very beautiful. It is not, however, always 'comfortable' to be with. It speaks with a deeply personal voice, and when that voice utters a cry of anguish, the effect can be extremely disturbing. He is a man of song and symphony. No operas here (three were destroyed by the composer), no concertos, no piano pieces and very little chamber music. His nine symphonies (and the unfinished tenth) embody what he had to say to the world, and are a remarkable mixture of the mystic, the childlike, the popular, the profound and the ironic. Each is memorable in its own way, no. 5 being arguably the best loved (its slow movement achieved additional fame when it was used for Visconti's film *Death in Venice*). The Second, Third and Eighth use a chorus in addition to the orchestra. The song cycles, with orchestra, contain what many believe to be the essence of Mahler. *Lieder eines fahrenden Gesellen* ('The Songs of a Wayfarer') are marvellous, as are the *Kindertotenlieder* ('Songs on the Death of Children'). Some think these are morbid, and they are certainly harrowing and extremely moving.

Das Lied von der Erde ('The Song of the Earth') (1909) is neither song nor symphony but lies in between. It is possible, as some conductors do, to treat it as a vast symphonic structure; it is equally feasible to perform it as a sequence of beautifully atmospheric songs. Sensitively handled, it will work superbly either way. In it Mahler sets six poems most strikingly for mezzo-soprano (or baritone), tenor and orchestra. The final sequence, 'Abschied' ('Farewell'), is impressive in a good performance; in a great one it is almost unbearably moving. Mahler himself once asked: 'Can this be endured. Will people not kill themselves afterwards?'.

● In addition to being a great composer, Mahler was a distinguished conductor with a wide range of interests. In the opera house he conducted performances of ▷Gluck's *Orfeo ed Euridice*, ▷Wagner's *Ring* and ▷Verdi's *Falstaff*. In the concert hall his repertory ranged from ▷Haydn symphonies to ▷Rakhmaninov's new Piano Concerto no. 3. Mahler also edited many works by other composers, including ▷Schumann's symphonies and ▷Mozart's *The Marriage of Figaro*.

MAKING WAVES
▷Benjamin Britten, 'Four Sea Interludes' from *Peter Grimes*
▷Claude Debussy, *La Mer* ('The Sea')
▷Edward Elgar, *Sea Pictures*
▷Maurice Ravel, *Un barque sur l'océan* ('A Boat on the Ocean')
Juventino Rosas, *Over the Waves*
▷Ralph Vaughan Williams, *A Sea Symphony*

MALIPIERO, Gian Francesco (1882–1973)
The Italian Gian Francesco Malipiero earned the gratitude of the musical word by editing the complete works of ▷Monteverdi at a time when little was known of that composer; it is generally considered that Malipiero's advocacy was largely responsible for the present-day interest in Monteverdi. He also produced valuable editions of music by ▷Vivaldi and ▷Frescobaldi. The idiom of Malipiero's own compositions is of our own century and sometimes owes much to the impressionism of ▷Debussy and to ▷Stravinsky. But underlying everything is his alle-

giance to 16th- and 17th-century music. The mixture makes for an unusual but undeniably attractive style and his music should be heard on the rare opportunities afforded to us. His 13 symphonies are descriptive of a variety of subjects, including the sea, bells, the Zodiac, death, the seasons and silence (!), and they have a great deal to commend them. Of the many concertos, the Violin Concerto no. 2 is especially striking, well worth investigating if you can find a recording. Malipiero wrote about 30 operas, one called *Don Giovanni* (though it is in no way modelled on ▷Mozart's).

● Other composers who have written works based on the amours of Don Giovanni (or Don Juan, to give him his more familiar title) are Franco Alfano (best known as the man who completed ▷Puccini's last opera *Turandot*), Alexander Dargomÿzhsky, ▷Delibes, Eugene Goossens, Giovanni Paisiello and ▷Richard Strauss.

MARTIN, Frank (1890–1974)

Frank Martin and ▷Honegger are the most important 20th-century Swiss composers. Martin's music is inventive, searching, often profound and requires a fair measure of concentration. Once the listener has found Martin's wavelength, however, his works offer a richly rewarding source of enjoyment. The *Petite symphonie concertante* is probably his most fascinating composition, playing with the sonorities of the harp, harpsichord and piano against a background of strings. His less-often played Concerto for seven wind instruments, timpani and strings is another unusual and interesting piece. The Ballades for saxophone, piano and strings gives further proof of this composer's delight in blending unfamiliar instrumental groupings. Martin's opera *Der Sturm* is closely based on Shakespeare's *The Tempest* and is sensitive and atmospheric. Two oratorios, *Le vin herbé* (inspired by the legend of Tristan and Isolda) and *In terra pax* (written to mark the end of World War II), are among Martin's most formidable scores, the latter being particularly moving.

- Martin's *Petite symphonie concertante* was commissioned by the Swiss conductor Paul Sacher for his Basle Chamber Orchestra. So were ▷Bartok's Music for Strings, Percussion and Celesta and his Divertimento. Other composers who received commissions from Sacher included ▷Berio, ▷Henze, ▷Hindemith, ▷Honegger, ▷Ibert, ▷Malipiero, ▷Richard Strauss, ▷Stravinsky and ▷Tippett.

MARTINŮ, Bohuslav (1890–1959)

In a just world, the music of the Czech composer Bohuslav Martinů would be performed more often than it is and would enjoy greater popularity than it does. His work is often said to be uneven and so it is. But at its best it is magnificent; and there never was a composer who wasn't prone to the odd lapse. Martinů's numerous compositions have a directness and freshness that are most appealing once the listener has absorbed something of his style and learnt to recognise his distinctive thumb prints. His six symphonies communicate a wide variety of moods from the sunniest gaiety to the darkest sorrow. But all are wonderfully vibrant and give off what the American composer and critic ▷Virgil Thomson called 'a shining sound'. No. 4 is probably the easiest to get to know quickly and, if it appeals, the others will provide no problems.

Martinů wrote concertos for various instruments. They contain much inspired material and again conjure up many different atmospheres. The Concerto for violin, piano and orchestra, for instance, is a dark, unsettled work of great strength. The Violin Concerto no. 2, on the other hand, is radiant and serene. One of Martinů's ballets, *Špalíček*, is particularly engaging: several of its dances remain in the mind even when you want them to go away! Most of his chamber music is worth investigating, notably the string quartets, and the piano works boast numerous gems, such as the *Bergerettes*, which have the same kind of charm as ▷Dvořák's *Slavonic Dances*.

Two of Martinů's operas are outstanding. *Julietta* is

NOW LISTEN ▷

Some works from Martinů's Czech heritage: ▷Antonin Dvořák, *Rusalka*; Zdeněk Fibich, *At Twilight*; Josef Foerster, symphonies; ▷Vítežslav Novák, *The Storm*; ▷Bedřich Smetana, *Má vlast* ('My Country'); Josef Suk, *Asrael*.

a strange but utterly absorbing work with little or no story, creating a world in which what appears to be fantasy is truth, and vice versa. *The Greek Passion* (1959) gave Martinů more trouble than any of his works and he died believing he had failed with it. In fact, it is probably his masterpiece. It's an adaptation of a novel by Nikos Kazantzakis (author of *Zorba the Greek*) and shows what happens when a village decides to stage a religious Passion and the people appearing in it begin to take on the characteristics of the biblical characters they are portraying. From the resplendent hymn-like Prelude with its carillon of bells to the tragic final pages, this offers a superb experience and is one of the great 20th-century operas.

MASCAGNI, Pietro (1863–1945)

The Italian Pietro Mascagni is remembered chiefly for one opera, *Cavalleria rusticana*, although he wrote more than a dozen. Its success over the years is not surprising. It has a strong story about a peasant girl whose bitter jealousy leads to the death of the man she loves. Mascagni's music is suitably passionate and conjures up skilfully the doom-laden atmosphere of a Sicilian village on Easter Day. The Easter Hymn which the villagers sing early in the opera has become a popular classic, as has the celebrated Intermezzo scored for strings and organ. *Cavalleria rusticana* is often staged as a double bill with ▷Leoncavallo's *Pagliacci*, another torrid tale of jealous emotions. Anyone curious to learn more of Mascagni's music may be able to find a recording of his comic opera *L'amico Fritz*, which is not unattractive and contains a lovely duet for soprano and tenor.

MASSENET, Jules (1842–1912)

Jules Massenet wrote two dozen operas, many of which enjoyed considerable success during his lifetime and for some years later. These included *Hérodiade*, which transformed Salome's lustful passion for John the Baptist into a very un-biblical Hollywood-style romance. *Le Cid* had the great Spanish hero as its central character (its ballet music is still played in the concert hall) and *Don Quixote* was a sensitive adaptation of Cervantes novel, composed specially for the talents of the Russian bass Chaliapin. Today, only three of Massenet's operas are staged with regularity. *Werther* is an affecting and effective study of a man's hopeless love and is based on Johann Wolfgang von Goethe's story. *Thaïs* focuses on a monk who is intent on saving a courtesan from damnation but who falls from grace himself.

The best of the three is *Manon* (1884), arguably Massenet's masterpiece. It's a reworking of Abbé Prevost's novel concerning the Chevalier Des Grieux and his love for Manon Lescaut, with whom he has a strong relationship. Eventually, she tires of him and goes to live with another man. The plot follows the attempts of Des Grieux (only partly successful) to win her back. Massenet's melodies flow effortlessly and copiously. They are often sweet but certainly not syrupy. The two main arias of Des Grieux, 'Ah, fuyez, douce image' and especially 'En fermant les yeux', are meltingly lovely. If sung really well and produced with sincerity and understanding, *Manon* can be as enjoyable as any opera written in the closing years of the 19th century.

Massenet's orchestral music is warm-hearted and most attractive. The *Scènes hongroises*, *Scènes alsaciennes* and *Scènes napolitaines* were composed following holidays in Hungary, Alsace and Italy. The *Scènes dramatiques* (sadly neglected) are a response to several of Shakespeare's plays. The Piano Concerto, rarely played, has much to commend it in a grand, ▷Lisztian manner. Massenet wrote more than 200 songs, some of which would make refreshing additions to the recitalist's repertory. No less a figure than ▷Debussy wrote of Massenet: 'He is the most beloved of contemporary musicians. His fame is a gracious one'.

● The story of Salome and John the Baptist has been used in opera or ballet by many composers, including ▷Maxwell Davies, Antoine Mariotte, Florent Schmitt and ▷Richard Strauss.

MATHIAS, William (born 1934)

The Welsh composer William Mathias is capable of writing accessible music such as the *Celtic Dances* (which owe something to the works of ▷Arnold) and pieces for royal occasions, such as the brilliant Fanfare composed for the tenth anniversary of the investiture of the Prince of Wales. But he can be tougher on the listener. His First Symphony of 1966 is quite an aggressive piece whose powerful rhythmic impulses sometimes suggest ▷Stravinsky. In between lie works like the splendid Harp Concerto (which shows the special understanding of the instrument one might expect of a Welshman), the Piano Concerto no. 3 and the short but attractive Sinfonietta, written for a school orchestra but not compromising on that account.

MAXWELL DAVIES, Sir Peter (born 1934)

Peter Maxwell Davies is one of the most significant, and least pretentious, of contemporary British composers. He has been described as 'English by birth, Scottish by inclination', following his acquisition of a cottage on the Orkney island of Hoy, where he spends much of his time. His work has been influenced by medieval and Renaissance music, the sights and sound of the sea and the performing skills of children (for whom he has written a large variety of compositions). His melodies are not the kind that one can whistle, though youngsters have little problem grasping his style. But the atmosphere he creates is often palpable and makes a deep impression.

Maxwell Davies's theatre pieces contain much of the best of this resourceful composer. *The Lighthouse* is a chilling essay in claustrophobia and restrained terror. *Eight Songs for a Mad King*, a nerve-jangling masterpiece, looks at the insanity of George III. *Miss Donnithorne's Maggot* concerns a crazy woman who could be second cousin to Miss Havisham in Dickens's *Great Expectations*. These, and other works, are immensely impressive.

Maxwell Davies is a prolific composer: many of his most recent compositions have been for the St Magnus Festival in Orkney, an event he founded. His symphonies are memorable, as are the two fantasias based on music by John Taverner, who was the subject of Maxwell Davies's only true opera, staged in 1972. His Violin Concerto is a work of the greatest beauty whose spirit occasionally puts the listener in mind of ▷Berg's concerto. It is music with which newcomers to Maxwell Davies's sound-world might well begin.

• When Maxwell Davies was studying at the Royal Manchester College of Music he was associated with a group that became known as the 'Manchester School'; other members were the composers ▷Birtwistle, ▷Goehr and the pianist John Ogdon.

MENDELSSOHN, Felix (1809–1847)
For a time after his death, it was felt that Felix Mendelssohn's music was the work of a dilettante whose privileged background was reflected in what he wrote. But his genius was rediscovered and acknowledged and the world was reawakened to the freshness of his melodies, the clarity and brilliance of his orchestration and the restrained poetry of his ideas. His symphonies reflect his wide experience: no. 2 ('Hymn of Praise') uses solo singers and a chorus and contains the famous sequence 'I waited for the Lord'. No. 3 ('Scotch') was begun during a holiday in Edinburgh and has decidedly Scottish elements. No. 4 ('Italian') ends appropriately with a saltarello (the dance which originated in southern Italy). No. 5 ('Reformation') quotes the Dresden Amen and the Lutheran hymn *Ein Feste Burg*. Mendelssohn's Violin Concerto, with its sublime slow movement and dazzling finale, is one of the most frequently performed violin concertos. The two piano concertos are attractively entertaining, though they need discerning performances to make them work really well.

Mendelssohn was only 17 when he composed his overture to *A Midsummer Night's Dream*, an amazingly atmospheric picture of Oberon's fairy kingdom. Years later he added several items of incidental music for a production of Shakespeare's play, and recaptured completely the magic of his original inspiration. (The Wedding March composed for the Duke of Athens in the play became so well loved that it is still used all over the world to accompany the exit of the bride and bridegroom after the marriage service.) The Octet for strings, another youthful work, is one of the finest in the repertory: not the work of a prodigy but of a genius. The many piano pieces collected under the title *Songs without Words* are polished gems (they include the celebrated 'Spring Song' and 'Bees' Wedding'). At one time, Mendelssohn's massive oratorio *Elijah* was one of the most popular choral works in Britain. Over the years it fell from favour, but it contains a wealth of fine music; the choruses are particularly memorable.

- Incidental music has been written for productions of *A Midsummer Night's Dream* by ▷Ibert and ▷Orff. ▷Purcell composed music for an adaptation of the play entitled *The Fairy Queen*. ▷Britten's opera *A Midsummer Night's Dream* stays close to the original. ▷Weber's opera *Oberon* is not based on Shakespeare, though it shares some of the same characters.

MENOTTI, Gian Carlo (born 1911)
The Italian-American composer Gian Carlo Menotti has always been popular with the public and criticised by those who feel that his music is not strong enough to sustain the lively ideas that lie behind it. His popular acceptance is because he has not lost touch with the world of melody. Menotti can write a good tune, and does. He composes mostly for the stage, and like his fellow Italians before him, ▷Verdi and ▷Puccini, is a true man of the theatre. His first opera, *Amelia Goes to the Ball*, written when he was in his 20s, is a delightful comedy; *The Telephone* extracts much humour out of a garrulous woman who can't put her phone down; and *The Old Maid and the Thief* is likewise amusing. Menotti's light touch is evident, also, in his most famous work, the television opera *Amahl and the Night Visitors*, about a crippled boy whose adventures with the Three

NOW LISTEN ▷

Other operas involving the capture and imprisonment of those seeking freedom of thought include: ▷Ludwig van Beethoven, *Fidelio*; ▷Luigi Dallapiccola, *Il prigioniero* ('The Prisoner'); ▷Leoš Janáček, *From the House of the Dead*; ▷Giacomo Puccini, *Tosca*.

Wise Men during the first Christmas lead to his cure.
But Menotti has tackled stronger subjects: *The Medium* is a chilling study revolving round a fake spiritu-
alist and *Maria Golovin* has a blind hero tormented by
jealousy.

The Consul (1950) is Menotti's masterpiece. It is set
in a nameless European police state and concerns the
frustrations of a group of people trying desperately to
obtain a visa to leave the country. The consul never
appears; only his businesslike secretary deals with in-
quiries. The heroine, Magda, is the wife of a freedom
fighter. When he is caught by the authorities, she kills
herself. The opera is a passionate denunciation of
man's inhumanity to man and is skilfully wrought.
Magda's great aria, 'To this we've come', is as powerful a musical statement as Menotti has made.

Menotti has written orchestral and choral works including a Violin Concerto which is full of fine tunes
and would become popular if performed, and a witty
and attractive Piano Concerto with a marvellously
jazzy finale. His music is influenced by many: the
march of the Three Kings in *Amahl* has strong echoes
of ▷Prokofiev's *The Love for Three Oranges*. Puccini can
be detected, too, and ▷Gershwin. But the product is
recognisably Menotti. He lives today in a gracious
mansion a few miles outside Edinburgh (whose annual
festival scarcely seems aware of his existence).

MESSAGER, André (1853–1929)
The Frenchman André Messager was a highly successful conductor who had charge, at different times,
of both the Opéra-Comique in Paris and Covent Garden in London. He introduced much ▷Wagner to his
native France and gave first performances of many operas, including ▷Debussy's *Pelléas et Mélisande*, which
is dedicated to him. But Messager is best known today
as the composer of the charming and popular ballet *Les
deux pigeons* ('The Two Pigeons'), with its tale of a
young artist's adventures among the gypsies. Two of
his many operettas, *Véronique* and *Monsieur Beaucaire*,
are still performed occasionally and contain some of
his most delightful ideas. The most popular number in
Véronique is the duet 'Trot here and there', sung as the

heroine is enjoying a donkey ride; *Monsieur Beaucaire* has the lovely song 'Philomel' (one of Messager's prettiest melodies). All Messager's works are highly polished and supremely elegant; his melodies are fresh and memorable.

● Some other French operettas written around the time Messager was working are Henri Christine's *Phi-Phi*, Charles Cuvillier's *The Lilac Domino*, Louis Ganne's *Hans, the Flute-Player*, ▷Hahn's *Malvina* and Maurice Yvain's *La-haut*.

MESSIAEN, Olivier (born 1908)
The French composer Olivier Messiaen has created a sound-world that some will instinctively resist. It is unlike anyone else's, absorbing a wide variety of ideas including birdsong, oriental percussion, Indian music and the legacy of such composers as ▷Franck, ▷Bartók, ▷Debussy and ▷Stravinsky. Now and again it even approaches the honest vulgarity of Hollywood. But to ignore Messiaen is to miss what can be a fascinating and richly rewarding experience. Messiaen is a devout Roman Catholic and his faith informs every bar he writes, not in the sense that it is all church music but in that his works are celebrations of God's creativity and of life itself. He is also much preoccupied with the mysteries surrounding Christ's birth and Resurrection.

There are certain of Messiaen's works that can be recommended as starting-points for those wishing to explore his remarkable musical kingdom. *L'ascension*, *Hymne au Saint Sacrement* and *Les offrandes oubliées* are early orchestral works which are highly atmospheric and emotionally charged. They are comparatively static but powerful and very personal. Messiaen's bird pieces, which include *Oiseaux exotiques* and *Catalogue d'oiseaux*, contain music as varied and colourful as the plumage on the feathered creatures he is depicting. *Chronochromie* also has its roots in birdsong but is a tour de force of percussive rhythm, with a rather amazing 'dawn chorus' for the strings.

NOW LISTEN ▷

Music by pupils of Messiaen: ▷Pierre Boulez, *Le marteau sans maître*; ▷Alexander Goehr, *Metamorphosis Dance*; ▷Karlheinz Stockhausen, *Gruppen*; ▷Iannis Xenakis, *Antikhthon*.

The *Turangalîla Symphony* (1948) is one of Messiaen's largest works and probably his most immediately impressive. It makes a strong impression, even on first hearing. In Sanskrit, 'Turanga' means 'time' and 'lîla' means 'love': the work is a love-poem on an epic scale, inspired by the ancient legend of Tristan and Isolda. Some of the music is sensuous in a very earthy way; some is otherworldly, whose beauty is enhanced by the composer's use of the ondes martenot, an electronic keyboard instrument whose oscillating waves make a haunting sound. Other sequences are vigorous and life-enhancing. *Turangalîla* is unquestionably a work of genius which demands a proper hearing – and many subsequent ones. It will win through to all but the most biased ears.

The *Quatuor pour la fin du temps* ('Quartet for the End of Time') was written when Messiaen was interned by the Nazis and is scored for violin, cello, clarinet and piano; it was first performed by the composer and three fellow prisoners. Messiaen's piano music has a special magic about it. *Vingt regards sur l'Enfant Jésus* is another work for 'beginners' to hear. The organ pieces include the magnificent *La nativité du Seigneur*, a stunning set of pieces describing the Christmas story; the movement depicting the appearance of the Angels is probably the closest anyone will ever get to portraying a dazzling white light in musical terms.

MEYERBEER, Giacomo (1791–1864)
Giacomo Meyerbeer thought on a grand scale. The German composer who spent nearly all his working life in France wrote massive operas which are mostly too expensive to stage effectively today. But their music is not lost, thanks to recordings and occasional concert performances. His finest work is probably *L'africaine* (which lasts for six hours): its hero is the explorer Vasco da Gama and the plot involves his ship being wrecked on the African coast. He falls in love with a native girl and takes her back to Portugal, with unhappy results. The celebrated tenor aria 'O Paradiso!' comes from this opera. *Les Huguenots*, about the notorious massacre, and *L'étoile du nord* ('The North Star'), about Peter the Great of Russia, are two

of Meyerbeer's other epic operas. *Le prophète* provided
▷Lambert with some of the music for the ballet *Les
patineurs* ('The Skaters') which was produced in
London in 1937. Some of Meyerbeer's music is rather
four-square and unimaginative. But at its best it is impressive and memorable.

- *L'africaine* is not alone in dealing with the problems of a 'mixed' relationship. ▷Puccini's *Madam
  Butterfly* concerns the tragic marriage of an American sailor to a Japanese Geisha girl. ▷Delibes's
  Lakmé links a British soldier and an Indian priestess with dire results. ▷Lehár's *The Land of Smiles*
  sees heartbreak result from the marriage of a Chinese prince to a Viennese socialite. The same idea
  is also at the root of the Rodgers and Hammerstein musical *South Pacific*.

MEZZO-SOPRANO

The mezzo-soprano voice, as its name suggests, lies
between those of a soprano and a contralto. Its quality
can be warm and romantic or dark and tragic, as required, and the world of opera gives it many opportunities with such roles as ▷Bellini's Adalgisa, ▷Bizet's
Carmen, ▷Gluck's Orpheus, ▷Mozart's Dorabella
and Cherubino, ▷Purcell's Dido, ▷Richard Strauss's
Oktavian and ▷Verdi's Amneris. In the concert hall
there are many openings for the mezzo-soprano. The
Sea Pictures of ▷Elgar, for example, the song cycles of
▷Mahler (*Das Lied von der Erde* and *Kindertotenlieder*),
and the oratorios of ▷Handel (including *Messiah*) are
wonderfully suited to the range. Some of the most famous mezzo-sopranos of this century are Dame Janet
Baker, Agnes Baltsa, Fedora Barbieri, Teresa Ber-
ganza, Fiorenza Cossotto, Marilyn Horne, Christa
Ludwig, Giulietta Simionato and Ebe Stignani.

MILHAUD, Darius (1892–1974)

Darius Milhaud was a member of the group of French

composers known as ▷'Les Six'. For a time, though, he was a diplomat in Rio de Janeiro and some of his music has a strong South American flavour, notably the *Saudades do Brazil*, a suite of orchestral pieces evoking places in that city. Milhaud composed 12 symphonies of varying sizes which are interesting but have never excited much interest. His ballets *La création du monde* ('The Creation of the World') and *Le boeuf sur le toit* ('The Ox on the Roof'), on the other hand, are well liked for their jazzy rhythms and catchy tunes. Milhaud was born in Aix-en-Provence and three of his best works reflect his birthplace: the *Suite provençale* has a wonderfully sunny, folky atmosphere, the *Carnival d'Aix* for piano and orchestra is lively and appealing, and *La cheminée du roi René* for wind quintet is named after a street in Aix and is delightful. There are no fewer than 18 string quartets among Milhaud's chamber output. A number of operas includes *Christophe Colomb*, which uses a cinema screen and moving images. The piano music is lively and enjoyable, especially the suite *Scaramouche* (for four hands). Just before his death, Milhaud, who spent many years in a wheelchair, declared: 'I have had a happy life'. That happiness comes through in most of his music.

NOW LISTEN

Some works by other members of 'Les Six': Georges Auric, *Phèdre*; Louis Durey, *L'occasion*; ▷Arthur Honegger, *Pastorale d'été*; ▷Francis Poulenc, *Les biches*; Germaine Tailleferre, Harp Concerto.

MOERAN, Ernest John (1894–1950)
E. J. Moeran, as he is always known, was an English composer of Irish descent, and it is his Celtic side that shows through the more strongly. Melody came easily to him: his tunes are unforced and effortless. The nuts and bolts of composition, a work's construction, gave him more problems. But however hard he may have struggled, his music is warm-hearted, lyrical and often very lovely. It is plain that Moeran admired such composers as ▷Sibelius, ▷Bax and ▷Walton. But he was no plagiarist; his style is very personal and one to which the listener will respond at once or not at all. I heard the Symphony in G minor as a boy of 12 and have loved all of it ever since. It is a marvellous outpouring, one glorious melody following another, and is certainly able to take its place alongside many better-known and much-lauded 20th-century British works. Moeran's Violin Concerto is a moving, bitter-sweet work of great

NOW LISTEN

▷Arnold Bax, *The Garden of Fand*; ▷Frank Bridge, *Enter Spring*; ▷Frederick Delius, Violin Concerto; ▷Jean Sibelius, Symphony no. 4; ▷Ralph Vaughan Williams, *A Norfolk Rhapsody*; ▷William Walton, Symphony no. 1.

beauty (it shares a vital musical phrase with the song cycle *Seven Poems by James Joyce*, whose words give some clue to the concerto's significance). The Cello Concerto, written for his wife Piers Cotemore, is only slightly less inspired. Moeran wrote chamber music and several piano pieces, ranging from the impressive Theme and Variations to an amusing little trifle called *Bank Holiday*.

MONCKTON, Lionel (1861–1924)

The music of Lionel Monckton conjures up, more effectively than almost anything else, the spirit of Edwardian England. He was destined for a career as a barrister but after practising law for a short time, his hobby – of providing songs for other people's musical shows – took firm hold, and he began composing his own light operas. These were an instant success and three of them *The Arcadians*, *A Country Girl* and *The Quaker Girl* are still staged regularly by amateur societies up and down the British Isles. Several of the songs from Monckton's shows (including 'The Pipes of Pan' and 'Come to the Ball') are classics of the musical theatre. Monckton, who married the music-hall star Gertie Miller, is generally considered to have been the man who laid the foundations for British musicals in the 20th century.

MONTEVERDI, Claudio (1567–1643)

The Italian Claudio Monteverdi was to music what Shakespeare was to literature. He achieved a revolution not by particularly revolutionary means but by taking traditional forms and raising them to another sphere by sheer imagination and creative genius. He is the man who put what we call 'theatre' into opera. His operas, among them the celebrated *Orfeo*, have recognisably human characters instead of the symbolic figures of his predecessors. They are full of bold, dramatic strokes and the music flows in a way that can sound remarkably modern to our ears. Even his madrigals gradually became more and more theatrical: some of the last he wrote were meant to be staged, like mini-operas. In the last period of his life, Monteverdi took

> **NOW LISTEN** ⟩
>
> Lionel Bart, *Oliver*; ▷Noel Coward, *Bitter Sweet*; Vivian Ellis, *Bless the Bride*; Frederic Norton, *Chu Chin Chow*; ▷Ivor Novello, *The Dancing Years*; H. Fraser Simpson, *The Maid of the Mountains*.

holy orders and his sacred music is no less arresting than his secular works.

His first opera, *Orfeo*, was already breaking new ground in 1607 and remains adventurous. But it's generally considered that Monteverdi's masterpiece is *L'incoronazione di Poppaea* ('The Coronation of Poppea'), a strong, impressive piece about the Roman Emperor Nero's love for a lady of his court and his wife's plans to thwart the affair. The intrigues and counter-intrigues that take place as the story unfolds are handled with a brilliance that is far ahead of its time.

● Many musicians and scholars have been fascinated with Monteverdi's music and have prepared editions of his work aimed at helping performers understand it. They include ▷Malipiero and ▷Respighi in Italy; in Britain, Raymond Leppard has made performing versions of the operas.

MOSZKOWSKI, Moritz (1854–1925)

Moritz Moszkowski made no pretensions to greatness. He wrote a good deal of entertaining and brilliant piano music which was much loved by virtuoso pianists of the day – and by their audiences. It's still possible to hear the occasional Moszkowski piece in recitals: the dazzling *Etincelles* ('Sparks') for instance, or the attractive *Spanish Dances*. But his large-scale works have been virtually forgotten, which is a pity. Many listeners would be agreeably surprised at the quality of the Piano Concerto, to name but one, which contains much charming material and has a finale of infectious gaiety. It was not for nothing that no less a figure than ▷Liszt expressed profound admiration for this undervalued composer. Moszkowski, who was German-born but of Polish extraction, lost all his money during World War I. He was saved from penury by some of the world's greatest musicians, who gave a special concert for him in New York and raised 10,000 dollars.

MOZART, Wolfgang Amadeus (1756–1791)

Many music-lovers, asked to name the greatest composer ever, would unhesitatingly pronounce the name of Wolfgang Amadeus Mozart. The man who transformed the piano concerto, the symphony, the string quartet, opera – indeed, every musical form he touched; the man of whom a famous critic once wrote: 'Mozart is music'. He simply did everything better than anyone had done it before. He took well-trodden paths and turned them into highways leading to a new musical world. Mozart looked at the work of many other composers, including ▷J. C. Bach, ▷Handel, ▷Gluck and ▷Haydn. But it was the way he used the knowledge he gained that made him such a gigantic figure.

The mature piano concertos probably contain the most characteristic elements of Mozart's style. They are all different but each is perfect: now light as thistledown, now heart-rendingly poignant. No-one has written such eloquent woodwind parts in a piano concerto; their contribution is often as important as the soloist's. No-one has written melodies that are so simple and yet so far-reaching. (Movie-buffs will admit that a feeble film called *Elvira Madigan* is remembered today simply because it used a Mozart piano concerto, no. 21 in C major, as background music.) Mozart wrote fine concertos for other instruments including the violin, the clarinet and the bassoon. But those he created for his beloved piano are in a world of their own.

Mozart's operas, likewise, occupy a special place in musical history. His understanding of the theatre and of human emotions allowed him to portray characters whose depth and humanity were previously unimagined in the opera house. *Le nozze di Figaro* ('The Marriage of Figaro'), *Don Giovanni* and especially *Così fan tutte* have their surface brilliance; but they frequently probe uncomfortably beneath that surface and the music, as much as the libretto, tells us a great deal about ourselves. *Die Entführung aus dem Serail* ('The Abduction from the Seraglio') has disturbing aspects but was composed in a lighter tradition. *Die Zauberflöte* ('The Magic Flute') with its trials of the human spirit remains a puzzle, capable of numerous interpretations (I have seen it produced as a comic pantomime, as a serious psychological drama and as a colourful pageant).

Mozart's symphonies, particularly the later ones, are powerful, personal statements which become an indispensable part of every listener's life (the haunting theme of the first movement of the Symphony no. 40 once made it into the British pop charts). Equally significant are the string quartets and his other chamber works, and the piano sonatas. It is through one of these that most people come to know Mozart: the celebrated one in C major whose opening melody is sometimes known as 'In an 18th century Drawing Room'. Many youthful pianists try their skills on its pages, just as young string players attempt the serenade *Eine kleine Nachtmusik* ('A Little Night Music'). But however Mozart enters a music-lover's life, he will undoubtedly take root there.

- Composers since the early 1800s have acclaimed Mozart and his significance and magnificence. Recently a young composer told me that the greatest single influence on his life had been Mozart. It's fascinating to note that one of the greatest 20th-century composers, ▷Britten, spent many years studying and performing the works of Mozart and said that a lifetime was not sufficient to fathom all his mysteries.

MUSGRAVE, Thea (born 1928)
The Scottish composer Thea Musgrave has a highly original mind and writes music full of interest which challenges the listener in an exciting and usually enjoyable way. Her style is very much of the present day, but it attracts rather than alienates. Her operas *Mary, Queen of Scots* and *The Decision* (about a mining disaster and its effect on the community) are striking works, showing an unerring feel for the stage. But her theatrical instincts are not confined to the opera house. In her Clarinet Concerto, the soloist wanders among the orchestra, joining this group and that and improvising

in opposition to the conductor. In her Horn Concerto, it is the orchestral horns that move about the hall, responding to the urgent blandishments of the soloist on the platform. The Chamber Concerto no. 2 has a maverick viola player who seems intent on disrupting the smooth progress of the work. Musgrave's ballet *Beauty and the Beast* is a marvellous, richly atmospheric score whose effect remains in the memory long after the stage action has been forgotton.

● There is another example of an orchestral player apparently trying to sabotage a concert performance. In ▷Nielsen's Symphony no. 5, the side-drummer is directed by the composer to play 'ad lib' and do everything he can to halt the music.

MUSORGSKY, Modest (1839–1881)

Modest Musorgsky died an alchoholic a few days after his 42nd birthday, a wreck of a man whose instability had made it impossible for him to work steadily or to complete most of the music he had begun. Yet it is not for nothing that he was once described as 'Russia's most individual and human musical genius'. What Musorgsky left is adventurous and progressive and more imaginative than a good deal of what his more sober fellows were producing. His *Pictures at an Exhibition*, musical descriptions of drawings exhibited by a friend, make up the first truly great solo piano work by a Russian. It gained wider popularity in various orchestral versions, the best by ▷Ravel. But the original still carries by far the greatest punch.

Boris Godunov (1869, revised 1873) is Musorgsky's masterpiece, the only one of several operas that he managed to finish. The story of a Russian tsar, who murdered for his throne and is haunted by guilt, suited the dark side of the composer's personality. The singers did not enjoy their music, which followed the pattern and inflection of speech; they were looking for more conventional arias. The orchestra could not get to grips with some of Musorgsky's strange harmonies, and were discomfited by the stark colours they were asked to produce. But in 1874 it was successfully staged in its revised version. (Later, Musorgsky's friend ▷Rimsky-Korsakov smoothed out the score and watered it down in a version that became commonly used). But over the years many experts began to see what Musorgsky was doing and the real nature of the score was understood. The composer's use of the chorus as living beings with thoughts and ideas of their own was perceived as particularly impressive.

One of Musorgksy's most popular orchestral pieces, *St John's Night on the Bare Mountain*, is usually played today in a version prepared by Rimsky-Korsakov. But again, the composer's original score is far more interesting. Musorgsky wrote some splendid songs. The cycle *Songs and Dances of Death* is very striking; *The Nursery* shows a delightful and unexpected awareness of the world of the very young (one song allows us to eavesdrop on the hilarious evening prayers of a little child).

- Besides Ravel's orchestration of *Pictures at an Exhibition*, there are versions by three conductors, Walter Goehr, Leopold Stokowski and Henry Wood; Elgar Howarth has arranged the music for brass ensemble.

MYASKOVSKY, Nikolay (1881–1950)
The Russian composer Nikolay Myaskovsky wrote, among other works, 27 symphonies, one of them for military band – not surprisingly, perhaps, since he trained for a military career. Just before his death, he was denounced by the Soviet authorities for introducing 'inharmonious' elements into his compositions and acting as a bad influence on the rising generation. It was a 'crime' of which ▷Prokofiev, ▷Shostakovich and others were also accused. But anyone listening to Myaskovsky's music will find few discordant elements and instead a strong vein of bitter-sweet nostalgia and melancholy which are wholly Russian. The Symphony no. 21 is arguably Myaskovsky at his finest.

- The British composer ▷Brian wrote 32 symphonies; sadly, he had died before anyone took a serious interest in them.

NICOLAI, Otto (1810–1849)

Otto Nicolai numbered two symphonies, a piano concerto and five operas among his compositions. Today all have been forgotten save one of the operas, *The Merry Wives of Windsor*, which is still popular in continental houses. It's amusingly based on Shakespeare and glories in showing how the fat knight Falstaff gets his come-uppance at the hands of a bunch of wily ladies. Nicolai, who was German despite his name, studied and worked in Rome for a time and his music combines the more solid German qualities with an Italianate fluency and grace.

● There is an opera about Falstaff by Antonio Salieri, the man once thought to have poisoned ▷Mozart out of jealousy; but the best-known operas on the subject are by ▷Vaughan Williams (*Sir John in Love*) and ▷Verdi.

NIELSEN, Carl (1865–1931)

The Danish composer Carl Nielsen has for many years been bracketed with Finland's ▷Sibelius, presumably because they were born in the same year, were Scandinavian and wrote symphonies. In fact their music could scarcely be more different. Nielsen's strong, individual voice demands our fullest attention. While he was always recognised in his native land, it wasn't until the 1950s that his powerful musical statements

NOW LISTEN ▷

Some music by other composers from northern Europe: ▷Edvard Grieg, *Holberg Suite*; ▷Johan Halvorsen, *Maskarade*

were heard in other parts of the world. His six symphonies are indispensable to anyone anxious to encompass the most important aspects of 20th-century music. No. 1 is among the earliest symphonies to begin in one key and end in another; no. 2 is sub-titled 'The Four Temperaments', no. 3 is called *Sinfonia espansiva* because of the expansive nature of its content, particularly the main theme of its finale; no. 4 is called 'The Inextinguishable' and progresses from an anxiety-ridden first movement to a last one that ends with supreme optimism; no. 5 is magnificently powerful with its war-like side-drum (which at one point is directed to attempt to stop the orchestra's progress); no. 6, *Sinfonia semplice*, is strangely bitter and ironic.

Nielsen's concertos are less often played but no less fascinating. The Violin Concerto has a mellow warmth which is all-engulfing; the Flute Concerto and the Clarinet Concerto exploit their respective instruments with skill and character (the jazz clarinettist Benny Goodman recorded the concerto with considerable success). Nielsen's operas are undervalued masterpieces. *Saul and David*, based on the biblical story of a great man's fall, engages our sympathies and attention throughout; the writing for chorus is particularly imaginative and moving. *Maskarade* (1906) could be on everyone's list of favourites if it were staged regularly in countries outside Denmark. It has been described as 'a Scandinavian *Fledermaus*', and there is something in that. The score bubbles with wit and good humour, its melodies are often catchy and memorable and the piece is constructed by an expert. The story concerns a pair of secret lovers who go to a masked ball and discover that their respective parents have arranged for them to be married. The piece should be translated into other languages forthwith.

Nielsen's chamber music includes some fine string quartets and a particularly interesting wind quintet; there is a wealth of unknown but well-written piano music and at least one splendid organ solo, *Commotio*. Easy access to Nielsen is through the *Helios* overture (describing the progress of the sun from dawn to dusk) and the music written for the play *Aladdin* (not typical but very enjoyable).

Suite; ▷Jean Sibelius, Violin Concerto; Christian Sinding, Suite for violin and orchestra; Johan Svendsen, *Four Norwegian Rhapsodies*; Wilhelm Stenhammar, Symphony no. 2.

NONO, Luigi (born 1924)

Anyone tackling the music of the Italian Luigi Nono will find it hard to avoid becoming embroiled in politics. His commitment to left-wing ideals is reflected in his compositions, which often use political texts. Those unsympathetic to the message may find this an insuperable barrier; others may attempt to come to terms with an idiom which is extremely difficult. If, as some writers have suggested, there is a vein of Italian lyricism running through Nono's music, it is well disguised. His opera *Intolleranza* (1960) was received with intolerance by the public who could not relate to its mixture of live and recorded singing, straight acting and film sequences. Other works include *Epitaph for Federico Garcia Lorca*, for speaker, singers and orchestra, and *On the Bridge at Hiroshima* for soprano, tenor and orchestra.

NOVÁK, Vítežslav (1870–1949)

Not much of Vítežslav Novák's music is known outside his native Czechoslovakia. But enough has filtered through for us to realise that he was a composer of considerable gifts, capable of communicating rapidly with an audience. He was a pupil of ▷Dvořák, though it was the music of ▷Brahms and ▷Schumann which most influenced him early in his career. Later he became fascinated by the experiments of ▷Janáček, and his own style changed. If you compare two of his string quartets, the one written in 1899 and the one of 1938, the difference is apparent. Novák's most delightful work is the *Slovak Suite* whose five movements include 'Two in Love', a ravishing picture of a young couple flirting and sparring in the village square. Why this piece (and the rest of the suite) is not in every orchestra's repertory is a mystery to me. Novák's cantata *The Storm* is a wonderfully atmospheric description of tragedy at sea, containing a haunting sequence in which a boy, sitting high in the rigging of a sailing ship, warns of the approaching turbulence. The Autumn Symphony, for chorus and orchestra, is striking, deserving much more attention. Perhaps concert promoters should look much more to 20th-century Czechoslovakia for their programmes.

> **NOW LISTEN** ⟩
>
> Jan Cikker, *Resurrection*; Josef Foerster, *Cyrano de Bergerac*; ▷Leoš Janáček, *Ballad of Blanik Hill*; ▷Bohuslav Martinů, Violin Concerto no. 2; ▷Josef Suk, *Fairy-Tale Suite*.

NOVELLO, Ivor (1893–1951)

Ivor Novello was a Welshman whose real name was David Ivor Davies. He composed a song which was a big hit during World War I, *Till the Boys Come Home* ('Keep the Home Fires Burning'). But it is for his romantic musicals that he is celebrated. Between 1935 and 1945, Novello had a string of successes, *Glamorous Nights*, *The Dancing Years*, *King's Rhapsody* and *Perchance to Dream*. Songs like 'We'll gather lilacs', 'Love is my reason for living', 'Waltz of my Heart' and 'Fly home, little heart' are sung to this day. Novello invariably appeared in his own shows, not as a singer but in an acting role (he once appeared in a silent film of *The Lodger* as Jack the Ripper). His musicals have been described as 'lavish hokum' and have been derided by the sophisticated. But as a melodist he had few equals in the theatre: a Novello tune remains resplendent!

NOVEL OPERAS

▷Arthur Benjamin, *A Tale of Two Cities* (Charles Dickens)
▷Benjamin Britten, *The Turn of the Screw* (Henry James)
▷Bernard Herrmann, *Wuthering Heights* (Emily Brontë)
▷Leoš Janáček, *From the House of the Dead* (Dostoyevsky)
▷Sergey Prokofiev, *War and Peace* (Tolstoy)
▷Arthur Sullivan, *Ivanhoe* (Scott)

OFFENBACH, Jacques (1819–1880)

Jacques Offenbach, that most French of composers, was born in Cologne to a German family called Eberst. He took the name we know from a station he happened to be passing through. Henceforth he liked to be known as 'O. de Cologne'. Offenbach gave us operetta, 'the flighty daughter of grand opera'. The appeal of his tunes, immediate and lasting, defies analysis. Some of his operettas are satires on society, but always disguised. (The characters in *Orphée aux enfers*, 'Orpheus in the Underworld', are gods and goddesses on Mount Olympus.) He wrote one serious opera, *Les contes d'Hoffmann* ('The Tales of Hoffmann'), which contains three bizarre stories after the writings of E. T. A. Hoffmann. It has a host of marvellous melodies including the 'Song of the Mechanical Doll', the languorous and erotic Barcarolle and the lively Legend of Kleinsack. But, as a whole, it is curiously unsatisfactory.

La Belle Hélène (1864) is arguably Offenbach's finest achievement: an hilarious send-up of the events leading to the Trojan wars. The characters of Greek mythology (Agamemnon, Achilles, Menelaus and the rest) emerge as buffoons and the beautiful Helen has no trouble managing her affair with the handsome Paris under her husband's very nose. There are brilliant patter-songs, a splendid love-duet and a world-beater of a waltz.

Other Offenbach operettas include *La vie parisienne*, *La grande duchesse de Gérolstein*, *La Périchole*, and *Robinson Crusoe*. He wrote a fine Cello Concerto (which he played himself) and one ballet, *Papillons*,

NOW LISTEN >

The Gilbert and ▷Sullivan operas; ▷André Messager, *Veronique*; ▷Johann Strauss, the younger, *Die Fledermaus*; ▷Franz von Suppé, *Boccaccio*.

which is worth investigating. His music was used by Manuel Rosenthal for the ballet *Gaité parisienne* (1938).

ORFF, Carl (1895–1982)

Carl Orff's opera-cantata *Carmina burana* is one of the most-performed choral works written since 1930. Whether audiences experience it in a staged version in the theatre or in a formal account in the concert hall (its more usual home), they are mesmerised by its urgent, pulsating rhythms and earthy, rumbustious tunes. The work is made up of a number of songs by medieval monks, students and minstrels; most of the verses are concerned with love in its most basic form and are sung – perhaps mercifully – in Latin. Orff, who was born and died in Munich and is one of Bavaria's few composers, has been concerned with stripping away operatic conventions and traditions. What is left is a direct assault on the ear and the emotions: vibrant, dramatic and often excitingly raw. *Carmina burana* is one of three works gathered under the title *Trionfi* ('Triumphs'); the other two are rather arid and distinctly less enjoyable. Those taken with *Carmina burana* should try another pair of Orff theatre pieces, *Der Mond* ('The Moon') and *Die Kluge* ('The Clever Woman'). The first tells of four lads who steal the moon and plunge the world into darkness: the second is about a woman who is a good deal too smart for her husband, the king, but wins his love in the end. Again the music is basic and free from frills and fancies, but most of it (notably in *Der Mond*) is very attractive and thoroughly alive. In addition to composing, Orff made a study of ▷Monteverdi's music and edited some of it. He also produced an impressive body of work for school children.

ORGAN

The organ was nicknamed 'the king of instruments' as early as the 14th century, not merely because of its size but also because of its versatility and range of expression. It remains mighty and unassailable. The sound of a great organ, superbly played in a vast cathedral, takes

NOW LISTEN ▷

Masterly 20th-century works for chorus and orchestra include: ▷Benjamin Britten, *War Requiem*; ▷Leoš Janáček, *Glagolitic Mass*; ▷Francis Poulenc, *Gloria*; ▷Sergey Prokofiev, *Alexander Nevsky*; ▷Sergey Rakhmaninov, *The Bells*; ▷Michael Tippett, *A Child of our Time*.

the breath away. The most profoundly magnificent organ music ever written came from the pen of ▷Bach; he wrote many works, the best known being probably the Toccata and Fugue in D minor, popularised – ironically – in an orchestral version by Leopold Stokowski in Walt Disney's cartoon film *Fantasia*. Many of the greatest composers thereafter produced few, if any, important organ works. But a new tradition of organ composition sprang up at the end of the 19th century. Its composers include ▷Franck, Sigfrid Karg-Elert, ▷Reger, Louis Vierne and Charles Widor. Try Vierne's *Carillon de Westminster*, based on the chimes of Big Ben. The Toccata from Widor's Organ Symphony no. 5 sprang into prominence when it was played as Princess Margaret left her wedding at Westminster Abbey. The most remarkable and original composer of organ music today is ▷Messiaen. His numerous works, which include the amazing *La nativité du Seigneur*, explore the organ's sonorities in an adventurous and exciting way.

PADEREWSKI, Ignacy Jan (1860–1941)

Paderewski is the only internationally famed musician to become a prime minister. He took charge of the Polish government immediately after World War I but resigned a year later following disagreements with other politicians. Paderewski was a great pianist who also wrote a number of attractive works, mostly for the piano. His *Concert Humoresques* include his most famous composition, the Minuet in G, but some of Paderewski's best ideas are in the *Tatra Album*, arrangements of songs and dances of Polish mountain-dwellers. The Piano Concerto, occasionally played today, is unpretentious and enjoyable, with a particularly lovely slow movement. A symphony and an opera (*Manru*) have disappeared. Paderewski supervised an edition of the complete works of ▷Chopin, a composer with whom he shared musical and patriotic sympathies.

• The former British prime minister, Edward Heath, is an enthusiastic amateur conductor and has appeared with several leading orchestras, including the London Symphony Orchestra.

PAGANINI, Nicolò (1782–1840)

Everyone was convinced that the Italian violinist Nicolò Paganini was in league with the devil. His playing was so brilliant that it was thought to go beyond the

NOW LISTEN

Some works written by virtuoso performers for

bounds of human capability; in addition, his tall, skeletal frame and wild, jet black hair gave him a Mephistophelean appearance. The way he actually attacked the violin was described as 'demonic'. But poor Paganini was human. He died of throat cancer after a protracted illness; and, contrary to public expectations, he did not rise out of his grave. Most of his music was designed to exploit his mastery of the violin. His six concertos tax the capabilities of even the finest players, as do the 24 *Caprices* for solo violin. (It is the second of these that has been used as a basis for compositions by many composers, including ▷Brahms, ▷Lloyd Webber, ▷Lutoslawski and ▷Rakhmaninov.) But Paganini's works are not empty showpieces. They are well constructed and by no means short of good tunes. Several chamber works involving the guitar are unusual and attractive.

themselves to play: ▷Fryderyk Chopin, 24 Preludes; ▷Louis Moreau Gottschalk, *Grand Tournament Galop*; ▷Fritz Kreisler, *Liebesfreud*; ▷Ferenc Liszt, *Transcendental Studies*; ▷Ignacy Jan Paderewski, Piano Concerto; ▷Sergey Rakhmaninov, *Etudes tableaux*; Pablo Sarasate, *Zigeunerweise*.

---

* Paganini was the hero of a romantic operetta by ▷Lehár. He was also the central character of a British film *The Magic Bow* in which the actor Stewart Grainger pretended to do the fiddling.

PALESTRINA, Giovanni Pierluigi da (?1525–1594)
The Italian Palestrina may not have shown the wide-ranging inventiveness or imagination of his contemporaries ▷Byrd and Orlande de Lassus. But his church music frequently reaches sublime heights and left an indelible mark on history. Its smooth, flowing lines and the rich way in which it blends voices give it a splendid character which has made it greatly admired. The *Missa 'Assumpta est Maria'* is particularly beautiful. The *Missa Papae Marcellae* is full of interest not least because it is said to have convinced the Council of Trent that sacred music could be elaborate and complex yet quite understandable to worshippers. Palestrina held many important musical posts in Italy.

---

* The German composer ▷Pfitzner wrote an opera,

Palestrina, based on the story of the *Missa Papae
Marcellae* and the Council of Trent – which may
or may not be true.

PANUFNIK, Andrzej (born 1914)

For a time Andrzej Panufnik was best known as a conductor. He conducted the Warsaw Philharmonic
Orchestra before he left his native Poland in 1954;
after he had settled in Britain, he conducted the City of
Birmingham Symphony Orchestra for three years. But
he is now encountered most as a composer. His earliest works were destroyed during the Warsaw Uprising
of 1944, but since the 1960s he has been quite prolific.
Panufnik's scores are often uneven; at his best,
though, he is a composer of great power and compelling originality. His music is basically accessible: his
idiom is modern but by no means abstruse. His music
ranges from the *Rustic Symphony* (based on folk melodies from his homeland) to the *Universal Prayer*, a setting for singers and orchestra of lines by Alexander
Pope. It was described by the conductor Leopold
Stokowski as 'one of the most original creations of
middle 20th-century music'. Panufnik's *Metasinfonia*
for organ, timpani and strings is a strangely affecting
work, strongly dramatic in a restrained way. This interesting composer is fascinated by geometric shapes,
which dominate his musical thinking. But the listener
need not be alarmed: it is possible to enjoy a Panufnik
score without a slide-rule.

NOW LISTEN >

Some music by other
distinguished 20th-
century Polish
composers: Tadeusz
Baird, *Sinfonia brevis*;
▷Witold Lutoslawski,
Concerto for Orchestra;
▷Krzysztof Penderecki,
St Luke Passion.

● ▷Poulenc wrote a Concerto for organ, timpani
and strings.

PARRY, Sir Hubert (1848–1918)

The music of the English composer Hubert Parry is
largely unfashionable today. Yet it has a great deal to
commend it, particularly to those who enjoy 19th-cen-
tury Romantic music as exemplified by ▷Brahms and
who seek something less familiar. The symphonies are

NOW LISTEN >

Music by Parry's British
contemporaries
includes: ▷Edward

beautifully constructed and full of fine melodies. No. 5 is probably the most arresting, with its movements called 'Stress', 'Love', 'Play' and 'Now'. Parry wrote a lovely *Elegy* for Brahms in memory of his idol and a set of fine Symphonic Variations. The *Lady Radnor's Suite* and the little *English Suite* for strings are charming and delightfully fresh. Parry's most memorable writing is in his choral works, notably his setting of Milton's *Blest Pair of Sirens* and of Blake's *Jerusalem*, which has established itself as a kind of national song in Britain, akin to ▷Elgar's tune for *Land of Hope and Glory*.

PENDERECKI, Krzysztof (born 1933)

Krzysztof Penderecki is one of the most significant and arresting Polish composers to appear in the years following World War II. His techniques are advanced and his scoring is adventurous, sometimes including unusual effects like the sawing of wood or rustling paper. Yet Penderecki's music speaks plainly and directly to many people and several of his works have become widely known, notably the *St Luke Passion* (related to the Passions of ▷J. S. Bach) which was an instant success at its first performance in 1966. Penderecki is not averse to addressing himself, in musical terms, to issues of great injustice. One of his best works is a *Threnody for the Victims of Hiroshima*; another is a *Dies irae* dedicated to those who died in the concentration camp at Auschwitz. His Violin Concerto, written for Isaac Stern, is a brilliantly organised, clean-cut work in a single movement which has traces of a funeral march and a scherzo woven into its texture. The opera *The Devils of Loudon* is immensely powerful, dealing with a 17th-century incidence of demonic possession and hysteria in a convent (the story was made into a notorious film by Ken Russell).

● ▷Prokofiev's opera *The Fiery Angel* has a plot that also culminates in an orgy of possession and hysteria in a nunnery.

Elgar, Serenade for strings; ▷Gustav Holst, *First Choral Symphony*; William Sterndale Bennett, Piano Concert no. 4; ▷Charles Villiers Stanford, *Songs of the Fleet*; ▷Ralph Vaughan Williams, *Job*.

PERCUSSION
The percussion instruments in the orchestra are struck or rattled. The most important are ▷timpani. The following are some of the other main ones, with pieces in which they can be heard. Tubular bells (▷Tchaikovsky, *1812 Overture*), vibraphone and wind machine (▷Vaughan Williams, *Sinfonia Antartica*), glockenspiel (▷Dukas, *Sorcerer's Apprentice*), cymbals (▷Tchaikovsky, *Romeo and Juliet*), xylophone (▷Kabalevsky, *The Comedians*), marimba (▷Milhaud, Concerto), triangle (▷Liszt, Piano Concerto no. 1), gong (▷Ravel, *Mother Goose*), castanets (▷Falla, *The Three-Cornered Hat*), whip (▷Arnold, *Tam O'Shanter*), anvil (▷Verdi, *Il trovatore*), side-drum (▷Ravel, *Boléro*), bass drum (▷Kodály, *Háry János*), tambourine (▷Delius, *La Calinda*). Any unusual effects required by a composer are normally provided by the percussion section of an orchestra.

PERGOLESI, Giovanni (1710–1736)
The Italian Giovanni Pergolesi died just after his 26th birthday, it is said from tuberculosis, and would have gone on to become a great figure in 18th-century music. He left behind some splendid music, including a *Stabat mater* of infinite variety and interest and a little operatic 'intermezzo' called *La serva padrona* which was designed to be performed between the acts of a larger opera, now forgotten. It shows him to be a master of comic opera. Many works attributed to Pergolesi have been found to be by others.

- In 1919 ▷Stravinsky took music by Pergolesi and 'recomposed' it for his ballet *Pulcinella*; the British conductor Sir John Barbirolli was another who raided Pergolesi's works to create a lovely Oboe Concerto for his wife, Evelyn Rothwell.

PFITZNER, Hans (1869–1949)
Hans Pfitzner must be one of the few composers, if not the only one, ever to be 'adopted' by an orchestra. Just

after World War II, he was living in penury in an old people's home in Munich. The president of the Vienna Philharmonic Orchestra found him there and the players saw to it that he lived in comfort for the rest of his days. Their action gives some indication of the esteem in which this dignified composer was held. His opera *Palestrina*, about the 16th-century Italian composer, recounts the possibly untrue tale of how a mass by Palestrina convinced the Council of Trent that it was possible to write elaborate church music in which the words were intelligible. But the opera is a fine one, nonetheless, full of warm-hearted and characterful music. Pfitzner's Symphony in C, one of his several orchestral works, was composed during World War II and appears to represent a release of tensions; it is attractive and undemanding. Pfitzner fought all his life against what he saw as the evil influence on music of modern experimentation. His own works belong to the world of ▷Richard Strauss and ▷Wagner.

PIERNÉ, Gabriel (1863–1937)

The French composer Gabriel Pierné is remembered for two engaging orchestral trifles, *March of the Little Lead Soldiers* and *Entry of the Little Fauns*. They are charming, in the best sense of the word. But someone ought to champion the piano music of this undervalued composer. There is a great deal of it – five long-playing records are required to accommodate it – and most of it is of high quality. Pierné has not the inspiration of ▷Fauré or ▷Ravel, but he writes most elegantly for the keyboard and most of his pieces fall refreshingly on the ear. He understands the world of children especially well and the works for young people or about childhood are enchanting.

PISTON, Walter (1894–1976)

The American composer Walter Piston is best known for the music he wrote for the ballet *The Incredible Flutist*, a score of great vitality and invention which deserves to be heard in the concert hall even more than it is. But Piston's greatest contributions to 20th-century music are his eight symphonies, of which no. 4 has been described as 'one of the finest works to be written in the United States'. His music can be dark and sombre, abrasive and exciting, or elegantly witty. It is almost always gripping.

PONCHIELLI, Amilcare (1834–1886)
The Italian Amilcare Ponchielli was a respected and effective teacher whose pupils included ▷Mascagni and ▷Puccini. He composed many operas, only one of which has endured. *La Gioconda* is still staged regularly in the major opera houses of the world and is an impressive piece of melodrama. It involves the love of a street singer for a nobleman and the attempts of an evil spy of the Inquisition to win her for himself. Two arias, 'Cielo e mar' and 'Suicidio!', are often sung in recitals and the Act 3 ballet (Dance of the Hours) has become a popular concert piece. Ponchielli's music looks back to ▷Verdi in the big ensembles but in its quieter moments it points plainly to the paths taken by Puccini and his associates.

> **NOW LISTEN** ▷
>
> Some Italian operas that followed on from *La Gioconda* include: ▷Francesco Cilea, *Adriana Lecouvreur*; ▷Umberto Giordano, *Andrea Chenier*; ▷Ruggero Leoncavallo, *La bohème*; ▷Pietro Mascagni, *Iris*; ▷Giacomo Puccini, *Tosca*; ▷Ermanno Wolf-Ferrari, *The Jewels of the Madonna*.

PORTER, Cole (1893–1964)
Cole Porter wrote the words and music of some of the most memorable songs to come out of his native America this century. *Night and Day*, *Begin the Beguine*, *I get a kick out of you*, *Just one of those things*, *Let's do it*, *I've got you under my skin* – the list is endless. He even entered controversial territory with *Love for sale*, a prostitute's embittered cry from the heart. In *Give me a primitive man*, Porter quotes from ▷Verdi's *Aida*, ▷Saint-Saëns's *Samson et Dalila* and ▷Beethoven's Fifth Symphony. His most successful Broadway show was *Kiss me Kate*, a musical version of *The Taming of the Shrew*; its many hit numbers include the witty duet 'Brush up your Shakespeare', sung by a pair of tough gangsters.

POULENC, Francis (1899–1963)
Francis Poulenc is one of the most lovable French

composers. It is difficult to hear his music and not be touched – either by its wit and gaiety or by its vein of deep seriousness, for both are present in his very considerable output. He was probably the most successful of the group of young composers known as ▷Les Six, particularly in the many works he wrote for the voice. His songs, though difficult to perform really well, are a gift to singers who wish to make the effort. The opera *Dialogues des Carmélites*, about the martyrdom of some nuns during the French Revolution, is among his most moving works and reaches unexpected depths of emotion. Poulenc's concertos are, without exception, thoroughly enjoyable. The Piano Concerto is cheekily attractive (it quotes *Way down upon the Swanee River* in its finale). The Organ Concerto is in direct contrast: a solemn, darkly impressive work. The *Concert champêtre* for harpsichord uses the solo instrument brilliantly, looking back to the past but in a modern idiom; the Concerto for two pianos is charming, with a winning slow movement. The *Aubade* for piano and 18 instruments (described as 'a choreographic concerto') is mischievously engaging, sending up various composers, including ▷Mozart and ▷Stravinsky.

Poulenc's Sinfonietta is a little gem whose neglect in the concert hall is hard to fathom. The music he wrote for the ballet *Les biches* in the 1920s is among his most charming and typical, being elegant, sophisticated, melodic (the 'Adagietto' is a hit) and brittle in a manner entirely suited to a tale involving young girls who are not as innocent as they appear. His *Gloria* (1959) is a late work which, like much of Poulenc's religious music, is joyous in a way that recalls the warmth of ▷Haydn. Its high spirits, however, give way from time to time to passages which are impressively grave and sincerely felt. It is the work of a man who obviously believes in a life to come. (The section beginning 'Laudamus te' is obstinately memorable with its jazzy, syncopated rhythms and simple melody.) Poulenc's piano music bespeaks the composer's intimate knowledge of the instrument (he was a fine pianist), the suite *Les soirées de Nazelles* containing some of his most imaginative ideas. The first of the *Trois Mouvements perpétuels* was used as the haunting theme tune for Alfred Hitchcock's thriller *Rope*.

NOW LISTEN ▷

Ballets which, like Poulenc's *Les biches*, were first staged in the 1920s: ▷Lord Berners, *The Triumph of Neptune*; ▷Constant Lambert, *Pamona*; ▷Darius Milhaud, *Le train bleu*; ▷Sergey Prokofiev, *The Prodigal Son*; ▷Maurice Ravel, *Boléro*; Igor Stravinsky, *Apollon musagète*.

PREVIN, André (born 1929)

André Previn is best known as a conductor, pianist and as a television communicator on musical matters. He has written some diverting music, however, which deserves to be more frequently performed, notably a Guitar Concerto and more recent Piano Concerto. The Guitar Concerto was composed for the virtuoso John Williams and is highly entertaining. It is tuneful, showing considerable understanding of the instrument's colours and capabilities. In the last movement, the soloist is joined by an electric guitar, an electric bass guitar and extra drums, which burst in every so often but don't affect the work's continuity. The Piano Concerto is an even finer work, written for Vladimir Ashkenazy. It sounds like an affectionate tribute to Previn's countryman ▷Barber, with dashes of ▷Bartók, ▷Prokofiev and ▷Shostakovich thrown in – all of it bound together by the experience Previn gained working for Hollywood for years. It makes special use of the cor anglais, the alto saxophone and the cello. Ashkenazy asked Previn to provide him with a good tune and Previn has done so, right at the beginning.

● Previn is a superb pianist. Other conductors who might have pursued a career as pianists are ▷Bernstein, ▷Harty, Sir George Solti, Walter Susskind and Bruno Walter. Lorin Maazel is a brilliant violinist and Sir John Barbirolli was a fine cellist.

PROKOFIEV, Sergey (1891–1953)

Sergey Prokofiev is one of the most popular of the great 20th-century Soviet composers. His music is often brittle, witty and pungently dramatic. But he could also be a real romantic and he wrote some of the most sumptuous melodies to be found in 20th-century scores. Two of his ballets, *Romeo and Juliet* and *Cinderella*, have attained classic status, containing wonderful music for dancing which can stand happily on its own in the concert hall. *Romeo and Juliet* especially is a magical response to Shakespeare's tragedy. Another ballet, *The Prodigal Son*, has a pithy score which underlines strongly the biblical tale of the boy who leaves home but is forced to crawl back to his father; the music associated with the son's sojourn among crooks and whores is superbly sleazy.

The seven symphonies are essential Prokofiev. No. 1, the 'Classical', is frequently heard in concerts; it is intended to invoke the atmosphere of a symphony from the age of ▷Haydn. No. 5 is a particularly fine work, dazzling and heart-wrenching by turns. No. 7 is a curious piece, sometimes serious, sometimes light-hearted, an odd symphonic swan-song. Prokofiev's five piano concertos are marvellously written and very effective – Prokofiev himself was a brilliant pianist. No. 3 is the most popular (with a meltingly lovely opening clarinet theme and a middle movement of typical grotesquerie). No. 4 is interesting in that the piano part is for the left hand only. His two violin concertos are completely dissimilar but equally enjoyable, the first being spiky, the second more lyrical.

His cantata *Alexander Nevsky* was an inspired rearrangement of a score Prokofiev wrote for an Eisenstein film; the Battle on the Ice is so vividly depicted in the music that the mind's eye can re-create it easily. The well-loved suite *Lieutenant Kijé* was likewise culled from a film score; its fourth movement, the sleigh-ride called 'Troika', is often played on its own. *Winter Campfire*, a suite for chorus and orchestra, is seldom performed but is worth tracking down on disc. It combines elegance and charm with a memorable childlike simplicity. The *Scythian Suite*, from an unsuccessful ballet, conjures up gods, goddesses and mighty deeds from ancient times: it is raw and dynamic. The orchestral fairy-tale *Peter and the Wolf* for narrator and orchestra has rightly earned the premier place among pieces for children.

Prokofiev's operas include an impressive version of the novel *War and Peace* (with some tremendous ballroom music). *The Love for Three Oranges* is a folktale which is deliciously amusing, its hero being a prince whom nobody can make laugh. The tiny March from the first act has become a concert-hall 'pop'. *The Fiery Angel* is a rather nasty tale about possession in a nunnery: in one scene the Devil eats a boy alive, then resurrects him from a nearby rubbish dump. Some nude nuns in an Edinburgh Festival production in the 1960s brought, ironically, strong Calvinist protests from the City Fathers. Prokofiev's piano sonatas are vital to a full understanding of this most strikingly original of composers; his chamber music adds a further dimension.

- Other works based on the parable of the prodigal son are by ▷Britten (church parable), ▷Debussy (cantata), ▷Joplin, arranged by Grant Hossack (ballet) and ▷Sullivan (oratorio). ▷Penderecki's opera *The Devils of Loudon* is also about possession in a nunnery.

PUCCINI, Giacomo (1858–1924)

Giacomo Puccini left a dozen operas to posterity. Of these, three are among the most popular ever composed; *La bohème*, *Tosca* and *Madam Butterfly* are performed all over the world, probably more often than any others. Puccini was always drawn to vocal music; his teacher ▷Ponchielli recognised in him a real theatrical flair and encouraged him to compose opera. From that time Puccini wrote virtually nothing not intended for the stage. His first two operas are interesting and show promise but are far from being masterpieces. *Le villi* is about a girl who becomes a spirit of the forest and joins the Wilis, familiar to ballet lovers from *Giselle*; *Edgar* is about a young nobleman who can't make up his mind between a respectable lady and a fiery gypsy called Tigrana.

With *Manon Lescaut* (based on Abbé Prevost's tale of the downfall of a courtesan) Puccini began to show his originality and skill at writing for the theatre. His personal style is clearly evident and we are given some of the first samples of Puccini's characteristic tunes. *La bohème* confirmed everyone's hopes. Puccini warmed to this tale of impoverished artists working, and loving, in a garret. There is not a superfluous bar in the score, which includes one gem after another, notably the tenor aria 'Che gelida manina' ('Your tiny hand is frozen') and the soprano's 'Mi chiamano Mimi' ('They call me Mimi'). The powerful *Tosca* followed with its exciting story of freedom fighters attempting to avoid the retribution of an evil police chief (a story which is still, sadly, relevant today). Tosca's aria 'Vissi d'arte' ('Love and music') and the tenor's 'È lucevan le stelle' ('The stars are shining brightly') are only two highlights.

Madam Butterfly was a failure initially but its study of a Japanese Geisha girl abandoned by her American sailor-husband quickly caught on and became probably the most effective tear-jerker in the operatic repertory. Puccini used some Japanese melodies in his score. 'Un bel di' ('One fine day') is one of the great soprano arias. *La Fanciulla del West* ('The Girl of the Golden West') is set in California during the Gold Rush. Its heroine is a tough, gun-toting saloon keeper who falls for a wanted bandit, and saves his life by cheating the local sheriff at poker! The plot is just about as absurd as you will find. But the opera somehow manages to be most endearing, and the score contains many marvellous passages. *La rondine* ('The Swallow') was a favourite of Puccini's but it never took off and probably won't do so until someone has the imagination to give it the kind of staging it deserves. It has certain similarities to ▷Verdi's *La traviata* in that its heroine gives up the man she loves rather than have his reputation besmirched; its music is gloriously and unashamedly sentimental.

Il trittico is three operas in one, all of them good. The first, *Il tabarro* ('The Cloak'), is a thriller about a bargee who suspects, correctly, that his wife is being unfaithful; *Suor Angelica* ('Sister Angelica') is set in a convent and concerns a nun with a past; *Gianni Schicchi* is a comedy about a family willing to go to any lengths to secure the fortune of a recently dead relative. Puccini manages brilliantly to conjure the right atmosphere for each of these widely different subjects.

Puccini died before he could complete *Turandot* but it is his most adventurous and imaginative opera, set in ancient China where the oppressed people are ruled by the icy, arrogant Princess Turandot. She will marry only the man who can answer three riddles she poses;

failure elicits instant death. The Prince Calaf tries his luck and wins but has a grim time trying to make the princess keep her side of the bargain. The last, long duet was completed from Puccini's sketches by Franco Alfano and is an anticlimax. But so much marvellously inventive and exciting music has gone before that one can accept the falling away of the score. Puccini used the orchestra and chorus even more stunningly than previously. Turandot's difficult opening aria 'In questa regia' and the tenor's 'Nessun dorma' ('None shall sleep') are the hits from this wonderful opera.

Puccini was one of the world's greatest melodists. His tunes linger long in the memory. His dramatic gifts are such that he can grip and hold an audience in the palm of his hand within a few short bars. His concern with helpless women, allied to a fondness for a touch of sadism, may not appeal to everyone. But the mixture is a proven success in the opera house. Puccini may not have the depth or the intensity of Verdi, but he understood the theatre in a way that few could ever claim to have done.

- The Frenchman ▷Massenet based his opera *Manon* on Prévost's story. The Italian ▷Leoncavallo's version of *La bohème* was staged shortly after Puccini's. ▷Busoni was another who used the *Turandot* story for an opera. In the middle of the 19th century, the English composer Edward Loder wrote an opera called *The Night Dancers* which has the same plot as *Le villi*.

PURCELL, Henry (1659–1695)
During his lifetime, the English composer Henry Purcell was a popular figure, both in musical and non-musical circles, and his music was well liked. But for the next two centuries it fell out of favour and only began to attract the attention it deserved in the early 1900s. Purcell composed all manner of music. He wrote many stage spectacles, including *The Fairy Queen*, an imaginative series of masques based on

NOW LISTEN ▷

String music composed by some of Purcell's English 'successors': ▷Arthur Bliss, Music for Strings; ▷Benjamin Britten, Variations on a

Shakespeare's *A Midsummer Night's Dream*. His sacred and secular songs are masterly examples of how to set words effectively to music. No less impressive are his instrumental compositions, notably the Chacony for strings. (Purcell was one of the first of many English composers to demonstrate an unusual sympathy with string instruments.)

Dido and Aeneas (1689) is usually reckoned to be the first true English opera, composed as a continuous piece of music without spoken dialogue and showing again Purcell's ability to fuse words and music to perfection. Dido's famous lament, 'When I am laid to earth', sung as her lover Aeneas is leaving her, touches a vein of emotion. Purcell's church music and his many odes testify to the versatility of a remarkable composer.

▷Britten, a 20th-century composer who did much to popularise Purcell, based his *Young Person's Guide to the Orchestra* on a stirring melody from the incidental music Purcell wrote for the play *Abdelazer*.

Theme of Frank Bridge; ▷Edward Elgar, Introduction and Allegro; ▷Michael Tippett, Fantasia Concertante on a Theme of Corelli; ▷Ralph Vaughan Williams, Fantasia on a Theme of Thomas Tallis; ▷Peter Warlock, *Capriol Suite*.

R

RAFF, Joachim (1822–1882)

The Swiss composer Joachim Raff was fascinated by the idea of writing 'music for the future', and taught his pupils, who included the American ▷MacDowell, to look ahead rather than backwards when they were composing. Ironically, Raff's music is regarded today as being very traditional. His operas and concertos are almost never performed, though one does hear occasional performances of the Fifth of his 11 symphonies (a work that has also been recorded); it is sub-titled 'Lenore' and is a ▷Lisztian piece describing an ill-fated love-affair in which the hero is killed and goes on a ghostly ride with the Devil. Raff may not be the greatest composer, but his music is by no means unattractive and does not, perhaps, deserve its virtual banishment from the concert hall.

● The Devil is depicted in many musical works. He is a leading protagonist in the various operatic versions of Goethe's *Faust* (by ▷Berlioz and ▷Gounod among others). He plays the violin for a bunch of dancing skeletons in the *Danse macabre* of ▷Saint-Saëns; and he sits on God's throne for a short spell in ▷Vaughan Williams's ballet *Job*.

RAKHMANINOV, Sergey (1873–1943)

Sergey Rakhmaninov was the last of the great Russian Romantic composers, with a seemingly inexhaustible store of marvellous melodies that are instantly memorable. It is surprising that Hollywood never made a fanciful film out of an episode in his life when he lost confidence in his ability to compose and had to be hypnotised by a psychiatrist to regain it. Rakhmaninov was a superb pianist, probably the greatest of the 20th century, and his solo piano music is arguably his best. The 24 Preludes (individually more substantial than those of ▷Chopin), the *Etudes-tableaux*, the two sonatas and the Variations on a Theme of Corelli are indispensable in the concert pianist's repertory. (The Prelude in C sharp minor quickly became immensely popular and acquired a story involving coffins and burial grounds; the composer came to hate it so much he tried to avoid playing it.) Rakhmaninov transcribed for the piano a good deal of music by other composers, including ▷Mendelssohn's *A Midsummer Night's Dream* Scherzo and ▷Schubert's song *Erlkönig*.

Rakhmaninov's four piano concertos are wonderfully effective. No. 1 is short and full of vitality and imagination, though without any of the big tunes found in no. 2 (the work composed as a result of his psychiatric treatment). No. 3 is the finest, terrifyingly hard to play but superbly constructed and cumulatively exciting. No. 4 has never been popular, some say because its slow movement has a theme that sounds like 'Three Blind Mice', but it has some splendid moments and repays attention. The Rhapsody on a Theme of Paganini for piano and orchestra is both a brilliant showpiece and an extremely clever set of variations, the 18th of which has become something of a 'pop' because of its supremely beautiful melody. Rakhmaninov composed three excellent symphonies which, after years of neglect, are now frequently heard on the concert platform; the Second is particularly memorable if handled carefully and paced properly by an intelligent conductor. The *Symphonic Studies*, both in their orchestral and two-piano versions, are thoughtful and rewarding and the symphonic poem *The Isle of the Dead* is a haunting piece, suggested by Böcklin's painting of a coffin aboard a boat which is sailing across calm waters towards a distant island; Death stands in the bows. Rakhmaninov's choral masterpiece is *The Bells*, a setting of Edgar Allen Poe's poem.

● Rakhmaninov, whose piano concertos sparked off a host of imitations by lesser composers, is always depicted as a serious, unsmiling figure. But in fact he had a Puckish sense of humour. Once he was giving a recital in New York with the violinist ▷Kreisler. Suddenly Kreisler lost the place. 'Where are we?', he whispered urgently to his colleague. Rakhmaninov, continuing to play impassively, whispered back: 'Carnegie Hall'.

RAMEAU, Jean-Philippe (1683–1764)

The life of Jean-Philippe Rameau falls neatly into two. He was first an organist in Paris and other French cities; from this period come the many harpsichord pieces which established Rameau as successor to the great ▷Couperin. But when he was 50, Rameau became a theatre composer. His chief works, notable for their colourful orchestration and bold harmonies, were *Castor et Pollux*, *Dardanus* and *Les Indes galantes*, and these led to his being hailed as the new ▷Lully and a master of French opera. His skills attracted the attention of King Louis XV who appointed him a royal chamber music composer.

RAVEL, Maurice (1875–1937)

The French composer Maurice Ravel had to work hard for recognition. His forward-looking ideas, particularly in his writing for the piano, were not liked by the Establishment in turn-of-the-century France. But he triumphed and is now regarded by many – though not all – as one of France's greatest musical figures. ▷Stravinsky described Ravel as 'a Swiss clockmaker' because of the meticulous way he composed. Ravel's best known but by no means best work is the ballet *Boléro*, with its one tune, repeated over and over again to the insistent tap of a side-drum. Much finer is *La valse*, a colourful lament for the gay, swirling Vienna lost after World War I. The lovely children's suite *Ma mère l'oye* (Mother Goose) and the atmospheric *Rapsodie espagnole* are fine, much-played concert works.

> **NOW LISTEN**
>
> Some music by composers who influenced and were admired by Ravel:
> ▷Emmanuel Chabrier *Le roi malgré lui*;
> ▷George Gershwin, *Rhapsody in Blue*;
> ▷Jules Massenet, *Scènes pittoresques*;
> ▷Modest Musorgsky, *Khovanshchina*;
> ▷Camille Saint-Saëns,

But they yield to the sad little suite *Le tombeau de Couperin*, which contains some of Ravel's most poignant music. He was an ambulance driver during World War I and was appalled by what he saw; *Le tombeau* pays tribute to friends killed in action and to ▷Couperin, the French composer most admired by Ravel.

The jazzy Piano Concerto in G and the Piano Concerto for the left hand (composed for a pianist who lost an arm in the war) are contrasting masterpieces. The ballet *Daphnis et Chloé* (1912) is, perhaps, Ravel's most adventurous and exciting score. It is set in mythological Greece and shows what happens when Chloe is kidnapped by pirates and returned to her lover Daphnis thanks to the intervention of the god Pan. Ravel's music, for a huge orchestra and wordless chorus, is full of atmosphere and ranges from miraculous delicacy to blazing brilliance. The depiction of dawn, with its rippling streams, bird-calls and gradually increasing light and warmth is magical; the final orgy is a tour de force. The music stands perfectly well as a concert suite.

Two one-act operas are superb theatre pieces: *L'heure espagnole* ('The Spanish Hour'), about the flighty wife of a Spanish clockmaker, and *L'enfant et les sortilèges* ('The Child and the Spells') based on Colette's tale of a naughty boy and the strange punishment he receives. Some splendid songs, including *Shéhérazade*, a marvellous cycle for soprano and orchestra, and several chamber works, notably a beautiful string quartet and the Introduction and Allegro for string quartet, harp, flute and clarinet, show Ravel's versatility. But it was Ravel's beloved piano that brought out the best in him; most of his orchestral works started life as piano pieces and were later fully scored. Of those he never turned into orchestral works, *Gaspard de la nuit*, the *Sonatine* and the early *Jeux d'eau* (a marvellous suggestion of a fountain) are outstanding. In 1922, Ravel orchestrated ▷Musorgsky's piano work *Pictures at an Exhibition*, still regarded as a model of orchestration.

Le rouet d'Omphale; ▷Erik Satie, *Gnossiennes*; ▷Richard Strauss, *Don Quixote*.

RAWSTHORNE, Alan (1905–1971)

There was a time when the music of the British composer Alan Rawsthorne could be heard fairly frequently in the concert hall. Now, sadly, he seems to
have faded completely. His work deserves much better. Rawsthorne's musical voice is highly individual;
his way with a melody is instantly recognisable and by
no means 'difficult' to absorb. Whether it be an overtly
popular piece like the bustling *Street Corner* overture or
the inventive and imaginative Symphonic Studies for
orchestra, Rawsthorne's personality shines through.
His two piano concertos (especially the second) are
excellent, superbly crafted works, and would make
ideal additions to the repertory of an adventurous solo
pianist. The three symphonies have plenty to say, and
do so strongly and with character. The ballet *Madame
Chrysanthème* contains a great deal of charming music,
suitably oriental in flavour. *Practical Cats* for speaker
and orchestra takes a refreshing look at T. S. Eliot's
famous poems. Rawsthorne wrote a fair amount of
chamber music and a handful of fine piano pieces,
including the Four Bagatelles which helped to make
his name known. It was his music that enhanced the
war film *The Cruel Sea*.

REGER, Max (1873–1916)

The German composer Max Reger did not believe in
writing 'programme music', or music that tells a story.
Most of his work is 'absolute music', to be heard for
itself alone. His orchestral works are often fairly heavy
going; even his Variations and Fugue on a Merry
Theme by J. A. Hiller isn't too merry and is very long.
Reger's numerous organ works are much played and
admired by lovers of the king of instruments.

RESPIGHI, Ottorino (1879–1936)

If Ottorino Respighi had lived just a little longer, he
would undoubtedly have made a fortune composing
for Hollywood. His three biggest scores, *The Pines of
Rome*, *Roman Festivals* and *The Fountains of Rome*, seem
to have been made for the cinema with their sumptuous orchestration and vivid colours. Most listeners

NOW LISTEN

The might of ancient
Rome, and the city
itself, have been
depicted by a number of

must be able to visualise Roman legions marching down the Appian Way at the end of *The Pines of Rome*. The fame of these pieces, however, has obscured for many the fact that Respighi also wrote very different works which reflected his fascination with the composers of the past. The *Ancient Airs and Dances* are brilliant and tasteful reworkings of lute pieces from the 16th and 17th centuries. *Gli Ucelli* ('The Birds') takes as its starting-point compositions dating from the 17th and 18th centuries and is a sheer delight. Gregorian chant was the inspiration of the *Concerto gregoriano* for violin and orchestra, an attractive work ignored by soloists partly because it is not 'showy' enough. The *Trittico botticelliano* ('Three Botticelli Pictures'), the *Impressioni braziliane* ('Brazilian Impressions'), prompted by a holiday in Rio de Janeiro, and the *Vetrate di Chiesa* ('Church Windows') are all sadly undervalued orchestral works.

Respighi's ballet *La boutique fantasque* ('The Fantastic Toyshop') is a highly successful arrangement and amplification of some salon pieces by ▷Rossini. The orchestration is masterly (as might be expected of a pupil of ▷Rimsky-Korsakov). Respighi once said to someone who was accusing him of not being modern or progressive: 'Why should I use new techniques when there is still so much to say through the language of conventional music?'. In his works you will find nothing of the 'chaos and absurdities' he so disliked in contemporary scores.

RIMSKY-KORSAKOV, Nikolay (1844–1908)

Nikolay Rimsky-Korsakov trained as an officer in the Russian navy. However, he was a keen amateur composer. He met ▷Balakirev, who introduced him to other leading composers of the day. When only 27 he was appointed professor of composition and instrumentation at the St Petersburg Conservatory, for which he had to teach himself harmony and counterpoint. (In his autobiography, he admitted that for a while he was only two textbook pages ahead of his students.) But he became the most influential teacher, counting ▷Stravinsky and Prokofiev among his pupils. Rimsky was soon renowned for his brilliant colourful

composers including:
▷Hector Berlioz,
Roman Carnival;
▷Georges Bizet; *Roma*;
▷Gabriel Faure,
Caligula; ▷Aram
Khachaturian,
Spartacus; ▷Giacomo
Puccini, *Tosca*.

NOW LISTEN ▷

Some works by pupils of Rimsky-Korsakov which show his influence:
▷Anton Arensky, Suite no. 1; ▷Alexander Glazunov, Symphony no. 5; ▷Anatol Lyadov, *The Enchanted Lake*;
▷Ottorino Respighi, *The Fountains of Rome*;

scores. He was a member of 'The Five', the group of nationalist Russian composers.

The suite *Sheherazade* (1888) is the most popular of his orchestral works. It's a rich piece of Arabian Nightery, full of memorable melodies and exotic orchestration. The Princess Sheherazade herself is represented throughout the work by a sinuous tune played by a solo violin. The tales she tells the sultan, to prolong her life, are represented by the most sensuous music, rich in oriental atmosphere. Another of the composer's most exciting creations is the *Capriccio espagnol*, a tribute to sunny Spain of dazzling virtuosity which ends in a whirlwind of orchestral fireworks. There's a piano concerto of passing interest and three symphonies of uneven quality. Of his chamber music a wind quintet, which deserves to be more often played, is great fun.

Rimsky composed many operas. Concert suites have been taken from some of them, notably *Legend of the Invisible City of Kitezh* and *Tsar Saltan*. The most frequently staged is *The Golden Cockerel*, a delicious fairy tale involving a lazy king who relies on a pet cockerel to warn him of impending danger. Rimsky was involved in the completion of ▷Borodin's unfinished opera *Prince Igor* and made his own performing versions of much music by ▷Musorgsky, including the opera *Boris Godunov*. His efforts were well intended but are now thought in some cases to have done the originals a disservice.

▷Igor Stravinsky, *The Firebird.*

• 'The Flight of the Bumble Bee', from the opera *Tsar Saltan*, has been arranged for practically every instrument including the tuba.

RODGERS, Richard (1902–1980)
The career of Richard Rodgers fell into two distinct parts. Until 1940 he worked with Lorenz Hart, producing a string of successful musicals including *On Your Toes* (which included the famous ballet 'Slaughter on Tenth Avenue'), *The Girlfriend*, *The Boys from Syracuse* and *Pal Joey*. From 1940 until his final years, Rodgers collaborated with Oscar Hammerstein II, which

resulted in *Oklahoma!*, *Carousel*, *The King and I* and *The Sound of Music* among others.

South Pacific (1949) is arguably their finest achievement – a more serious musical than most with something to say on the insidious problems of racism and on the futility and waste of war. It involves a nurse working among the troops on a Pacific island during World War II. She falls for an older man, a Frenchman, and is set to enjoy a relationship with him until she discovers he was once married to a Polynesian girl and had children by her. The score contains many great songs, notably 'Some enchanted evening', 'This nearly was mine', 'Younger than Springtime' and 'Bali Ha'i'. Rodgers possessed the gift of memorable melody. The songs from his shows are often sung out of their theatre contexts. His score for the television documentary 'Victory at Sea' won him many plaudits.

- Other musicals set against a background of war are Joan Littlewood's Theatre Workshop production *Oh, what a lovely war!*, Lionel Bart's *Blitz* and ▷Straus's *The Chocolate Soldier*, based on Bernard Shaw's *Arms and the Man*.

RODRIGO, Joaquin (born 1901)

The Spanish composer Joaquin Rodrigo was responsible for what is probably the most popular guitar concerto ever written. The *Concierto de Aranjuez* has a slow movement that is so ear-catching it even entered the pop charts. Its success, of course, has had its drawbacks. With the exception of the *Fantasía para un gentilhombre*, a guitar work written as a tribute to earlier Spanish music, Rodrigo's music is largely unperformed today – regrettable since much of it is colourful and most attractive. There is, for instance, the piquant *Pastoral Concerto* for flute, the *Summer Concerto* for violin, with a ravishing slow movement, the splendidly virile *Concerto in Galant Style* for cello, and a beautiful Serenade for harp and orchestra – not forgetting the brilliant *Concerto andaluz* for four guitars and composed for the remarkable Romero family. Some purely orchestral works, including *For the flower of the Blue Lily* (about a prince who goes in search of a rare bloom), are worth investigating. Rodrigo's music is distinctly but not aggressively Spanish – always melodic and admirably stylish.

- Since the age of three, Rodrigo has battled against the handicap of total blindness. The 18th-century Austrian pianist and composer Maria Theresia von Paradis was also blind, as was the 20th-century Englishman ▷Delius in the last years of his life; he suffered the additional tragedy of paralysis, but continued to compose with the help of an amanuensis, Eric Fenby. ▷Beethoven and ▷Smetana both composed masterpieces after they had become deaf.

ROGUES' GALLERY
Opera offers a generous selection of rogues, some villainous, some charming:
▷Malcolm Arnold, *Tam O'Shanter*
Daniel Auber, *Fra Diavolo*
▷Claude Debussy, *Danse de Puck*
▷Wolfgang Amadeus Mozart, *Don Giovanni*
▷Richard Strauss, *Till Eulenspiegel*
▷Giuseppe Verdi, *Falstaff*

ROMBERG, Sigmund (1887–1951)
Sigmund Romberg was the Hungarian-born composer of a number of highly successful American musicals, notably *The Student Prince*, *The Desert Song* and *The New Moon*. He based one of his shows, *Blossom Time*, on the melodies of ▷Schubert. Most of Romberg's best work was done between 1917 and 1928, but he had another hit as late as 1945, with *Up in Central Park*. Today if theatre managements need to make money quickly, they only have to mount a revival of *The Desert Song* and the queues will form.

ROSSINI, Gioachino (1792–1868)

Gioachino Rossini's life is as remarkable as one of his own opera plots. For 20 years he composed operas which were the toast not only of Italy but far beyond. Then, when he was only 37, he virtually stopped writing music. The next 30 years saw him compose only two religious works (the fine *Stabat mater* and the delightful *Petite messe solennelle*) and some entertaining but trivial piano pieces which he called *Péchés de vieillesse* ('Sins of Old Age'). Ill-health is one reason given for his early retirement; another is terminal disappointment at the lack of interest shown in his last opera, *Guillaume Tell* (William Tell). But if such a state of affairs was sad for the musical world, at least he left behind a number of masterpieces. *La Cenerentola* ('Cinderella') is a witty and colourful interpretation of the familiar fairy story; *Le comte Ory* is the hilarious study of a lecherous nobleman who invades a nunnery with his pals; *La gazza ladra* ('The Thieving Magpie') involves a peasant girl wrongly accused of stealing; and *L'italiana in Algeri* ('The Italian Girl in Algiers') is looking for a missing lover.

Il barbiere di Siviglia ('The Barber of Seville', 1816), the peak of Rossini's achievement in comic opera, is based on the play by Beaumarchais. It tells of the successful attempts of the lively Figaro to help the Count Almaviva to win the hand of Rosina, who is closely watched by her guardian Doctor Bartolo. Additional comedy is provided by the sleazy music teacher, Don Basilio, whose unwelcome appearances punctuate the action. (These characters were already familiar from ▷Mozart's *The Marriage of Figaro* which, though composed before it, is a sequel to *The Barber*, being based on another Beaumarchais play.) Rossini's invention runs riot in a host of numbers, notably Figaro's famous song 'Largo al factotum' with its refrain, 'Figaro here, Figaro there' and Basilio's amusingly nasty 'Slander' song. Rosina's aria 'Una voce poco fa' is a popular showpiece.

Not all Rossini's operas are funny, however. His *Otello* may have been eclipsed by ▷Verdi's mighty version but it is worth hearing. So are *Semiramide*, and *Tancredi*. William Tell, the Swiss hero who had to shoot an apple off his son's head to satisfy his enemies, is a splendid creation. Those who know only the part of the overture used for the 'Lone Ranger' should try music from the opera itself: they will be delighted by its freshness.

Rossini's late piano pieces (mentioned above) were orchestrated and arranged by ▷Respighi for the ballet *La boutique fantasque*; they were also used by ▷Britten for his two orchestral suites, *Matinées musicales* and *Soirées musicales*.

- Rossini's wit was legendary, as was his contempt for the music of ▷Wagner. He once said: 'There are some fine moments in Wagner, but some terrible quarter-hours!'. When asked how he had enjoyed the opera *Tannhäuser*, Rossini declared: 'I can't say after hearing it only once – and I certainly don't intend to hear it again'.

ROTA, Nino (1911–1979)

The Italian Nino Rota achieved international fame as a composer of film music. He wrote the score for the successful romance *The Glass Mountain*, which introduced the up-and-coming baritone Tito Gobbi to a wide audience. He also composed a number of enjoyable concert works, including a charming Harp Concerto, and several operas, of which one is pure delight. *The Italian Straw Hat*, based on Eugene Labiche's farce, has an endless stream of catchy melodies and races along at a breathless pace; it's about a young man whose wedding plans are jeopardised by one unforeseen circumstance after another, and in an English translation, it would be a knock-out. Why no one has made one is a mystery.

- The French composer ▷Ibert wrote incidental music for a production of the original play *The Italian Straw Hat* and reworked it to form his much-loved orchestral *Divertissement*.

ROUSSEL, Albert (1869–1937)

The French composer Albert Roussel spent a number of years as a naval officer (as did ▷Rimsky-Korsakov). His tours of duty in far-off places clearly influenced him when he began composing: much of his music has more than a touch of oriental exoticism about it. The wonderful orchestral *Evocations*, for example, include a memorable sound-picture of the ancient Indian city of Jaipur. The listener can almost see its rose-red buildings glowing in the rays of the setting sun. Roussel, who was a pupil of ▷d'Indy, learnt much from his master about orchestral colour. His palette is rich and varied and his music is highly individual and forward-looking without being in the least difficult to listen to. It can be breathlessly vigorous (as in the final *Gigue* from the imaginative Suite in F): it can just as easily be rapt and reflective and extremely beautiful. The ballet *Bacchus et Ariane*, in similar vein to ▷Ravel's *Daphnis et Chloé*, contains some of its composer's most highly charged and absorbing music. The last two of Roussel's four symphonies are superbly constructed, tight and economical. The chamber works are best represented by the Serenade for flute, violin, viola, cello and harp – an enchanting piece. Roussel's experiments with orchestral textures and imaginative flights of musical fancy had great influence on later generations of French composers.

RUBBRA, Edmund (1901–1986)

Edmund Rubbra was a British composer whose strong, individual music has never been fully appreciated. His teachers included ▷Holst, and Rubbra's music is very much in the tradition of Holst and ▷Ireland. His works do not have immediate appeal but yield their treasures slowly. His huge output includes religious music, concertos, chamber works and some interesting piano music. But it is in the symphonies that the listener anxious to make his acquaintance will find the most rewarding material. The Fifth is probably the most impressive gateway to Rubbra's orchestral world. If you are won over by its unusual middle movement, you will undoubtedly wish to explore further.

NOW LISTEN ⟩

Music by other pupils of ▷d'Indy: ▷Georges Auric, *Imaginées*; ▷Albéric Magnard, Symphony no. 4; Roland Manuel, Piano Concerto; ▷Erik Satie, *Relâche*; ▷Joaquín Turina, *Danzas fantasticas*.

RUTTER, John (born 1945)

John Rutter wrote one of the most attractive modern carols, the *Shepherd's Pipe Carol*, now an indispensable part of most Christmas concerts. It is testimony to his ability to write tunes which are in a modern idiom but which are easy to sing and to remember. Rutter's style is accessible and aims to woo us. He has written excellent new tunes to some famous psalms and hymns (notably 'The Lord is My Shepherd' and 'All things bright and beautiful') and a number of fine church anthems, including a tiny, exquisite *Gaelic Blessing*. His larger works include an exciting *Gloria* for choir and brass which makes a joyful noise, even if it does owe much to the ▷Walton of *Belshazzar's Feast*. Rutter's music makes the most weary listener feel that life is good.

● Some other composers who have made settings of the *Gloria* include: ▷Poulenc, ▷Puccini, ▷Rossini, ▷Vivaldi and ▷Walton.

S

SAINT-SAËNS, Camille (1835–1921)

The French composer Camille Saint-Saëns was neither innovatory nor adventurous. But his music is elegant, well-crafted and appealing. It was admired by composers as widely different as ▷Liszt and ▷Ravel, and it survives today because it has many delights to offer the listener. His most popular work is *The Carnival of the Animals* for two pianos and small orchestra, written as a joke for some of his students to play. It is a witty look at the world of birds and beasts, the tortoise plodding along to a slow version of ▷Offenbach's 'Can-Can', and the elephant cavorting to the fairy Scherzo from ▷Mendelssohn's *A Midsummer Night's Dream*. The third of Saint-Saëns's three symphonies contains some marvellous music and makes effective use of the organ, an instrument the composer played with distinction. His five piano concertos have a lightness of touch and genuine charm; no. 5 quotes a song Saint-Saëns heard on the banks of the Nile in Egypt during one of his many visits to Africa. His other concert music includes several fine symphonic poems, of which the *Danse macabre* and *Le rouet d'Omphale* ('Omphale's Spinning Wheel') are the best: and there is a lovely Concert Piece for harp and orchestra.

Samson et Dalila (1877) is the only one of Saint-Saëns's operas regularly performed today, but it is arguably his finest work. It tells the familiar biblical tale of the Hebrew warrior whose great strength lies in his hair; when it is cut off by the treacherous Delilah, the enemy Philistines take him prisoner. But his faith in God allows him to find the power to pull down the temple of his foes and destroy them. The opera's most

NOW LISTEN ▷

Other musical works inspired by biblical stories: ▷Lennox Berkeley, *Ruth*; ▷Benjamin Britten, *The Burning Fiery Furnace*; ▷Andrew Lloyd Webber, *Joseph and the Amazing Technicolor Dreamcoat*; ▷Sergey Prokofiev, *The Prodigal Son*; ▷Arnold Schoenberg, *Moses und Aron*; ▷Ralph Vaughan Williams, *Job*; ▷Giuseppe Verdi, *Nabucco*.

famous aria is sung by Delilah as she begins her seduc-
tion, 'Softly awakes my heart'. But there are many
other highlights, notably Delilah's other big aria
('Spring which begins') which some find even more
moving and the exciting choruses and dances scattered
through the piece. The opera is the work of a man who
understood the theatre well and knew how to exploit
the human voice.

SATIE, Erik (1866–1925)

Erik Satie was a French composer of Scottish descent
who will be remembered as an eccentric – with good
reason. He had an obsession with green velvet; he was
absent-minded to the point where he frequently mis-
laid manuscripts he was writing and forgot them; and
he gave silly titles to some of his pieces, for example
'Three Pieces in the Form of a Pear', 'Flabby
Preludes', 'Shameless Idyll', 'Tiresome Peccadilloes'
and 'Waltz of the Chocolate with Almonds'. But there
was a good deal more to Satie than that. Not for nothing did ▷Debussy value his opinion and ▷Ravel play
Satie piano pieces at his recitals. Underneath the zany
façade, he had musical wisdom and was an experimenter whose work was to have far-reaching effects on
the group of Paris-based composers known as Les Six.
Some of his orchestral music is deliciously unusual.
His ballet *Parade*, about circus entertainers, includes a
typewriter in the score. *Relâche* was intended as background to a silent film depicting Satie crawling on the
façade of Notre Dame Cathedral.

But it is Satie's piano music which will ensure that
he is remembered. One of his *Trois gymnopédies*, gently
hypnotic little pieces of the utmost simplicity, has
achieved pop status and been arranged for almost every conceivable instrument or group. The *Trois gnossiennes*, inspired (it is thought) by the culture of ancient
Greece, are exquisite miniatures. The *Trois morceaux
en forme de poire* ('Three Pieces in the Form of a Pear'),
for piano duet, are among his most memorable works.
The French composer ▷Sauguet wrote of Satie: 'His
music must be got used to . . . it will echo your own
solitude and fill it with its magic song: friendly, calming
and pure'.

> **NOW LISTEN**
>
> Music by Les Six, the
> composers influenced
> by Satie: ▷Georges
> Auric, *Phèdre*; ▷Louis
> Durey, *L'occasion*;
> ▷Arthur Honegger,
> *Pastorale d'été*;
> ▷Darius Milhaud, *Le
> boeuf sur le toit*;
> ▷Francis Poulenc,
> *Novelettes*; ▷Germaine
> Tailleferre, Piano
> Concerto.

SAUGUET, Henri (born 1901)

Henri Sauguet is very much a man of the theatre with 25 ballets and half-a-dozen operas to his credit. His style is very French (he studied with ▷Canteloube and idolised ▷Satie); it is also sophisticated to the point of being chic. But it is effective and sometimes affecting. Sauguet is at his most serious in the opera *La chartreuse de Parme*, after Stendhal. But his best music is in his ballets. *Les forains* ('The Show People') is especially memorable, a tragi-comic little piece about a troupe of entertainers who set up their show in one village after another and get little return for their efforts. It is another, but quite intense, variation on the old 'laugh-while-your-heart-is-heavy' story. Another ballet, *La dame aux camélias* is a version of the same Dumas story used by ▷Verdi in his opera *La traviata*. Sauguet's piano concertos are undemanding and attractive; his First Symphony ('Expiatoire') is much tougher, dedicated to the memory of innocent war victims.

NOW LISTEN
▷Joseph Canteloube, *Triptyque*; ▷Charles Koechlin, *Seven Stars' Symphony*; ▷Francis Poulenc, *Les biches*; ▷Erik Satie, *La belle excentrique*.

SAXOPHONE

The saxophone is a wind instrument which comes in several sizes and was invented by a Belgian called Adolphe Sax around 1840. It was intended for, and soon used in, military bands but several French composers, including ▷Berlioz and ▷Bizet, took an interest in it and used its smooth, mellifluous sound to good effect in the orchestra. It did not take root in the world of serious music until this century. The saxophone represents the bleak, lonely Old Castle in ▷Ravel's orchestration of the *Pictures at an Exhibition* by ▷Musorgsky. It is prominent in ▷Prokofiev's ballet *Romeo and Juliet* and ▷Debussy showed real understanding of its capabilities in his *Rapsodie*. ▷Vaughan Wiliams included the saxophone in both his Sixth and Ninth Symphonies (he had earlier found its velvety tone ideal to suggest Job's wily comforters in his ballet *Job*). The Russian ▷Glazunov and the Brazilian ▷Villa-Lobos have composed excellent saxophone concertos; and in the 1930s, the British composer ▷Coates wrote a fairly substantial *Saxo-Rhapsody* for the virtuoso Sigurd Rascher (their recording of the work is still available). Jazz bands, of course, have al-

ways made use of the 'sax'; the big bands of Glenn
Miller and Tommy Dorsey had particularly impressive
sections.

SCARLATTI, Domenico (1685–1757)

The Italian composer Domenico Scarlatti wrote music
for the church and the stage, but his fame rests on his
keyboard sonatas. He was appointed to give keyboard
lessons to the Portuguese king's daughter, and his
years in Lisbon saw the composition of over 550 remarkable, imaginative sonatas, in which he exploited
and explored many aspects of playing technique, creating pieces of extraordinary brilliance.

His father Alessandro (1660–1725) composed a
vast amount of music in many forms, including over
700 cantatas and numerous operas.

• Another Italian composer, Vincenzo Tommasini,
  used Scarlatti's music when asked to provide a
  score for the ballet *The Good-Humoured Ladies*
  (1916).

SCHOENBERG, Arnold (1874–1951)

The Austrian Arnold Schoenberg has been described
as a revolutionary, but for whom music would have
followed a different path. It is certainly true that the
method he devised for organising his music (called the
12-note method, or 'serialism') has had far-reaching
influence on later composers; but the nature of that
method and Schoenberg's intentions are often misunderstood, chiefly because much of his music is gritty,
intense, has no keys and, with its elusive quality, is
difficult to listen to and understand. It is now appreciated, however, that Schoenberg was really a 'reluctant
revolutionary'.

His early music, following the traditions of his
teachers and influenced by Brahms, whom he deeply
admired, is melodic, even luxuriant. His tone poem
Pelleas und Melisande (based on the play ▷Debussy
used for his opera) is rich and colourful. *Gurrelieder*

('Song of Gurra') is scored for huge forces and is almost Wagnerian in scale and impact; *Verklärte Nacht* ('Transfigured Night') is a beautiful, romantic piece, originally for string sextet but better known in its arrangement for string orchestra.

By 1911 Schoenberg's music was taking a different turn. *Pierrot lunaire*, which dates from this time, is for an instrumental quintet and a reciter who uses *Sprechgesang*, a vocal technique halfway between song and speech. The work is a setting of 21 poems, intense, ambiguous and disturbing with no sense of 'key'; its sound-world is compelling and its originality cannot be ignored. By the time Schoenberg wrote his Variations for Orchestra he had developed his 12-note method: the 12 notes of a scale are arranged in a particular order, forming a 'series' or 'row' which becomes the basis of a composition. In the early 1930s Schoenberg wrote his opera *Moses und Aron*; it was unfinished at his death but is a powerful and moving piece about the problems of communication, a subject dear to the heart of a composer for whom artistic integrity was all-important.

Towards the end of his life, Schoenberg returned to composing in a more conventional manner, while at the same time developing serialism to greater complexity (notably in his Violin Concerto). A devout man, he wrote several religious choruses and *A Survivor from Warsaw*.

Schoenberg made many arrangements of works by other composers, including his beloved ▷Brahms, ▷Bach and ▷Johann Strauss.

● Schoenberg's two most devoted pupils and disciples were ▷Berg and ▷Webern. The three men, based in Vienna, became known as the 'Second Viennese School'. Berg married Schoenberg's ideas to a romantic, melodic style; Webern developed a spare, stark mode of expression, writing works of great brevity and intensity.

SCHUBERT, Franz (1797–1828)

Franz's Schubert's Ninth Symphony is nicknamed 'Great'. Yet that word could be fairly placed before any number of his works. The String Quintet, the piano quintet known as 'The Trout', several of the string quartets, the late piano sonatas and two of the finest song cycles ever conceived, *Die Schöne Müllerin* ('The Fair Maid of the Mill') and *Die Winterreise*, ('The Winter Journey'), are only some. The listener exploring Schubert's vast output (there are more than 600 songs alone) will make an exciting discovery every day. His gift of melody was sublime. He was only 31 when he died and many of his works remained unperformed and unpublished at his death, some not surfacing until as much as 40 or 50 years later.

Schubert's songs are at the heart of his genius. He set all manner of poems: some great (by Goethe and Heine among others), some quite trivial. But in Schubert's hands even the humblest verses were transformed into something memorable and wonderful. The two cycles referred to above are pinnacles in the art of song writing. *Die Schöne Müllerin* exudes much sunshine though it is ultimately sad; *Die Winterreise* is dark and lonely, a reflection of Schubert's frame of mind at the time he was writing it. In his songs the piano plays more than a mere accompanying role: Schubert raised its status so that singer and pianist become equal partners.

Schubert's symphonies hold a special place in the concert repertory, notably the small but perfect no. 3, the elegant and resourceful no. 5, the 'Unfinished' no. 8 (only two movements were completed), and, of course, the 'Great' C major, no. 9, one of the most magnificent of all symphonies. Schubert wrote no concertos and his operas failed to attract attention. But incidental music he wrote for the play *Rosamunde* is well loved and quite often performed.

Schubert was an accomplished pianist and his piano works are among the finest ever written. He brought a new and powerful dimension to the piano sonata; he composed 21, the last three of which represent a peak of achievement. The superb *Wanderer* Fantasy so impressed ▷Liszt that he arranged it for piano and orchestra. Even the less mighty pieces, such as the

NOW LISTEN ▷

Some works by other composers who have contributed greatly to the singer's repertory: ▷Benjamin Britten, *Winter Words*; ▷Gabriel Fauré, *La bonne chanson*; ▷Francis Poulenc, *Tel jour, telle nuit*; ▷Hugo Wolf, *Italian Songbook*.

impromptus and the *Moments musicaux*, not to mention the popular *Marches militaires* (for piano duet), are the work of a man who knew how to make the piano communicate to the full.

Schubert's chamber music is matchless. There are many who could not face existence without the string quartets (especially the impassioned 'Death and the Maiden'), the quintets and the wonderful Octet in F. That Schubert achieved so much before dying at such a tragically early age is one of the miracles of music.

SCHUMANN, Robert (1810–1856)

Robert Schumann was a tragic figure. When he was barely 44, he attempted suicide by throwing himself into the Rhine. Two years later he died in an asylum. His inner conflicts are apparent in some of his music. His legacy is a rich one: his piano music is masterly and his songs are pillars of the singer's repertory. There are two distinct sides to Schumann's musical personality, and he gave names to both. If he was writing impetuous, vigorous music, he was 'Florestan'; his gentler, dreamier self was 'Eusebius'.

Schumann's four symphonies were for long considered dense and unwieldy, the work of a pianist who didn't understand the orchestra. ▷Mahler was one composer who tried to 'improve' them by tinkering with their orchestration. Now, however, they are seen for the splendid pieces they are and are regularly played in concert programmes. Their characteristic sound is acknowledged. No. 1 (nicknamed 'Spring') is arguably the most immediately attractive, with its dance-like melodies and rhythms.

Schumann's Piano Concerto (1845) is his most popular composition. A single orchestral chord launches the solo piano into a brief cascade of notes which merges into the opening, meditative theme. In turn, this becomes the basis of the first movement. The second movement (like that of ▷Beethoven's Piano Concerto no. 4) is a brief argument between piano and orchestra which flows straight into the rumbustious, high-spirited finale. The concertos for violin and for cello are less inspired and less often played. But the *Konzertstück* for four horns and orchestra is imaginative and enjoyable.

The solo piano music is consistently imaginative. It includes *Carnaval*, a set of marvellously varied pieces in which the contrasting characters of 'Florestan' and 'Eusebius' appear, the enchanting *Kinderszenen* ('Scenes from Childhood') and the compelling *Symphonische Etuden*. The songs and song cycles are no less superbly conceived. Many of the world's greatest singers regard the cycle *Dichterliebe* ('A Poet's Love'), settings of poems by Heine, as the equal of any. Nor should the chamber music be overlooked, for it is frequently touched by Schumann's genius. The string quartets, for example, are not performed so frequently as those of other composers but are nevertheless worth hearing. His only opera, *Genoveva*, was only moderately successful and is rarely revived. Schumann was an astute music critic and was quick to spot the talents of many composers, notably ▷Chopin and ▷Brahms.

- Some composers who, like Schumann, wrote only one fine piano concerto: ▷Barber, ▷Grieg, ▷Hindemith, ▷Ireland, ▷Khachaturian and ▷Poulenc.

SHCHEDRIN, Rodion (born 1932)

Rodion Shchedrin is a Soviet composer with a sense of humour, apparent in many of his works. His Concerto for Orchestra, sub-titled 'Merry Ditties', is a riotous piece – tuneful, jazzy and more than a little zany. It prompts a smile with its hectic, cheeky assault on the senses. His ballet *Carmen* is a brilliant, witty reworking of ▷Bizet's opera, scored for strings and a vast array of percussion instruments. At one point, the accompaniment to the famous Toreador's Song is played, minus the tune itself, but an aural illusion makes us believe we are hearing it. Another ballet, *The Little Humpbacked Horse* is very popular in the USSR and contains charming music that reminds us of Shchedrin's intense interest in folksong. A third ballet, *Anna Karenina*, reveals the composer's more serious side; it is a dark, brooding, atmospheric score that uses some

NOW LISTEN ⟩

Works by some other contemporary Soviet composers: Murad Kazhlayev, *Gorianka*; Andrey Petrov, *The Creation of the World*; Alfred Shnitke, Violin Concerto No. 3; Sergey Slonimsky, *Choreographic Miniatures*; Loris Tjeknavorian, *Othello*.

avant-garde techniques but gives more than a few nods in the direction of ▷Tchaikovsky's great ballets. The opera *Not Love Alone* mixes sentiment with satire in an agreeable way; it is about a girl who leads a collective farming operation and finds true love by taking a straight and honest path. Shchedrin, whose music has always been 'acceptable' in the USSR, has also written symphonies, concertos and some interesting piano music (including 24 Preludes).

SHOSTAKOVICH, Dmitry (1906–1975)

The Russian composer Dmitry Shostakovich is one of the greatest 20th-century composers. His 15 symphonies and 15 string quartets are towering creations, sometimes described as the present-day equivalents of ▷Beethoven's symphonic and chamber output. Shostakovich's mastery is the more remarkable since it was achieved against a background of trouble with Soviet authorities. In the 1930s he was fiercely attacked for distortion, bourgeois sensationalism and formalism (writing 'difficult' music not in line with the ideals of social realism). Later, after World War II, he came under critical fire again, this time being deprived of his teaching post and all artistic privileges. Because his creative staying-power was enormous, Shostakovich came through it all. The inner tensions and agony he suffered may have led to triumphant masterpieces, but there is an unmistakable anguish and a bitterness in some of his works.

The symphonies (1925–1971) reflect the circumstances of Shostakovich's life. No. 1 is the work of a precocious teenager; it already contains many of the characteristics of his later works and attracted international attention. No. 5 followed the official attack on his music in the 1930s and is sub-titled 'A Soviet Artist's Practical Creative reply to Just Criticism'; it remains his most popular work. No. 7, the 'Leningrad', was begun during the Nazi siege of Leningrad, through which Shostakovich lived. No. 10 signifies magnificently his rebirth after Stalin had died and the 1950s criticisms had been laid to rest. No. 15 is death-haunted and enigmatic, with quotations from the work of other composers.

Shostakovich's string quartets (1938–1974) are autobiographical in an even more moving and involving way, because they are so much more intimate than the symphonies. Each is memorable and deeply impressive. But to hear the complete cycle, in sequence, is profoundly disturbing and can drain the listener physically and emotionally. The two piano concertos, by contrast, are easy on the ear and lightweight. The second contains an affectionate and very appealing tribute to ▷Rakhmaninov's romantic style. The two violin concertos are tougher but very typical and the two cello concertos include much of the best of Shostakovich.

The opera *Lady Macbeth of the Mtsensk District* was the work that first brought official criticism of Shostakovich. In 1936 the Soviet newspaper *Pravda* described it as discordant and chaotic. In 1963 it was revived, under the title *Katerina Izmaylova*, and shown to be powerfully dramatic and intense; it has since been staged many times. It is the story of a woman who murders her father-in-law and husband to be with her lover, only to discover he is unfaithful to her. Shostakovich's ballet *The Age of Gold*, about a Russian football team's visit to Europe, includes some of his most grotesquely amusing music. His piano works, notably the 24 Preludes and Fugues (a tribute to ▷Bach), are full of interest. Several film scores, too, show that he met the needs of the cinema with care and imagination. The music he wrote for the film of *Hamlet* in 1963 is particularly impressive. Shostakovich made arrangements of music by other composers (including ▷Johann Strauss, the younger) and made his own performing version of ▷Musorgksy's opera *Boris Godunov*. Shostakovich's works are a powerful mixture of tragic intensity, soaring nobility, savage energy, mordant wit and eccentric parody. His style was copied from no-one: it has been successfully imitated by no-one.

• Two leading Scottish composers have paid tribute to Shostakovich in recent years. Ronald Stevenson's massive piano piece, *Passacaglia on DSCH*, was espoused and recorded by John Ogdon. John

McLeod's orchestral work *The Shostakovich Connection* has been given many performances in Britain.

SIBELIUS, Jean (1865–1957)
The giant of Finnish music, Jean Sibelius, appeared to compose nothing for the last 26 years of his life. But the question remains whether he wrote another symphony, which may have been destroyed. There is much speculation on the matter. Sibelius's music used to be described as 'cold', 'austere', even 'impersonal': and there is certainly more than a draught of icy Scandinavian wind to be felt in many of his works. But much of it is romantic and appeals to the emotions if the listener cares to surrender to it. Sibelius was a fervent nationalist and influenced by Finnish legend and the folk music of Karelia.

Sibelius's seven symphonies (1899–1924) are central to a full appreciation of his art. No. 1 has a feeling of ▷Tchaikovsky about it, though Sibelius's fingerprints are already to be noted; no. 2, with its short scraps of melody building towards a bigger entity, is pure Sibelius; no. 3 is attractive and easy-going, apparently traditional but in fact quite unconventional in its plan; no. 4 is starker, more economical in gesture, uncompromising and the hardest to tackle; no. 5 is perhaps the easiest – emotional, colourful, melodic and with a strong vein of heroism; no. 6 is pleasant, pastoral and strangely withdrawn; no. 7 is in one movement, with all its elements compressed and distilled.

The Violin Concerto is a tour de force for the soloist but it's not a glittering showpiece in the accepted sense, and its melodies are not immediately memorable. In some ways its popularity is surprising. The symphonic poems, which include *En saga*, *Tapiola* and *The Oceanides* are vintage Sibelius, decisive, tight-reined and highly personal. The incidental music he wrote for various plays, notably *The Tempest* and Maeterlinck's *Pelleas and Melisande*, is of the highest calibre. Sibelius's biggest hits are *Finlandia*, a powerfully nationalistic orchestral work whose great central melody is sung in British churches as the hymn 'Be still, my soul'; the *Valse triste*, the last moments of a dying woman as she relives her past; *The Swan of Tuonela* which sings but once, just before its death; and the *Karelia* suite. Sibelius's lighter music is, like ▷Elgar's, finely crafted and not to be discounted. Nor are his many fine songs. The String Quartet ('Voces Intimae') is impressive and revealing, written when Sibelius feared he was suffering from cancer.

- Many composers wrote autobiographical music.
  ▷Elgar pictured himself in the last of his 'Enigma' Variations. ▷Janáček gave one of his string quartets the sub-title 'Intimate Letters' reflecting the correspondence he had for several years with a woman. ▷Smetana describes the onset of deafness in his string quartet 'From my Life'.
  ▷Richard Strauss is the hero of his tone poem 'A Hero's Life'.

SIX, Les

'Les Six' was the name given in 1920 to a group of French composers who gave concerts together and shared an anti-Romantic view of music. They were Georges Auric, Louis Durey, ▷Honegger, ▷Milhaud, ▷Poulenc and Germaine Tailleferre. They were strongly influenced at the outset by the eccentric composer ▷Satie and the poet and dramatist Jean Cocteau. But it was not long before they went their separate ways. Five of them (Durey was the odd one out) collaborated on the ballet *Les mariés de la tour Eiffel*, a zany story involving a wedding breakfast on top of the most famous landmark in Paris.

SKRYABIN, Alexander (1872–1915)

The early works of the Russian composer Alexander Skryabin are strongly tinged with the music of ▷Chopin and ▷Liszt. The Piano Concerto, with its beautiful slow movement, is an excellent example. But Skryabin turned into something of a mystic: his philosophical and musical ideas became strange and rari-

fied to the extent that even colleagues were baffled by
them. Ultimately, he was conceiving performances
embracing not only orchestral sounds but also dazzling
coloured lights and exotic perfumes – psychedelic effects, in fact, many years before they became part of
1960s culture.

The *Poem of Ecstasy* is Skryabin's most famous work,
a cross between a symphony and a tone poem bound
up with 'the soaring flight of the human spirit'. It has
been described as sounding like something which
might have been written by a Russian ▷Ravel – and
there is more than a grain of truth in that. Skryabin's
best music is for his favourite instrument, the piano.
His sonatas and preludes are of special interest and
have been played by many great pianists, including
Horowitz. When Skryabin died prematurely of septi-
caemia, he was working on a piece called 'Prefatory
Action', which was to have been the prelude to a monumental piece with the title *Mysterium*. He left some
sketches which the contemporary Soviet composer
Alexander Nemtin used as the basis of his piece *Uni-
verse*. It is a composition of genuine interest which
could well have met with Skryabin's approval.

---

* Some works abandoned or unfinished by their
  composers and completed by other hands include
  ▷Bartók's Viola Concerto (completed by Tibor
  Serly), ▷Mahler's Symphony no. 10 (rendered
  into a performing version by Deryk Cooke),
  ▷Puccini's *Turandot* (completed by Franco Alfano), ▷Schubert's Symphony no. 7 (completed
  and scored by Felix Weingartner), ▷Tchaikov-
  sky's Symphony no. 7 (reconstructed by Semyon
  Bogatyrev), and ▷Weber's *Die drei Pintos* (completed by Mahler).

SMETANA, Bedřich (1824–1884)
The Czech composer Bedřich Smetana played the violin in his father's amateur string quartet at the age of
five; by six he had given a piano recital and by eight he
had written his first compositions. He was to become

NOW LISTEN ▷

Music by Czech
composers who

the leading figure in Czech music, introducing a strong vein of nationalism built on by such figures as ▷Dvořák and ▷Janáček. For much of his life, Smetana was deaf; by the end of his life he could hear nothing. Indeed, unlike ▷Beethoven he had the additional disability of a high-pitched noise in his head. (It is this noise that he reproduced in the poignant last movement of his String Quartet no. 1 'From my Life': a chilling moment in the middle of some happy music-making.)

Smetana's orchestral music is colourful and falls easily and gratefully on the ear. His cycle of six symphonic poems *Ma vlast* ('My Country') includes one of his most popular concert pieces, *Vltava*, a musical trip down the great Czech river from its source to the sea. But if Smetana's fame were to rest on one work, it would be *The Bartered Bride* (1866), perhaps the finest comic folk opera ever written. Its plot is rather unpleasant, involving a joke played by a peasant on the girl he intends to marry: he makes her believe that she is really betrothed to his half-witted younger brother. But a happy ending is reached by way of a host of wonderfully warm and memorable melodies. The chorus plays an unusually important role in telling the story, as does the orchestra. Three dances from the score, along with the brilliant overture, have long since established themselves as concert pieces in their own right. Several of Smetana's other operas, notably *The Two Widows* (so loved by ▷Richard Strauss that he asked for it to be performed every time he visited Prague) and *The Kiss*, are well worth hearing if the chance presents itself.

followed in Smetana's footsteps: ▷Antonín Dvořák, *The Devil and Kate*; Josef Foerster, *From Shakespeare*; ▷Leoš Janáček, *Katya Kabanova*; ▷Bohuslav Martinů, *Julietta*; ▷Vítězslav Novák, *Slovak Suite*; ▷Josef Suk, *Fairy Tale*.

SONDHEIM, Stephen (born 1930)
Stephen Sondheim is the most imaginative and original of his generation of American composers of stage musicals. He writes his own words to highly distinctive melodies and has created a number of hits, notably *A Little Night Music* (which includes the song 'Send in the Clowns'), *Follies* and *Pacific Overtures* (which uses elements of Japanese music). In *Sweeney Todd*, Sondheim took a bizarre, even gruesome, theme and managed to make it entertaining. The show concerns

the 'demon barber' of Fleet Street in London and has a song about pies made from human flesh. *Into the Woods*, perhaps his best flight of fancy, mixes several popular fairy stories and cynically relates them to the kind of life we lead today (as soon as the show's two handsome princes have won Cinderella and Rapunzel, they are off chasing the Sleeping Beauty and Snow White). Sondheim's style is easily identifiable: his songs are usually bitter-sweet with haunting refrains and his lyrics deal frequently with infidelity and the weaknesses of marriage. Sondheim wrote the lyrics for ▷Bernstein's musical *West Side Story*.

SOPRANO

Sopranos have the highest female voices. In the opera world, the best of them are known as 'prima donnas', who invariably have wonderful roles to sing. ▷Mozart's Countess in *The Marriage of Figaro* and Fiordiligi in *Così fan tutte*; ▷Verdi's Gilda in *Rigoletto* and Violetta in *La traviata*; ▷Wagner's Brunnhilde in *The Ring*; ▷Puccini's Tosca, Madam Butterfly and Turandot; ▷Richard Strauss's Salome; ▷Janáček's Jenůfa; ▷Gershwin's Bess in *Porgy and Bess* and so on. The great sopranos of the past include Amelita Galli-Curci, Nelli Melba and Luisa Tetrazzini; more recent stars are Maria Callas, Mirella Freni, Birgit Nilsson, Jessye Norman, Elisabeth Schwarzkopf, Joan Sutherland and Renata Tebaldi.

SOUNDS ODD...

Over the years, many composers have introduced odd 'instruments' into the orchestra. These include sandpaper (Leroy Anderson, *Sandpaper Ballet*), teacups (▷Britten, *Noye's Fludde*), motor horns (▷Gershwin, *An American in Paris*), a police whistle (▷Ibert, *Divertissement*), Jew's harp (▷Ives, *Washington's Birthday*), recorded nightingale (▷Respighi, *The Pines of Rome*), iron chains (▷Schoenberg, *Gurrelieder*), short-wave radio (▷Stockhausen, *Spiral*), recorded heartbeat (▷Tippett, Symphony no. 4), four accordions (▷Tchaikovsky, Suite no. 2), wind machine (▷Vaughan Williams, *Sinfonia antartica*).

SOUSA, John Philip (1854–1932)

The American John Philip Sousa was nicknamed the 'March King' with good reason. No-one in the history of music wrote so many stirring marches, nearly all of them featuring fine, original and distinctive tunes. Sousa believed that 'a good march should make a man with a wooden leg want to get up and join the parade', and claimed he always worked to that end. He conducted his own famous band, with which he toured the world on several occasions, his concerts being sold out months in advance. (His love of baseball appears to have dictated which cities and towns he visited in his native America. It's said he would take the band only to places where a good game was to be played. The march *The National Game* is a tribute to all baseball players.)

Sousa's greatest marches are *The Stars and Stripes* (almost another national anthem in the USA), *Washington Post*, *Semper fidelis*, *El capitan* and *Liberty Bell* (used by the BBC to introduce the television comedy series 'Monty Python's Flying Circus'). But, as with the music of ▷Johann Strauss (the younger), there is much fun to be had investigating the unfamiliar pieces. One march called *New Mexico*, for instance, includes South American dance music, Red Indian folk tunes and the bugle calls of the US Cavalry. The sousaphone, a brass tuba made for his band, was named after him.

STANFORD, Sir Charles Villiers (1852–1924)

The music of Charles Villiers Stanford is out of fashion but it falls much more graciously on the ear than many scores currently favoured by concert promoters. The seven symphonies, for instance, have considerable strength and character, notably no. 3 ('Irish') which is a very attractive mixture of ▷Brahmsian elegance and the folk music of Erin's Isle, where Stanford was born. The Clarinet Concerto, one of many concertos Stanford wrote for various instruments, is a delightful work, unaccountably ignored by clarinettists. The best of Stanford, though, is to be found in two song cycles for baritone and orchestra, both settings of poems by Sir Harry Newbolt. *Songs of the Sea* contains the rumbustious 'Drake's Drum' and 'The Old Superb'.

NOW LISTEN ▷

Some great marches by other composers: ▷Kenneth Alford, *Colonel Bogey*; Henry Walford Davies, *RAF March Past*; ▷Julius Fučik, *Entry of the Gladiators*; Louis Ganne, *Marche lorraine*; Abe Holtzman, *Blaze Away*; Carl Teike, *Old Comrades*; Josef Franz Wagner, *Under the Double Eagle*.

NOW LISTEN ▷

Music by some of Stanford's pupils: ▷Arthur Bliss, Music for Strings; ▷Gustav Holst, *The Perfect Fool*; ▷Herbert Howells, *Hymnus paradisi*; ▷John Ireland, Piano Concerto; ▷Ralph Vaughan Williams, *A Sea Symphony*.

The even better *Songs of the Fleet* includes 'Sailing at Dawn', a wonderful evocation of tall ships leaving port at first light, and the 'Song of the Sou'wester' which has the listener almost sharing the bite of the wind and tasting the salt of the sea spray.

STOCKHAUSEN, Karlheinz (born 1928)
The works of the German composer Karlheinz Stockhausen were once disarmingly described as 'possibly masterpieces, but beyond the ken of most people!' The writer could also have remarked that many of them are undeniably fascinating. I attended an early performance of his *Gruppen* for three orchestras and three conductors; it may have been incomprehensible, but the sounds produced and the electric atmosphere of the event were the stuff of memories. A difficulty with much of Stockhausen's music is that the listener is unlikely to hear it played the same way twice. He seeks to encourage spontaneity and sometimes leaves certain elements of his compositions to chance. In *Zyklus* for percussion, the player may start on any page of the score he wishes; he may then play the music conventionally (from left to right) or turn it upside down and play it from right to left. Stockhausen's instructions to musicians transcend the physical. Before playing another of his works, *Gold Dust*, the players are asked to starve themselves of food and companionship for four days and nights; when they finally come on to the platform to perform, they are directed to play single notes, without thinking of what they're playing. Stockhausen's opera cycle, *Licht*, is a projected cycle of seven operas, intended for performance on the day of the week after which each is named.

STRAUS, Oscar (1870–1954)
The Austrian Oscar Straus composed a number of fine Viennese operettas in the first 30 years of this century. The most popular is *The Chocolate Soldier*, based on Shaw's play *Arms and the Man*, about an army officer who prefers to carry chocolate rather than a gun. Its hit song, beloved of sopranos, is 'My Hero'. Straus's best piece, though, is *A Waltz Dream*, the bit-

ter-sweet tale of a prince's love for a café singer. Straus hated being confused with the celebrated Strauss family and was forever pointing out that he spelt his name with a single 's'. In a desperate bid to reinforce the point he called his pet cat 'Pusy'.

STRAUSS family

The Strauss family made Vienna the capital of the dance for the best part of the 19th century. Johann the elder (1804–1849) led his own orchestra in cafés, dance-halls and ballrooms and composed more than 200 dances, more than 150 of them waltzes. Ironically, his most famous composition is a march, *Radetzky*, which traditionally ends all concerts of Viennese music today. He had three musical sons. Johann the younger (1825–1899) brought the composition of waltzes to a fine art. *The Blue Danube*, *Tales from the Vienna Woods*, *Roses from the South* and the great *Emperor Waltz* are among the most popular. But adventurous listeners should rummage among the lesser-known ones, which include *Memories of Covent Garden*, a marvellous pot-pourri of music-hall tunes heard by Strauss during a visit to London. The spirited polkas (like *Thunder and Lightning* and *Tritsch-Tratsch*) are brilliant miniatures. Johann wrote many works for commercial concerns (*Feuerfest*, for example, was a polka composed to mark the manufacture of a new fire-proof safe).

Johann the younger's greatest achievement in the theatre was the operetta *Die Fledermaus* ('The Bat') which has achieved classic status. Its lasting success was ensured by a host of marvellous melodies (including 'The Laughing Song', the ensemble 'Brother mine', the Hungarian Csárdás, and the 'Champagne Chorus'). But its story, about infidelity and deception at a glittering ball, had more to say than most operettas about the human condition. Another operetta, *The Gipsy Baron* brought its composer some plaudits, but has never rivalled *Fledermaus* in international appeal.

Josef (1827–1870) had enormous talent as a composer. His older brother said: 'He is the more gifted: I am simply the more popular'. Josef's waltzes are imaginative and superbly scored. *Music of the Spheres* is probably the best, but *Dynamiden* was the one chosen by ▷Richard Strauss (no relation) to include in his opera *Der Rosenkavalier*. One of Josef's polkas, *Plappermäulchen* ('Little Chatter Box') could become a real favourite if played more often.

Eduard (1835–1916) was the least impressive of the Strausses, though even he turned in some attractive and lively polkas. He made his name as a conductor, touring the world and directing performances of his family's music until well into the 20th century. His death marked the end of a dynasty of dance.

- The music of Johann Strauss the younger impressed numerous later composers. When ▷Brahms was asked to autograph a lady's fan at a ball, he noticed the fan carried the opening notes of *The Blue Danube*; underneath, he wrote: 'Regrettably not by Johannes Brahms'. ▷Schoenberg arranged the *Emperor Waltz* for six players, and ▷Shostakovich reorchestrated the polka *Vergnügungszug* ('The Pleasure Train'). ▷Gershwin composed a song in praise of the Viennese master which he called *By Strauss*.

STRAUSS, Richard (1864–1949)

Rockets to the moon brought the music of the German composer Richard Strauss into the world's living room. The first bars of his tone poem *Also sprach Zarathustra* were used to introduce television coverage of the Apollo space programme because they had been part of Stanley Kubrick's film *2001: A Space Odyssey*. But there's more to *Zarathustra* than the distant trumpets and pounding timpani we heard so often. Early in his career Strauss wrote a good deal of 'programme music' (music of a descriptive kind, or that tells a story), and although these early tone poems weren't always favourably received, they are now seen to be richly rewarding and are among Strauss's most popular pieces. *Till Eulenspiegels Lustige Streiche* ('Till Eulenspiegel's Merry Pranks') is a witty picture of a lovable rogue whose exploits lead to his end on the scaffold; *Don Juan* traces some of the affairs of the

NOW LISTEN ▷

Some operas inspired, like *Elektra*, by Greek mythology: ▷Hector Berlioz, *The Trojans*; ▷Christoph Willibald Gluck, *Orfeo ed Euridice*; ▷Wolfgang Amadeus Mozart *Idomeneo*; ▷Jacques Offenbach, *La belle Hélène*; ▷Henry Purcell, *Dido and Aeneas*; ▷Michael Tippett, *King Priam*.

world's most famous lover; *Don Quixote*, inspired by Cervantes' novel, is a gentle study of the chivalrous old knight who is out of touch with reality. *Ein Heldenleben* ('A Hero's Life') is a splendidly rounded self-portrait. Strauss himself is the hero, battling his way through life; there is a marvellous sequence devoted to his critics, whose music is sour and sniping! Some regard *Alpine Symphony* as great Strauss; others find it hardly worth the climb. There is a similar division of opinion over the *Domestic Symphony*, a look at the composer's marriage.

But there is unanimity about the operas, which are Strauss's greatest glories. *Der Rosenkavalier* is one of the most frequently performed 20th-century operas and is a marvellously opulent, melodious score. Its subject, an aging woman who gracefully surrenders her lover to a younger woman, is very affecting. *Capriccio*, his last opera is a 'conversation piece' in which the argument is whether the music or the words are more important in opera.

Many Straussians, however, are fatally attracted to the much less comfortable *Elektra* (1909) and *Salome* (1905). *Elektra* is the terrible Greek tragedy of a daughter's revenge on her father's murderer (who turns out to be her mother). It is a score of savage brilliance which makes for memorable theatre. *Salome* is based on Oscar Wilde's version of the biblical story in which Salome demands John the Baptist's head as a reward for dancing for her stepfather. Strauss's music conjures up an atmosphere heavy with evil and lechery and it is easy to understand why the opera attracted controversy in its early days. (When the Scottish soprano Mary Garden sang the role in Chicago in the 1920s, the police department's vice squad was in attendance at every performance.) The Dance of the Seven Veils has become a popular concert piece in its own right.

Strauss's two horn concertos and Oboe Concerto are splendid works. He wrote more than 200 songs, most with piano accompaniment but some with orchestra, and they are well worth investigating. His *Four Last Songs*, which are especially beautiful, may be thought of as virtually a summing up of his life's work. Since Strauss stayed in Nazi Germany during World

War II, he was vilified outside his native land. His *Metamorphosen* for 23 solo strings, however, was written as a lament for the German musical life Strauss had known and lost.

STRAVINSKY, Igor (1882–1971)

The Russian composer Igor Stravinsky is one of the outstanding musical figures of the 20th century: a composer whose head was crowned, metaphorically, with laurels only after having been pelted with rotten fruit by a violent public. His ballets, created for Diaghilev's famous company in Paris, contain much exciting music. *The Firebird*, a Russian fairy-tale, is the most accessible, influenced by his teacher ▷Rimsky-Korsakov but containing many of the characteristic elements that were to inform his later style. *Petrushka*, the tale of a puppet who has a soul and wants to be human, is enormously effective in the theatre; even heard as a concert piece, it is so colourful and brilliantly descriptive that the listener can follow the story.

Stravinsky's masterpiece is *The Rite of Spring* (1913), which caused a riot at its première. The music supports a story of ritual sacrifice in primeval times and the audience found it so brutal, so alarming and so unlike anything they had ever encountered, that they shouted it down. The dancers, at one point, could not hear the orchestra. In the concert hall today, it is still an overwhelming experience. It is a work of genius, in which rhythm plays a particularly compelling and hypnotic role, and it had a profound influence on other composers.

Rhythm, indeed, is vital to all Stravinsky's music. It is especially strong in the jazz-inspired works such as *The Soldier's Tale* for narrator and chamber ensemble (an engaging little off-shoot of the Faust legend), the *Ebony Concerto* (written for the clarinettist Woody Herman and his band) and the splendid *Ragtime* for 11 instruments. Strong rhythms also underpin some of Stravinsky's orchestral pieces: the Symphony in Three Movements, the Symphony in C and the *Symphony of Psalms* (which involves a chorus). These, like the splendid Violin Concerto, are not difficult works since some of them are deliberate explorations of the

NOW LISTEN ▷

Ballets commissioned by the impresario Sergey Diaghilev: ▷Manuel de Falla, *The Three-Cornered Hat*; ▷Francis Poulenc, *Les biches*; ▷Sergey Prokofiev, *Chout*; ▷Maurice Ravel, *Daphnis et Chloé*; ▷Erik Satie, *Parade*; ▷Richard Strauss, *The Legend of Joseph*.

styles and forms of the 18th century.

The opera *The Rake's Progress*, suggested by Hogarth's famous engravings showing the downfall of a man-about-town, is as elegant and sophisticated as *The Rite of Spring* is wild and untamed. It gives the listener a different perspective on Stravinsky. Perhaps even finer as a theatre piece is *Oedipus Rex*, a cross between an oratorio and an opera, which tells the Greek tragedy with an almost classical severity and power. For two ballets, *Pulcinella* and *The Fairy's Kiss*, Stravinsky reworked music by ▷Pergolesi and ▷Tchaikovsky respectively. But the end-products are very much his own.

SUK, Josef (1874–1935)

Josef Suk was a pupil of ▷Dvořák (whose daughter he married). His early music belongs unmistakably to the Czech nationalist school, which leans heavily on folk traditions. The *Fairy Tale* suite is delightful and deserves a place in any orchestra's repertory. The powerful symphony *Asrael* is a moving and impressive tribute to Dvořák, who had died shortly before its composition. Towards the end of his life, Suk began to use more advanced musical techniques and some of his later music is quite adventurous. He is a composer of more than passing interest.

SULLIVAN, Sir Arthur (1842–1900)

Arthur Sullivan composed a serious opera, *Ivanhoe*, a distinguished symphony, a fine Cello Concerto and some memorable music for productions of Shakespeare plays, notably *The Tempest* and *The Merchant of Venice*. But he is a household name today because of a song, a hymn and 11 operettas. The song is *The Lost Chord*, the hymn is 'Onward, Christian soldiers' and the operettas are those he wrote in collaboration with W. S. Gilbert. The partnership of Gilbert and Sullivan, which began with *Trial by Jury* (1875), had its ups and downs. It produced, however, a series of stage shows which have, to this day, a worldwide following, unique in the history of the musical theatre.

Nearly all the operas, first staged at the Savoy Thea-

NOW LISTEN ▷

Some British operettas which took the stage after the reign of Gilbert and Sullivan had ended: ▷Edward German, *Merrie England*; H. Fraser-Simpson, *The Maid of the Mountains*; Sidney Jones, *San Toy*; ▷Lionel Monckton, *The Quaker Girl*; Frederic

tre, London, take great pleasure satirising one British institution or another, or some movement fashionable at the time. The police are the butt of the humour in *The Pirates of Penzance*; the navy in *HMS Pinafore*; the law in *Trial by Jury*; women's rights in *Princess Ida*; the Victorian fascination with things Japanese in *The Mikado*; class consciousness in *The Gondoliers*; country life and manners in *The Sorcerer* and *Ruddigore*; the House of Lords in *Iolanthe*; and the aesthetic cult of Oscar Wilde in *Patience*. Only *The Yeoman of the Guard*, set in the 16th century against a background of the Tower of London, aims simply to tell a story.

The last two Gilbert and Sullivan operas are not included in this round-up because they have never captured the public imagination. But *Utopia Ltd* (a satire on the British way of running a country) and *The Grand Duke* (a send-up of the acting profession) have much more to offer than is generally supposed. The latter enjoys the distinction of having a song about sausage rolls, and a number in French. The level of inspiration in Sullivan's music for the Savoy operas is consistently high. Songs like 'Poor wand'ring one', 'Tit-Willow', 'I have a song to sing-o', and 'Take a pair of sparkling eyes' are known to everyone. The 'patter' numbers, such as the Major General's song from *The Pirates* or the Nightmare song from *Iolanthe*, have tunes brilliantly tailored to the rapid cascade of words provided by Gilbert. But Sullivan manages to bring real dignity and eloquence to many of the songs. Ironically, these are sometimes given to the least sympathetic character in the story.

For many years, the Gilbert and Sullivan tradition was closely guarded by the D'Oyly Carte Opera Company. But its productions ultimately became stale and the company was disbanded. It has now been reformed and looks set to give the operas a fresh look.

SUPPÉ, Franz von (1819–1895)

If the Austrian composer Franz von Suppé had used his real name, people would have had trouble remembering it. He was baptised Francesco Ezechiele Ermenegildo Cavaliere Suppé Demelli. But when he took up composing, he reckoned something snappier would be more appropriate. He specialised in ope-

Norton, *Chu Chin Chow*; Leslie Stuart, *Floradora*.

> **NOW LISTEN**

Operettas by other composers who worked in Vienna at the time of Johann Strauss: Richard

retta, writing more than 30, and his music was highly popular in a Vienna where ▷Johann Strauss, the younger, still held sway. Today, only two of his theatre pieces survive: *Beautiful Galathea* and *Boccaccio* (based on stories from the Italian writer's bawdy *Decameron*). However, the overtures to some of the forgotten operettas are often played as concert items, *Light Cavalry*, *Poet and Peasant* and *Pique Dame* being among the favourites. Suppé, a big bear of a man, was a well-loved Viennese personality. Before he began to conduct one of his operettas, he took a pinch of snuff; the resultant, enormous sneeze was the signal that the performance could begin.

Heuberger, *The Opera Ball*; Carl Millöcker, *The Beggar Student*; ▷Karl Zeller, *The Bird Seller*; Karl Michael Ziehrer, *The Tramps*.

SZYMANOWSKI, Karol (1882–1937)

The Polish composer Karol Szymanowski is not the force in 20th-century music that he perhaps deserves to be. His works have never gained universal acceptance and are appreciated by comparatively few people. It took some time for his style to mature. Szymanowski's early works are influenced by ▷Chopin and by ▷Skryabin. Later, he went through a period where the romanticism of ▷Richard Strauss and ▷Wagner can be discerned, followed by another in which he was influenced by ▷Debussy. But when Szymanowski finally discovered the music of his native Poland, and in particular the folk melodies of the Tatra mountains, his musical style crystallised.

Szymanowski's two violin concertos demand to be played as often as those of ▷Bartók; the first is French in atmosphere, the second undeniably Polish. His four symphonies are uneven but contain many marvellous and haunting things. No. 2 is scored for a soprano or tenor soloist and a chorus, no. 4 has a prominent role for a solo piano. Perhaps the finest of Szymanowski's scores is the ballet *Harnasie* (sometimes called 'The Highland Robbers'), a nationalist work of great colour and variety, brilliantly scored for a very large orchestra, a heroic tenor and a full chorus. The *Stabat mater* is a very beautiful setting and the opera *King Roger* (about a shepherd who creates havoc in the lives of a monarch and his queen) is full of dramatic music and has proved to be an effective theatre piece. Szymanowski's piano music and songs (many written for his sister, a professional singer) make stimulating listening.

● For a variety of reasons, the music of the ballet *Harnasie* was first heard in Poland not in a theatre but in the concert hall and it was some years before the work was staged. A similar fate befell a better-known ballet score, ▷Prokofiev's *Romeo and Juliet*. The Bolshoy Theatre turned it down as 'undanceable' and the composer made a concert suite of the music. When the Bolshoy finally came to its senses, the public already knew most of the music.

T

TAKEMITSU, Toru (born 1930)
The Japanese composer Toru Takemitsu uses avant-garde techniques and makes much use of tapes. His style is basically gentle and has been influenced by French composers such as ▷Debussy and ▷Messiaen. Most of his music falls easily on the ear as he is primarily concerned with creating pleasing, elegant sounds. *November Steps* is one of his best known pieces; it incorporates Japanese traditional instruments into an orchestral texture. Many of Takemitsu's compositions have picturesque titles, for example the piano piece *Far Away* and the orchestral work *A Flock Descends into the Pentagonal Garden*.

TCHAIKOVSKY, Peter (1840–1893)
There is a case for saying that the music of the Russian composer Peter Tchaikovsky is the most popular ever written. Many orchestras devote whole programmes to his works. Typically, the Piano Concerto no. 1 in B flat minor will be preceded by the fantasy overture *Romeo and Juliet* and probably followed by the *Capriccio italien*. After the interval will come the suite *Nutcracker*, and the event will be rounded off by the overture *1812*, with multifarious bells and cannons. The fact that audiences flock to such concerts is because he wrote wonderful, heart-filling, emotional melodies and was a master of brilliant, luxurious orchestration. His is the gift of immediate communication. To hear a Tchaikovsky tune is to want to hear it again and again. But studying Tchaikovsky's music closely reveals that it is often a good deal more cerebral and skilfully con-

NOW LISTEN ▷

Some great Russian ballets composed since the death of Tchaikovsky:
▷Alexander Glazunov, *Raymonda*; ▷Reyngol'd Glier, *The Red Poppy*; ▷Aram Khachaturian, *Gayaneh*; ▷Sergey Prokofiev, *Cinderella*; ▷Rodion Shchedrin, *The Little Humpbacked Horse*; ▷Dmitry

structed than it may appear on the surface.

The Piano Concerto no. 1 is so familiar we sometimes forget that it is highly unconventional. Its memorable opening tune is never played again as the work progresses. The splendid Violin Concerto and the Serenade for Strings, however, are almost as popular. His three ballets contain some of the most colourful and typical music composed by this remarkable man. *Swan Lake*, *The Sleeping Beauty* and *Nutcracker* are stupendous scores full of memorable dances, imaginatively orchestrated. Each has a big waltz and all three are concert favourites in their own right. Two of Tchaikovsky's operas have rightly held their place in the repertory. *Eugene Onegin*, based on Pushkin's poem, is the moving study of a young girl humiliated after declaring a teenage passion. The Letter Scene in which she pours out her feelings to an older man is a highpoint in Russian opera. *The Queen of Spades*, also inspired by Pushkin, involves a gambling soldier obsessed by the need to win at cards; it has a splendid streak of the sinister – even macabre – running through it.

The six symphonies are key works in Tchaikovsky's art. It used to be fashionable to dismiss the first three but they are now seen to be fine works and very representative of their composer. The last three are superb, no. 6, 'Pathétique', is especially passionate, with a searing, tragic final movement following a manic march. Tchaikovsky died a few days after its first performance. *Manfred*, an unnumbered symphony, is uneven but at its best is very exciting.

Music-lovers seeking less familiar Tchaikovsky should investigate his four suites for orchestra. No. 2 is unusual in featuring passages for four accordions; no. 4 is a tribute to ▷Mozart, the composer most loved and revered by Tchaikovsky. The incidental music he wrote for a production of *Hamlet* is full of atmosphere, notably the sequences dealing with the wretched Ophelia, and the Piano Concerto no. 2 is great fun. It has been overshadowed by the First, but its finale is as catchy as anything in Tchaikovsky's output. His many songs are often truly affecting (the most celebrated is 'None but the lonely heart') and the string quartets are the best of his chamber music (no. 1 contains the lovely

Shostakovich, *The Age of Gold*.

Andante Cantabile which enjoys an independent existence).

Tchaikovsky was a tragic figure who was forced to
repress his homosexuality and who suffered from
deeply rooted melancholia. He was said to have died of
cholera, but there is some evidence that he committed
suicide.

TENOR

It's often said that tenors get all the best tunes to sing;
and a look at the world of opera alone goes some way to
bearing that out. The Flower Song (▷Bizet's *Carmen*),
'M'appari' (▷Flotow's *Martha*), 'Your tiny hand is frozen' (▷Puccini's *La bohème*), 'La donna e mobile'
(▷Verdi's *Rigoletto*), the Prize Song (▷Wagner's *Die
Meistersinger*) – the list is endless. The tenor is a high
male voice; good tenors are much in demand. Some
tenor roles are extremely taxing; anyone singing Arnold in ▷Rossini's *William Tell* has to sing more top Cs
in one performance than he is normally called on to
tackle in a season. The Astrologer in ▷Rimsky-Kor-
sakov's *The Golden Cockerel* is positively stratospheric.
The tenor taking an ▷Offenbach role requires, in addition to a fine voice, a sense of humour. He is often
called on to perform tongue-twisting numbers and
may even be asked to imitate trumpet fanfares. In the
past, great tenors included Enrico Caruso, Tito
Schipa and Beniamino Gigli; today they are Luciano
Pavarotti, Placido Domingo, and José Carreras (in between were fine tenors like Heddle Nash, Julius
Patzak, Richard Tauber and Fritz Wunderlich).

THOMAS, Ambroise (1811–1896)

The Frenchman Ambroise Thomas wrote many operas for the Paris Opera. Today only two are remembered but they have much to commend them. *Mignon*
is an adaptation of a Goethe novel, and is about a girl
who is stolen by the gypsies and only discovers her true
identity when she grows to adulthood. The score contains many 'plums', including the lovely aria 'Connais-
tu le pays?' and the waltz song 'Je suis Titania'.
Thomas's other success, *Hamlet*, is a somewhat fanci-

NOW LISTEN ▷

Other 19th-century
French operas:
▷Georges Bizet, *The
Pearl Fishers*;
▷Emmanuel Chabrier,
L' Étoile; ▷Gustave
Charpentier, *Louise*;
▷Leo Delibes, *Lakmé*;

ful adaptation of Shakespeare's play. Too many people are left alive at the end – not least Hamlet himself. 'Long live Hamlet, our king!', sing the jolly courtiers at Elsinore. But the music is excellent and there is a particularly fine 'mad scene' for Ophelia. *Hamlet* is probably the first opera to include a saxophone in the orchestra.

THOMSON, Virgil (born 1896)
The American composer spent many years as a newspaper critic and writer on music, at the same time composing a large number of works. The most famous is the opera *Four Saints in Three Acts*, based on a libretto by Gertrude Stein showing how Theresa (surrounded by men) and Igantius (surrounded by women) help each other to become saints. Thomson's style is consciously American and can be heard at its most enjoyable in the scores he wrote for the films *Louisiana Story*, *The River* and *The Plow that broke the Plains*. The last, including a guitar and banjo in the orchestra, contains a number of cowboy tunes. A little piece for harp and orchestra called *Autumn* is most engaging.

TIMPANI
The timpani are sometimes called 'kettledrums' because of their bowl-shaped, copper bases. They are placed at the back of an orchestra, alongside the other instruments of the percussion department. They give rhythmic impetus to orchestral music and often provide it with a firm foundation. ▷Beethoven introduces his Violin Concerto with five taps on the timpani. They are made to suggest an approaching thunderstorm in the *Symphonie fantastique* of ▷Berlioz and conjure up a sinister atmosphere for Banquo's assassins in ▷Verdi's opera *Macbeth*. In the *Festival Overture* of ▷Smetana they go amiably berserk, and they offer some crisp, punchy comments in ▷Glinka's *Ruslan and Lyudmilla* overture. In ▷Nielsen's Symphony no. 4 ('The Inextinguishable') two sets of timpani engage in a pitched battle.

▷Jules Massenet, *Thaïs*; ▷Jacques Offenbach, *The Tales of Hoffmann*.

NOW LISTEN ▷

Other works featuring cowboys: ▷Aaron Copland, *Rodeo*; ▷Alberto Ginastera, *Estancia*; ▷Richard Rodgers, *Oklahoma!*; Elie Siegmeister, *Western Suite*.

TIPPETT, Sir Michael (born 1905)

Michael Tippett has great compassion for the plight of mankind, as did his contemporary ▷Britten. But their musical language is different, Tippett's not making the instant appeal of Britten's. It seems, on first acquaintance, altogether more gritty. But a little perseverance and the listener can easily become a Tippett fan. His work has a life-enhancing quality which is capable of lifting the most flagging of spirits. It's possible to hear many influences in Tippett's music. Madrigals from the 16th century, negro spirituals, blues from the world of jazz – even, quite plainly, the later works of ▷Beethoven. But they are taken on board and fused together in a style that is quite unlike any other.

Tippett's opera *The Midsummer Marriage* (1955) is, with Britten's *Peter Grimes*, a landmark in the history of British opera. It is a study of two people who believe they cannot enter into marriage until they have found themselves. The mundane aspects of 20th-century living, however, are placed against a series of magical and mystical happenings which lead the two main characters to a happy ending. Tippett's music is, by turns, scintillating, exciting and profoundly moving. It is music of the highest calibre and very accessible. Later operas, including *King Priam* and *The Knot Garden*, are tougher but study of these works can be recommended.

Tippett's concert works include a fine piano concerto, a brilliant Concerto for Orchestra, the Concerto for Double String Orchestra which first brought Tippett to the public eye, and a marvellous oratorio, *A Child of our Time* which is as good a gateway to this composer as any. The symphonies are fascinating; no. 4 must be unique in making use of a recorded, amplified heart beat. There is not much chamber music, but the string quartets are valuable to our complete understanding of Tippett.

● Sir Michael Tippett is a fine conductor of his own music. Unlike some composers, he is able to communicate his intentions clearly to an orchestra and achieve many nuances which escape others. What is not generally known is that, as a young man, he studied with two of Britain's most celebrated conductors, Sir Adrian Boult and Sir Malcolm Sargent.

TOWN AND COUNTRY
▷Arthur Bliss, *Edinburgh* overture
George Butterworth, *The Banks of Green Willow*
▷Frederick Delius, *Paris: the Song of a Great City*
▷Jacques Ibert, *Bostoniana*
Lars-Erik Larsson, *Pastoral Suite*
Hamish MacCunn, *Land of the Mountain and the Flood*
▷Johann Strauss the younger, *Tales from the Vienna Woods*
▷Ralph Vaughan Williams, *A London Symphony*

TROMBONE
The trombone is a brass instrument with a slide to vary its pitch. (Big band enthusiasts will recall Glenn Miller's prowess with it.) The three trombones normally used in the orchestra can add massive weight to a musical climax and, indeed, if not properly controlled can almost swamp the other 90 players on the platform. ▷Wagner's music often calls for the trombone, and its rip-roaring brilliance enhances the celebrated Prelude to Act 3 of his opera *Lohengrin*; it also carries the listener along in the invigorating 'Ride of the Valkyrie' from *The Ring*. The Italian composer ▷Respighi uses its impressive grandeur to represent a Roman legion marching down the Appian Way in his symphonic poem *The Pines of Rome*. ▷Mozart was one of the first to use the trombone effectively in an opera (*Don Giovanni*) and ▷Beethoven introduced it to the symphony in his Fifth.

TRUMPET
The trumpet is the most familiar member of the brass family; it is also the oldest (a variety of trumpet is supposed to have blown down the walls of Jericho). It adds glitter and panache to a vast array of orchestral works

but it can be piercingly menacing or, if muted, mysterious and sinister. Its natural ability to play fanfares has been exploited dramatically by ▷Mahler in his Symphony no. 1. ▷Debussy has trumpets approaching from afar in the second of his three *Nocturnes*, 'Fêtes'. ▷Prokofiev scored them chattering amongst themselves in the Scherzo of his Symphony no. 5. ▷Bach wrote a scintillating trumpet part in the Brandenburg Concerto no. 2 and both ▷Haydn and ▷Hummel composed the concertos which are in every professional trumpeter's repertory.

TUBA

Years ago, the comedian Danny Kaye made a children's record highlighting the plight of the bass tuba. Its central character, Tubby the Tuba, complained that all he ever got to play was 'oompah-oompah'. He was never given a melody. It has to be said that this heaviest, and most endearing member of the brass family does tend to underpin the orchestra or band and is generally short of tunes. But ▷Vaughan Williams took pity on it and composed a splendid Concerto for tuba, a piece full of melodies which are both jolly and, on occasion, beautiful. The smaller, tenor tuba fares rather better in the concert hall: you can hear it, for instance, in 'Mars' from ▷Holst's *The Planets*, striding out with one of the best themes. The so-called ▷'Wagner tuba', invented by Wagner to give him a special horn-like sound, is prominent in *The Ring*.

TUBIN, Eduard (1905–1983)

The music of Eduard Tubin has come to prominence outside his native Estonia only recently, thanks to the advocacy of the conductor Neeme Järvi. But Tubin's arrival on the scene is not a moment too soon. His works are a real find. His style is very much geared to our own time but is not difficult to listen to. There is a breadth and sweep about much of it that recalls ▷Sibelius, though there is nothing of the Finnish giant in the way Tubin handles melodies or orchestration. His symphonies are marvellous and well worth unhurried investigation; the curious should start with nos. 4

and 7. The Music for Strings is a fine, representative work. The suite of *Estonian Dances* is in frankly popular mould, with strong reminders of ▷Kodály's *Dances of Galanta* and ▷Bartók's *Romanian Dances*. Tubin composed what must be the only Balalaika Concerto, a delightfully unusual work. (Its dedicatee is a brilliant amateur who is one of Stockholm's most distinguished neuro-surgeons.)

TURINA, Joaquín (1882–1949)

The comparative neglect of Joaquín Turina's music is surprising. It is warm, colourful, tuneful and full of the atmosphere of the composer's native Spain. The flame of Turina's inspiration does not burn so brightly as that of his illustrious countryman, ▷Falla. But several of his orchestral works are well worth including in concert programmes. The *Fantastic Dances* are most attractive, sunny pieces. The *Sinfonia sevillana* is an affectionate and splendidly scored tribute to the great city of Seville, as in the *Canto a Sevilla*, a song cycle for soprano and orchestra of great charm. *The Bullfighter's Prayer*, originally for lute quartet but arranged for strings, is a fascinating curio, showing us not the arrogant, flamboyant side of the toreador but rather his quieter, more fearful moments before entering the arena.

NOW LISTEN ▷

▷Isaac Albéniz, *Iberia*; ▷Manuel de Falla, *Love the Magician*; ▷Enrique Grenados, *Goyescas*; Frederico Mompou, *Songs and Dances*.

V

VARÈSE, Edgard (1883–1965)

The music of Edgard Varèse was criticised in the 1920s, being described in the critical press as 'cacophonous', 'mad' and 'unendurable'. One writer even said, 'Gunpowder explosions might similarly overawe the ear'. Varèse, a French-born American, was not a whit dismayed. He continued his musical experiments for another 40 years. When he died, he was a cult figure, regarded by many disciples as a visionary. His music was never intended to be comfortable, and it certainly is not, even today. But it is enormously stimulating and the challenging sounds he produces are undeniably exciting. Varèse once said, 'I like music that explodes into space', and that is what much of his work does. *Arcana*, for a huge orchestra, is a good example of his 1920s style; if it appeals to the musical explorer (and I suspect it might) then some of his other works can be broached, notably *Amériques* ('New Worlds'), which uses sirens and whistles, though not in an incongruous way. *Ionisation* is for percussion only, but it is not in the least arid. Varèse's most famous work is also his purest: *Density 21.5*. It is for solo flute and the title refers to the density of platinum, the metal from which the flute is often made. Latterly, Varèse composed electronic music which is no less arresting and original than what he wrote for more conventional forces.

• In the 1920s, Varèse founded a group of composers who had similar aims, called the International

Composer's Guild (succeeded by the Pan American Association of Composers); among its members were ▷Chávez, Henry Cowell, ▷Ives and Nicolas Slonimsky. It tells us much more about Varèse that when he attended the première of ▷Stravinsky's ballet *The Rite of Spring* and heard it howled down by a furious audience, he commented, 'The music seemed very natural to me'.

VAUGHAN WILLIAMS, Ralph (1872–1958)

Folk music and the works of Ralph Vaughan Williams are virtually inseparable. This most English of composers began collecting folksongs and folk-dances when quite young, and their influence on his music remained to the very end. His most popular work is an arrangement of one of England's oldest folk melodies, 'Greensleeves'; and another of his often played pieces, the overture *The Wasps*, abounds in what sound like traditional tunes.

The symphonies are the essential VW (as he is often affectionately called). No. 1, *A Sea Symphony*, is a massively impressive choral work setting texts by Walt Whitman; no. 2, *A London Symphony*, is an evocation of London by night; the third, *Pastoral Symphony*, was inspired by the composer's beloved countryside; no. 4 is a fearful presage of war, harsh and violent, no. 5 – quiet, reflective and beautiful – is linked musically to the opera *The Pilgrim's Progress*; no. 6 is again warlike but peters out in an enigmatic finale which fades into infinity; no. 7, *Sinfonia antartica*, is icy and remote, using music written originally for the film *Scott of the Antartic*; no. 8 is a jolly 'little' work, perhaps the equivalent of ▷Beethoven's Eighth; and no. 9 is valedictory but shows no signs of any diminution of strength or power. The music in all these is direct, honest, accessible and enjoyable.

The ballet *Job* (actually described as 'a masque for dancing') is a distillation of VW. All the elements of his music are here – robust jollity, brutality and mysticism – and the score mirrors superbly the biblical story of Job's battle to subdue Satan. The composer's use of saxophones to represent Job's insincere comforters is masterly. VW composed concertos for various instruments, notably the oboe and the bass tuba (a richly witty work, this); and he wrote a Romance for harmonica and orchestra at the behest of Larry Adler, the virtuoso harmonica player. *The Lark Ascending* is a wonderfully imaginative flight of fancy; as we listen, we can almost visualise the bird disappearing into the clear air.

VW's operas have never gained great popularity, but *Hugh the Drover* and *Sir John in Love* (both heavily inspired by folk music) are delightful, one about a lovable rogue who has the lasses in a spin, the other revolving round Shakespeare's Falstaff and his misadventures in Windsor. Vaughan Williams's many songs include a fine cycle *On Wenlock Edge* and the exquisite *Linden Lee*. The *Serenade to Music* for 16 solo voices and orchestra sets words from Shakespeare's *The Merchant of Venice*. His output also includes much fine church music, the splendid *English Folk Song Suite* for military band and several highly skilled film scores, including one for the wartime propaganda thriller *49th Parallel*.

- Some other composers who collected folk music and were influenced by it: ▷Bartók (Hungary), ▷Canteloube (France), ▷Dvořák (Czechoslovakia and the USA), ▷Ginastera (Argentina), ▷Grainger (Britain), ▷Grieg (Norway) and ▷Tchaikovsky (Russia).

VERDI, Giuseppe (1813–1901)

The Italian composer Giuseppe Verdi lived for opera. With the exception of his magnificent Requiem, he wrote nothing of lasting significance that was not for the theatre. Even the Requiem, with its emotional arias and offstage trumpets, is operatic in style and flavour. Verdi composed 26 operas. At least 16 of them are still performed regularly in houses all over the world. Their huge success and the warm affection in which they are held by almost all music-lovers make Verdi among the greatest composers for the theatre.

NOW LISTEN ▷

Some other operas based on plays by Shakespeare: ▷Ernest Bloch, *Macbeth*; ▷Benjamin Britten, *A Midsummer Night's Dream*; ▷Charles Gounod, *Roméo et*

One of his earliest winners, *Nabucco*, drew on the biblical story of the tyrannical Nebuchadnezzar and his fall from grace; it contains one of Verdi's best-loved choruses, 'Va pensiero', the lament of the Hebrew slaves. But if its characters have a somewhat pasteboard look about them, the later operas are filled with very real people whose situations and problems can be understood and shared by all of us: the crippled jester in *Rigoletto* whose unfeeling master seduces his daughter; Violetta, the heroine of *La traviata*, who gives up her lover rather than see him become a social outcast; the slave girl in *Aida* who dares to love the same man as her all-powerful mistress; the king in *Un ballo in maschera* ('A Masked Ball') who falls for the wife of his best friend; the Doge of Venice, the central character of *Simon Boccanegra*, locked in a political and personal struggle which destroys him; the hero of *Don Carlos* who has to stand by and watch his father marry the woman he loves. Some of Verdi's operas have plots which are extraordinarily complex. It is a bold man who tries to give a quick summary of *Il trovatore* (The Troubadour) or *La forza del destino* ('The Force of Destiny'). But the music is so marvellous that the listener is carried along.

Verdi raided Shakespeare three times. *Macbeth* was one of his own favourites – and no wonder. It is a treasure-house of melody, keenly attentive to the nuances of the play, even if the Bard's three weird sisters become a whole chorus! *Otello* is considered by many to be an even finer work than the original play. It is certainly tighter, and in places more sharply dramatic. *Falstaff* showed that in his last years Verdi was able to compose a comic opera of stunning brilliance. The fat knight and his misadventures are portrayed in music that is witty, elegant and warm-hearted. The composer had so much to say in this work that wonderful melodies come and go almost before we have had time to savour them. Verdi grew in stature as he advanced in years. But he never lost the attribute that made him stand out in his early days: a love of life which he translated into music.

Juliette; ▷Otto Nicolai, *The Merry Wives of Windsor*; Aribert Reimann, *King Lear*; ▷Gioachino Rossini, *Otello*.

VILLAINY
▷Arrigo Boito, *Mefistofele*
▷Aaron Copland, *Billy the Kid*
▷Gaetano Donizetti, *Lucrezia Borgia*
▷Stephen Sondheim, *Sweeney Todd*
▷Richard Strauss, *Salome*
▷Giuseppe Verdi, *Macbeth*

VILLA-LOBOS, Heitor (1887–1959)
Heitor Villa-Lobos is Brazil's leading composer and is best known today for a set of pieces which he called *Bachianas brasileiras*. There are nine, some for full orchestra, others for smaller instrumental groups. No. 2 contains the delightful 'Little Train of the Caipira', a trip down the line in the Brazilian interior amid much squeaking, clanking and hissing. No. 5, the most often played, is for soprano and eight cellos. The pieces were written 'in homage to the great genius of ▷Johann Sebastian Bach'. They are a fascinating attempt to fuse the atmosphere of Bach's music with that of Brazilian folk traditions. Villa-Lobos wrote a large number of works of all kinds, his Guitar Concerto and Harp Concerto being especially colourful and attractive. His piano music includes the suite *Prole do bebe* ('The Baby's Family') which the great Artur Rubinstein often played.

VIOLA
The viola looks like a violin but is slightly larger and makes a deeper sound. It has an important inner role to play in most orchestral pieces but tends not to be given many opportunities to shine. ▷Mozart gave the viola a solo part in his *Sinfonia concertante*, K364 and it figures prominently in *Harold in Italy* by ▷Berlioz. Nearer our own time, composers who have written viola concertos include ▷Bartók and ▷Walton.

VIOLIN
The violin has the highest voice of the orchestral string instruments and is generally the hardest worked. Oc-

> **NOW LISTEN** ▷
>
> Some other music inspired by locomotives or trains: ▷Richard Rodney Bennett, *Murder on the Orient Express*; ▷Benjamin Britten, *Nightmail*; Vivian Ellis, *Coronation Scot*; ▷Arthur Honegger, *Pacific 231*; ▷Hans Christian Lumbye, *The Copenhagen Steam Railway Galop*; ▷Johann Strauss the younger, *Excursion Train*.

casionally in orchestral scores composers have written parts for a solo violin, for example ▷Rimsky-Korsakov in *Sheherazade* and ▷Tchaikovsky in his ballet *Swan Lake*. Most of the great composers have composed violin concertos, including ▷Mozart, ▷Beethoven and ▷Brahms. The most frequently heard are probably those by ▷Bruch, ▷Mendelssohn and ▷Tchaikovsky. From nearer our own time, the concertos by ▷Berg, ▷Bartók and ▷Elgar are among the finest.

VIOLONCELLO

The violoncello, usually called simply 'cello', is a string instrument played between the knees, pitched between the viola and the double bass. Its rich, warm sound is well loved by composers but is difficult to project successfully over the sound of a full orchestra. Its concerto repertory is smaller than the violin's. The concertos by ▷Elgar, ▷Dvořák, ▷Shostakovich and ▷Walton are noteworthy and there are fine cello solos in many orchestral pieces. The cello plays a long, lovely duet with the piano in the Piano Concerto no. 2 by ▷Brahms and it portrays the hero in *Don Quixote*, the tone poem by ▷Richard Strauss. One of the most famous pieces for solo cello is 'The Swan' from *The Carnival of the Animals* by ▷Saint-Saëns.

VIVALDI, Antonio (1678–1741)

The Italian composer Antonio Vivaldi took holy orders when he was a young man and became known as the 'Red Priest' – not for political reasons but on account of his carrot-coloured hair. He composed a great deal of fine church music, including a *Gloria* which has become one of his most popular works. But it is his secular music that has made him a household name, in particular the group of brilliant concertos for solo violin and strings which he called *The Four Seasons*. Their depiction of the changing moods of the year, from icy winter to warm and lazy autumn, is masterly. Vivaldi composed numerous concertos for many different instruments. He was among the first to recognise the clarinet's solo possibilities. The bassoon, too, is ca-

tered for (to the extent of more than 40 works) and
even the mandolin is put in the spotlight.

- ▷J.S. Bach was a fervent admirer of Vivaldi and
  arranged a number of his concertos for the organ
  or the harpsichord.

W

WAGNER, Richard (1813–1883)

Richard Wagner was once described by the memorable phrase 'a dead-end in music'. In the sense intended by the writer, he was. What Wagner did was unique. But, of course, his influence was – and is – incalculable. In the last 100 years, scarcely a composer has not admitted being affected in some way by the German genius and his 'music of the future', as he called it. Wagner wrote almost exclusively for the theatre. But he not only changed opera; he changed music itself, and he had a profound effect on all aspects of intellectual and philosophical life.

By the time he was writing his mature operas, Wagner had formulated his concept of the 'total art work'. In his 'music dramas', as he preferred to call them, he aimed to give music, drama and spectacle equal roles, uniting them into a significant whole that could powerfully convey psychological and emotional issues, as well as narrative, on a large scale. One of the ways he found of unifying these big works was by using *leitmotifs* ('leading motifs'): themes associated with a significant idea, character or emotional state recur in subtle and modified ways, establishing links and adding another musical layer to the drama. There are no separate songs or arias in Wagner's mature operas: the music is continuous, requiring a new approach to singing; and the orchestra, usually a huge one, plays a vital part in unfolding the drama, not acting merely as accompanist.

The earliest of Wagner's successes, *Der Fliegende Holländer* ('The Flying Dutchman'), immediately shows the composer's consuming interest in legend as a subject for musical treatment: it tells the supernatural story of the accursed, haunted sailor who must forever sail the seas until redeemed by the love of a woman. But it is in *Tannhäuser* and *Lohengrin* that we are given the first real intimation of Wagner's way ahead, the former with its song contest and strong religious overtones, the latter with its knight in shining armour and deeds of chivalry. By the time he came to compose *Tristan und Isolde*, a passionate love story, Wagner's musical language had expanded and intensified, reaching the point where all feeling of key and direction is lost and moving towards the paths that would be followed this century by ▷Schoenberg and others. His next work, however, was a comedy – if a somewhat serious one – the warm and richly human *Die Meistersinger von Nürnberg* ('The Mastersingers of Nuremberg'). With *Parsifal*, described by the composer as a 'sacred festival drama', he became involved with the search for the Holy Grail and returned to the world of Lohengrin (who is Parsifal's son).

But Wagner's masterpiece is *Der Ring des Nibelungen* ('The Nibelung's Ring'), four interlinked music dramas based on ancient sagas dealing with a struggle for power among gods, dwarves (Nibelungs), giants and humans. Power is symbolised by gold, stolen from the bed of the River Rhine and fashioned into a magical ring. In its four parts (*The Rheingold*, *The Valkyrie*, *Siegfried* and *Twilight of the Gods*) we are shown how that most human of sins – greed – destroys everything and everyone it touches. But this extraordinary, long work has been interpreted in many ways, touching as it does on crucial moral and philosophical issues. Wagner's music unfolds on an unprecedented scale, displaying his brilliant sense of theatre and masterly handling of *Leitmotifs*. Obviously a lot of homework – and a score – are a help in tackling *The Ring*. But it's quite possible to take it as it comes: as one of the great experiences in the world of the theatre. Over the years, what the famous critic Ernest Newman described as 'bleeding chunks' have been hacked from *The Ring* and used as concert pieces, notably the rumbustious 'Ride of the Valkyrie', 'Siegfried's Journey to the Rhine' and 'The Entry of the Gods into Valhalla'.

For many years after World War II, Wagner's music

had Nazi connotations because of his anti-semitic views, and *The Ring* was seen and interpreted as sympathetic to Hitler's racial policies. Today, however, it is almost unreservedly accepted for what it is, without political overtones.

- In order to stage his music dramas effectively and precisely in the ways he wanted, Wagner, with an architect, designed a special theatre at Bayreuth. The first complete performance of *The Ring* was given there in 1876. It is still used for annual festivals of his works, but it is in no sense a museum dedicated to old ways of staging them. *The Ring*, for instance, has been given several modern interpretations, one recent production beginning not in the Rhine, as tradition dictates, but in the shadow of a power station.

WALDTEUFEL, Emile (1837–1915)
Emile Waldteufel is sometimes called 'the French ▷Johann Strauss' but the description is misleading since it suggests that Waldteufel was merely imitating the Viennese master. In fact, Waldteufel's waltzes and polkas are highly original, their melodies fresh and invigorating and very much his own. He was court pianist to the Empress Eugénie for some years. His best music is in the celebrated *The Skaters' Waltz* but some of his others are equally enjoyable, especially *Pomone*, *Mon rêve*, *The Grenadiers* and *España*.

- Waldteufel must be one of the few pianists who knew the instrument inside out – literally: he spent several years testing pianos at a factory near Paris.

WALTON, Sir William (1902–1983)
William Walton is perhaps the composer upon whom

▷Elgar's mantle fell. It is not simply that he was able to produce 'Pomp and Circumstance' music, as he demonstrated superbly in the coronation marches *Crown Imperial* and *Orb and Sceptre*. There is a certain Englishness about his style that directly reflects the older composer. Walton's music sometimes makes gestures in the direction of the world of ▷Prokofiev and ▷Stravinsky but changed little during his composing career. The man thought of as an *enfant terrible* in his early days ultimately became an establishment figure (rather like ▷Bliss).

Walton's Second Symphony is a glossier extension of the First, composed 25 years earlier, but both are richly scored, imaginative works whose impact is considerable. The three concertos, one each for violin, viola and cello, are as fine as anything written in Britain this century. The Viola Concerto is perhaps the most personal and intimate of all Walton's works and was first played by a fellow composer, ▷Hindemith. (Later Walton wrote a set of superb Variations on a Theme of Hindemith.) Two concert overtures are vintage Walton: there is *joie de vivre* in plenty in *Scapino* and jazzy elements in *Portsmouth Point*. Jazz can also be heard in the witty and dexterous entertainment *Façade*, in which some of Edith Sitwell's poems are read (preferably through a megaphone) against Walton's score, played by a chamber ensemble.

Belshazzar's Feast (1931), one of Walton's most-performed works, is a dramatic cantata with a biblical text set for solo baritone, chorus and large orchestra. It is emotional, thrilling, chilling and exultant by turns, with music that is immensely colourful and ear-catching. There's a jazz influence here, too, with saxophones denoting the decadence and profanity of Belshazzar the king. Two operas *Troilus and Cressida* and the one-act *The Bear* show Walton to have a fine sense of theatre. The first has a stream of lovely melodies, old-fashioned arias if you like, plus impressive set-piece choruses. In the second, based on Chekhov's comedy about an uncouth landowner, Walton's music pokes gentle fun at the style of several other composers. His film music is in a class of its own. *The First of the Few*, a wartime film about the invention of the Spitfire, brought out all Walton's patriotism. The Shakespeare

NOW LISTEN ▷

Some works by English composers writing in the earlier years of Walton's career: ▷Lord Berners, *Fantaisie espagnole*; ▷Arthur Bliss, *Rout*; Eugene Goossens, Sinfonietta; Gavin Gordon, *The Rake's Progress*; ▷Constant Lambert, *Pomona*; Gerrard Williams, *Valsette brut*.

films of Olivier, *Henry V*, *Hamlet*, and *Richard III*, owe a fair measure of their success to Walton's scores (just sample the Battle of Agincourt from *Henry V*). The undervalued chamber music includes a splendid string quartet (which the composer later expanded for full string orchestra) and a haunting violin sonata. Walton arranged some of the music of ▷Bach for the 1940 ballet *The Wise Virgins*.

WARLOCK, Peter (1894–1930)
The English composer Peter Warlock is remembered by one short work, the *Capriol Suite*, which exists in versions for strings and for full orchestra. It's based on a set of 16th-century French dances and shows a consistently delicate touch and sensitivity. Anyone seeking to investigate this interesting composer more fully should try his song cycle *The Curlew* for tenor, flute, cor anglais and string quartet. It is charming, as is the Serenade for strings which Warlock composed to mark the 60th birthday of his friend and mentor ▷Delius. Warlock's real name was Philip Heseltine and his use of two names was possibly significant. One side of his nature was ebullient and good-natured; the other tortured and withdrawn. He took his own life at the age of 36.

WEBER, Carl Maria von (1786–1826)
For some time, the influence of Carl Maria von Weber was considered to be of greater importance than his music. His freedom of writing and the brilliance of his orchestration left their mark on such composers as ▷Chopin, ▷Berlioz, ▷Liszt and even ▷Mahler. ▷Wagner spoke the oration at Weber's funeral and ▷Debussy wrote that Weber understood the soul of every instrument. As the years went by, however, Weber's works began to be played more and gradually assumed their true position in the concert hall. The clarinet concertos and the Bassoon Concerto are loved dearly by both players and public and they explore the instruments as effectively as anyone has ever done. The piano concertos and the accomplished little *Konzertstück* for piano and orchestra are also charming

and show clearly Weber's mastery as a keyboard composer. His two symphonies, once rarely played, have been shown to be excellent and enjoyable.

Two of Weber's operas, *Oberon* and *Euryanthe*, suffer from dismal librettos but are musically very strong; the latter is fairly said to be the inspiration for ▷Wagner's *Lohengrin*. *Der Freischütz* is his finest operatic achievement. Its tale of a marksman who enlists the help of an evil spirit to help him win a shooting contest relies on the supernatural but Weber clothes it with such marvellous music that the listener can but sit back and enjoy it unreservedly. It was in this opera that Weber showed how folk-type melodies could be effective, if used skilfully, in an operatic context, and in effect he created the first real Romantic Garden opera.

- An unfinished opera by Weber, *Die drei Pintos*, was completed by ▷Mahler and performed in 1888; it's about a simpleton named Pinto who has his name used by two other men to further their ends.

WEBERN, Anton (1883–1945)
If brevity is the soul of wit, it is also the essence of the compositions of the Austrian composer Anton Webern. His works, which are relatively few, are pared down to the barest musical essentials and are often extremely short. His Six Bagatelles for string quartet last just over three minutes. The Five Pieces for small orchestra consist of a mere 76 bars. Webern was a pupil of ▷Schoenberg and a member of the Second Viennese School who followed his teacher's compositional methods very seriously. Because most of Webern's music is so spare and highly controlled, it is often held to be tough and difficult; to reap rewards from his output, it is necessary to persevere. But do so – and discover that the purity of the music is often very expressive and even tender. Webern met his end through a tragic accident: he was shot in error by an American soldier after the end of World War II.

- Webern arranged music by some other composers including ▷J.S. Bach, ▷Schubert and ▷Wolf.

WEILL, Kurt (1900–1950)

The German composer Kurt Weill was 28 when he composed his masterpiece, *The Threepenny Opera*, on which he worked with the great German dramatist Bertolt Brecht. It's an updated version of ▷Gay's English classic *The Beggar's Opera*, in which Macheath, the highwayman hero of the original, becomes Mack the Knife, a cheap crook. The music – stark, brash, jazzy and sentimental by turns – is considered now to be the epitome of Berlin in the 1920s. Weill worked with Brecht on other theatre pieces, among them *The Rise and Fall of the City of Mahagonny* and *Happy End*. Mahagonny is the city of eternal pleasure where death is the penalty for failing to pay your whisky bill. *Happy End* is about gangsters and a Salvation Army girl (as is ▷Loesser's musical *Guys and Dolls*). The barbed shafts that Weill and Brecht loosed on the politics and society of the day infuriated the Nazis who drove them from Germany. Weill settled eventually in the USA and, though he wrote other fine works, including *The Seven Deadly Sins*, *Lady in the Dark* (about a woman who tells her dreams to her psychiatrist) and *Knickerbocker Holiday* (from which comes the famous 'September Song'), he never again achieved the sharpness and brilliance of the Brecht shows. Those interested in hearing another side of Weill should seek out his two symphonies, well-constructed and interesting works, and the Concerto for violin and wind instruments. His style leans towards that of ▷Schoenberg but is considerably more melodious.

- Weill married the singing actress Lotte Lenya, whose unique personality and highly individual way of putting songs across contributed greatly to the success of his musicals. Film buffs will recall Lenya's performance as the evil Rosa Klebb in the James Bond adventure *From Russia with Love*.

WILLIAMS, John (born 1932)
The composer John Williams, not to be confused with the eminent guitarist of the same name, has written the music for some of the most successful films of recent times, most notably *Star Wars*, *Superman*, *E.T.*, *Raiders of the Lost Ark* and *Close Encounters of the Third Kind*. His big, broad tunes, sumptuously orchestrated, are instantly identifiable as his work, and if one is pretty much like another, so be it.

WILLIAMSON, Malcolm (born 1931)
Malcolm Williamson is the present Master of the Queen's Music, a post with the responsibility of writing music for state occasions and previously held by ▷Bliss. Williamson is an Australian whose music is extremely accomplished, unpretentious and likable. His is not the most original of voices but his works have the merit of refreshing the ear. Like ▷Britten and ▷Maxwell Davies, Williamson has written a great deal of music for children, and one of his operas for young people *The Happy Prince*, based on Oscar Wilde's fairy tale, contains some of his most charming ideas. His Piano Concerto no. 2, which has an accompaniment only for strings, is a most enjoyable piece, completed in only eight days but showing no signs of hurry; its finale betrays Williamson's love of jazz. The Piano Concerto no. 3 is even finer and its catchy melodies and bouncy rhythms could make it a concert pop if it were better known. Some of Williamson's purely orchestral work is striking (the symphonies are well worth a listen) and his church music is of a high level of inspiration. The Easter piece *Procession of Palms* is lovely. Williamson is a splendid organist and has written a considerable amount of effective music for the instrument (the Organ Concerto is gripping). His operas are *Our Man in Havana* (based on Graham Greene's novel), witty and attractive, while *The Violins of Saint-Jacques* has an

abundance of good tunes (it was described by one critic as 'the thinking man's *South Pacific*', but that might commend it to some listeners!).

- The office of Master of the King's (or Queen's) Music originated in the reign of Charles I, when the holder not only wrote music at the royal behest but also directed the monarch's orchestra; 18 composers have since been appointed to the post, including William Boyce, John Stanley, ▷Elgar, Henry Walford Davies, ▷Bax and ▷Bliss.

WILSON, Thomas (born 1927)

Thomas Wilson, unlike his fellow Scots ▷Musgrave and ▷Hamilton, has remained in his native land and is now a distinguished professor in Glasgow. His music is direct, finely crafted and in an idiom to which most people will be able to relate – that's to say modern but not outrageously avant garde. His output is quite large and strays into many areas including ballet, and music for church and brass band. His opera *The Confessions of a Justified Sinner* is an impressive and atmospheric interpretation of James Hogg's dark novel. The Piano Concerto, alternatively introspective and virtuoso, is consistently fascinating. *Touchstone*, an orchestral portrait of Shakespeare's celebrated clown, is suitably enigmatic and intriguing.

WIRÉN, Dag (1905–1986)

Dag Wirén is included here on two counts. He is one of the few Swedish composers to gain performances outside his native land; and the single work for which he is known, the Serenade for strings, is a little gem. The final March has one of those tunes which, once heard, is never forgotten (it was used during the earlier days of British television as the signature tune of an arts programme called 'Monitor'). Wirén's many other compositions, including symphonies, string quartets and an opera inspired by Winston Churchill's 'Blood,

NOW LISTEN ▷

Some composers who have written Serenades for strings: ▷Lennox Berkeley; ▷Benjamin Britten; ▷Antonín Dvořák; ▷Edward Elgar; ▷Wolfgang Amadeus Mozart; Wilhelm

tears and sweat' speech during World War II, are not performed.

Stenhammar; ▷Peter Tchaikovsky.

WOLF, Hugo (1860–1903)

The Austrian composer Hugo Wolf has often been described as the true successor to ▷Schubert in the realms of song writing. He spent most of his life composing for the voice and produced a vast number of songs, many of them collected in the Italian Songbook and the Spanish Songbook. Some of his best are settings of verses by the poet Mörike. Wolf wrote superb vocal lines. But his songs are equally interesting for their piano accompaniments. Often these seem almost to have a life of their own and tell us as much about the subject of the song as the words. Wolf, a tormented man who died insane, composed an opera *Der Corregidor* and the charming *Italian Serenade* for string quartet, later orchestrated. But the songs are his glory.

● ▷Falla's ballet *The Three-Cornered Hat* is based on the story used by Wolf in his opera *Der Corregidor*, about an official in a little Spanish town who makes the mistake of flirting with the local miller's wife.

WOLF-FERRARI, Ermanno (1876–1948)

As his name suggests, Ermanno Wolf-Ferrari was part-German, part-Italian. But so far as his music is concerned it is his Italian side that dominates. Much of his work was for the opera house, and it is melodious and warm-blooded. His greatest achievement is *I gioielli della Madonna* ('The Jewels of the Madonna'), well known for a tuneful, light-hearted little Intermezzo which gives no idea of the opera's real nature. It is actually a strongly dramatic piece about the tragic consequences that ensue after a young man robs a church so that he can give a present to his lover. In contrast *I quattro rusteghi* (translated for a London performance as 'The School for Fathers') is a charming, amusingly written opera about a group of bully-boy

husbands who get their comeuppance when their
wives rebel. Wolf-Ferrari's best-known opera,
though, is *Il segreto di Susanna* ('Susanna's Secret'), a
one-acter of the utmost wit and polish about a woman
who goes to inordinate lengths to stop her husband
finding out that she smokes! One day, he smells cigarette smoke, but assumes there has been a man in the
house . . . The overture, often played in the concert
hall on its own, has a ▷Mozartean delicacy and sophis-
tication.

● Smoking occurs in several musical works.
▷Bizet's *Carmen* has a chorus of Cigarette Girls;
Minnie, the heroine of ▷Puccini's *The Girl of the
Golden West*, offers cigars to the Wells-Fargo
agent, Ashby; and there is a 'Waltz of the Cigarette' in ▷Lalo's ballet *Namouna* (banned at the
first performance because of fire-risk to the theatre). ▷Kern's musical *Roberta* includes the hit
song 'Smoke gets in your eyes'.

WOMEN COMPOSERS
Women composers, even in this enlightened age, are
thin on the ground. This state of affairs is not encountered in the fields of literature or the visual arts. Over
the centuries, women have been accomplished singers
and instrumentalists, but their role in society has not
fostered the art of composition. There are notable ex-
ceptions. The abbess and mystic Hildegard of Bingen
(1098–1179) wrote music; Barbara Strozzi (1619–
1664) was a pupil of Cavalli and an able composer;
Elisabeth-Claude Jacquet de la Guerre (*c*1666–1729)
was the only woman to write a lyric tragedy opera and
among the earliest to publish collections of harpsichord music. Schumann's wife Clara, as well as being an internationally known pianist, composed;
▷Mendelssohn's sister Fanny wrote songs and piano
music. The best-known women composers from earlier this century include Dame Ethel Smyth, Germaine Tailleferre, Amy Beach, Ruth Crawford (See-
ger) and Cécile Chaminade: and, more recently,

Elisabeth Lutyens, Elizabeth Maconchy, Priaulx Rainier, Phyllis Tate, Grace Williams, ▷Musgrave and Judith Weir.

XENAKIS, Iannis (born 1922)

Mathematics and music go hand in hand in the world of the Greek Iannis Xenakis. He studied as an engineer and worked with the architect Le Corbusier, and he has employed computers to create the structures he has applied to his compositions. Sometimes he has used electronics, but mostly he writes for conventional instruments. What does it all sound like? It is actually easier on the ear than much other avant-garde music. The titles of Xenakis's pieces are often daunting: *Terretektorh* for orchestra deployed among the audience; *Hibiki-hana-ma* for 12 tapes distributed over 800 loudspeakers, and so on. But try the hypnotic atmosphere and strange, elusive colours of the ballet *Antikhthon*, which has been recorded. Better still, hear some Xenakis live if you get the chance. It is unquestionably an experience.

Z

ZANDONAI, Riccardo (1883–1944)

The Italian composer Riccardo Zandonai wrote his finest opera, *Francesca da Rimini*, in 1914, and for a while was seen as a talented successor to ▷Puccini. But he never surpassed *Francesca* and is regarded as an also-ran; nevertheless it is an opera of merit, full of lovely melodies and beautifully orchestrated. The story is taken from Dante's *Inferno* and concerns the girl who falls in love with the brother of the man she is supposed to be marrying. Zandonai composed several other operas, including one with the intriguing title *Siberia*, which makes use of the 'Song of the Volga Boatmen'.

- Many composers wrote operas on the tragic tale of Francesca da Rimini, notably the Frenchman ▷Ambroise Thomas and the Russian ▷Rakhmaninov (his version, interestingly, has a libretto by Modest Tchaikovsky, brother of Peter, the celebrated composer).

ZELLER, Carl (1842–1898)

The German composer Carl Zeller wrote one operetta which many believe to be touched with the muse that visited ▷Johann Strauss (the younger) and ▷Lehár. *Der Vogelhändler* ('The Birdseller') is one of the most-performed musical works on the Continent today and regularly shares billboards with *Die Fledermaus* and

The Merry Widow. Zeller was an amateur, in that he never left his job as a senior official in the Austrian Ministry of Culture. But the skill and imagination of *The Birdseller*, with its procession of singable tunes, spell nothing but professionalism. Its plot is pleasantly silly, about the love-affair between a village postmistress in the Tyrol and a young lad who catches birds (à la Papageno). But if there is little substance in the story, there is not a weak bar in the music: the song 'When you give roses in the Tyrol' is one of the loveliest in Viennese operetta. Zeller had some success with *Der Obersteiger* ('The Mine Foreman'), whose principal song 'Don't be cross' has been recorded by many leading sopranos (most notably Elisabeth Schwarzkopf), but the work has not stayed in the repertory. Zeller's life came to a sad end. He was involved in a lawsuit, convicted of perjury and died of a stroke.

ZEMLINSKY, Alexander (1871–1942)

The Austrian composer Alexander Zemlinsky is a somewhat shadowy figure in music. But earlier this century he was an influential composer who taught ▷Schoenberg and the man who was to become the king of Hollywood's musical empire, ▷Korngold. Zemlinsky's own works deserve to be much better known. His two Oscar Wilde-inspired operas, *Eine florentinische Tragödie* ('A Florentine Tragedy') and *Der Zwerg* ('The Dwarf'), have in recent years been shown to be highly effective when well staged. But anyone curious to discover music that is both absorbing and refreshing should try his *Lyric Symphony* for two voices and orchestra: it was inspired by ▷Mahler's *The Song of the Earth* and inhabits that world, without being a copy of it. The attractive Sinfonietta is melodious and skilfully put together. The Six Songs to poems by Maeterlinck are lovely, the vocal line being supported by an orchestral accompaniment of rapt intensity. The second of Zemlinsky's four string quartets carries a quotation from ▷Schoenberg's *Verklärte Nacht*, a sincere tribute to his gifted pupil.

● Oscar Wilde's decadent play *Salome* was used as a basis for ▷Richard Strauss's exotic opera of the same name; the Wilde fairy tale *The Happy Prince* provided ▷Williamson with the libretto for his children's opera.

ZIMMERMAN, Bernd Alois (1918–1970)
The German composer Bernd Alois Zimmerman composed many works, including a symphony, concertos and orchestral pieces, before taking his own life in a fit of depression. He will be remembered for an opera which some people consider one of the most original and far-reaching of the 20th century, *Die Soldaten* ('The Soldiers'). Its story is simple and sordid: a girl becomes the mistress of a high-ranking army officer; when he rejects her, she becomes the regimental whore. Zimmerman uses film, jazz, speech, electronic sounds and dance, as well as conventional singing and orchestral playing, to make his impact – and quite an impact it is.

INDEX